SOCIAL WORK IN NORTHERN IRELAND

Conflict and change

Deirdre He~~~~ ~ ~~rek Birrell

This edition published in Great Britain in 2011 by

The Policy Press
University of Bristol
Fourth Floor
Beacon House
Queen's Road
Bristol BS8 1QU
UK

Tel +44 (0)117 331 4054
Fax +44 (0)117 331 4093
e-mail tpp-info@bristol.ac.uk
www.policypress.co.uk

North American office:
The Policy Press
c/o International Specialized Books Services (ISBS)
920 NE 58th Avenue, Suite 300
Portland, OR 97213-3786, USA
Tel +1 503 287 3093
Fax +1 503 280 8832
e-mail info@isbs.com

British Library Cataloguing in Publication Data
A catalogue record for this book is available from the British Library.

Library of Congress Cataloging-in-Publication Data
A catalog record for this book has been requested.

ISBN 978 1 84742 332 0 paperback
ISBN 978 1 84742 333 7 hardcover

The right of Deirdre Heenan and Derek Birrell to be identified as authors of this work has been asserted by them in accordance with the 1988 Copyright, Designs and Patents Act.

The statements and opinions contained within this publication are solely those of the authors and contributors and not of The University of Bristol or The Policy Press. The University of Bristol and The Policy Press disclaim responsibility for any injury to persons or property resulting from any material published in this publication.

The Policy Press works to counter discrimination on grounds of gender, race, disability, age and sexuality.

Cover design by The Policy Press
Front cover image is of the Northern Ireland Children's Friendship Project Mural, by artist Xavier Cortada. The mural was created in October 2000 in collaboration with Irish and Protestant young people. Reproduced by kind permission of the artist. www.cortada.com
Printed and bound in Great Britain by Hobbs, Southampton.
The Policy Press uses environmentally responsible print partners.

Contents

Detailed contents   iii
List of tables   vii
List of abbreviations   viii
Acknowledgements   ix

one   Introduction   1
two   Historical context   7
three   Sectarianism and social work   23
four   Violence and social work   37
five   The integration of health and social work   55
six   Social work and community development   73
seven   Cross-border social work   91
eight   Poverty and social work   109
nine   Devolution and social work   129
ten   Conclusions   151

References   154
Index   175

Detailed contents

one   **Introduction**   1

two   **Historical context**   7
          The creation of Northern Ireland   7
          State welfare from 1921 to 1948   8
          Voluntary action   11
          Beginning of a probation service   15
          The role of the almoner service   16
          Establishment of the welfare state 1945–50   17
          Mental health services   20
          Social work education   21
          Conclusion   22

three   **Sectarianism and social work**   23
          The impact of sectarian attitudes   23
          Sectarianism and discriminatory practices   24
          Social work representing a sectarian state   24
          Sectarianism as segregation   25
          Sectarianism and paramilitarism   27
          Sectarian values   27
          Agency approaches of neutrality and avoidance   28
          Response of educators and trainers   29
          Anti-discriminatory measures   30
          Post-1988: The good relations strategy   33
          Anti-racism   34
          Anti-oppressive practice   35
          Conclusion   36

four   **Violence and social work**   37
          The nature of violence   37
          Response to civil emergencies   40
          Mental health and trauma   43
          Social services responses   45
          Trauma and staff   48
          The impact of the Northern Ireland experience   49
          Support for victims   50
          Conclusion   53

five	**The integration of health and social work**	**55**
	The development of integrated services	55
	The operation of integrated services	59
	Internal assessment of integration	63
	UK perceptions of the integrated structure	65
	The lessons from Northern Ireland	66
	Integration and innovation	68
	The problem of protecting social services	70
	Conclusion	71
six	**Social work and community development**	**73**
	Introduction	73
	What is community development?	74
	Community social work	76
	History of social work and community development	77
	Policy developments since the 1990s	83
	Community-oriented services	86
	Conclusion	89
seven	**Cross-border social work**	**91**
	Context	92
	Background to cooperation	93
	Development of collaboration	94
	Identifying cross-border cooperation in the social services	95
	Classification of cross-border cooperation	96
	The nature and focus of cooperative projects	101
	The funding of cross-border work	103
	Compatibility of professional qualifications in social work	104
	Obstacles to cooperation	105
	Conclusion	106
eight	**Poverty and social work**	**109**
	Poverty in Northern Ireland	109
	Policy responses to poverty	119
	The implications of poverty and disadvantage for social work	125
	Social work initiatives to address poverty	127
	Conclusion	127
nine	**Devolution and social work**	**129**
	Programmes for government	130
	Organisational position of social care in the devolved administration	131
	Delivery by quangos	132
	Structures for registration, training and inspection	133

Policy innovation and development 135

Departmental strategies 137

Child protection reforms 137

Older people and care 139

Mental health and learning disability 140

Personalisation 141

User and public involvement 142

Policy copying 144

The role of social work 144

Conclusion 148

ten **Conclusion** **151**

List of tables

5.1	Structures for health and social care delivery	59
8.1	Poverty type among children (2008)	112
8.2	Severe child poverty	113
8.3	Comparison of worklessness (2009)	114
8.4	Pensioners at risk of poverty in different geographical locations	117
8.5	Children on the Child Protection Register, per 10,000 (2008)	125
9.1	Forms of government in Northern Ireland	129
9.2	Expenditure on health and personal social services	136
9.3	Expenditure per child on personal social care	136
9.4	Strategic points	146

List of abbreviations

ACYPC	Area Children's and Young People's Committee
BIC	British Irish Council
BMUA	Belfast Metropolitan Urban Area
CAWT	Cooperation and Working Together
CCBS	Centre for Cross Border Studies
CCETSW	Central Council for Education and Training in Social Work
CERT	Community Emergency Response Team
DH	Department of Health
DHSSPS	Department of Health and Social Services and Personal Safety
DSD	Department of Social Development
ECNI	Equality Commission Northern Ireland
ESRC	Economic Social Research Council
EU	European Union
GB	Great Britain
JMC	Joint Ministerial Council
NAO	National Audit Office
NHS	National Health Service
NIA	Northern Ireland Assembly
NIAO	Northern Ireland Audit Office
NICTT	Northern Ireland Centre for Trauma and Transformation
NIHE	Northern Ireland Housing Executive
NIO	Northern Ireland Office
NISCC	Northern Ireland Social Care Council
OFMDFM	Office of the First Minister and Deputy First Minister
PTSD	Post-Traumatic Stress Disorder
RPA	Review of Public Administration
TAP	Trauma Advisory Panel
TSN	Targeting Social Need
UK	United Kingdom
UNOCINI	Understanding the Needs of Children in Northern Ireland

Acknowledgements

Many thanks to everyone who provided the support to make this book possible. We would like to express our gratitude to colleagues at the University of Ulster and practitioners who provided comments on earlier drafts of chapters. Thanks to staff at The Policy Press for their guidance and support. Finally, we are indebted to Gemma Thornton for her diligence and patience in the production of the book; her good humour and expertise were invaluable.

ONE

Introduction[1]

Since the introduction of devolution more attention has been paid to social work divergence throughout the UK. Brodie et al (2008) suggest that social work in Scotland is distinct in many important respects from social work elsewhere in the UK. Scourfield et al (2008) have asked how distinctive social work is in Wales and inquired into the 'Welsh context' of social work. This book investigates how distinctive social work is in Northern Ireland.

Social work in Northern Ireland has developed along broadly similar lines to Great Britain. Since the development of the welfare state, social work has expanded in terms of its role and functions in ways generally mirroring England, Scotland and Wales, with increasing access to resources. Professional training has also developed along broadly similar routes in terms of what is required in order to gain professional recognition, the status of a social worker and with some similar developments of the social care workforce. Social work in Northern Ireland has, however, a number of distinctive contexts that set it aside from Great Britain and have led to significant and interesting differences.

The distinctive context can be differentiated in terms of its impact on social work:

1. the highly distinctive features of communal conflict, political violence and a long history of devolved governance;
2. lower-profile distinctive features of integrated delivery structures and a land border;
3. less divergent aspects relating to socio-economic needs and the significance of community development approaches.

Within these contexts the book sets out to examine perspectives that have been unique in the delivery of social work services, the responses adopted, the formulation of policy and strategies, the development of practice, and the outcomes for the well-being of the population.

The first highly distinctive context has been the impact of the conflict on the operation of social work, and the delivery of services in a society marked by violence, sectarianism, intimidation and social disruption against a backdrop of social and political division and polarisation. This brought with it a number of unique challenges, where social workers were forced to develop mechanisms to cope with the demanding circumstances.

Also identified as a highly distinctive characteristic is the issue of sectarianism in Northern Ireland and the multidimensional ways in which it has impacted on social work delivery and the training of social workers. Along with sectarianism were issues of segregation between the two communities, especially working-class Protestant and Catholic communities and also discrimination in service provision and employment, leading to a focus on the need for anti-discriminatory practice, the challenge of diversity and the need to promote community relations.

Social workers in Northern Ireland have also found themselves after 1969 in localities where they faced a situation of violence and civil disturbances, which at its worst resembled a civil war. This was marked by a prolonged period of bombings, shootings, security operations, civil disturbances and intimidation, resulting in extensive household displacement. Associated with the political and inter-communal violence was the operation of paramilitary groups, especially in working-class housing estates. The patterns of violence changed over the years, but even with the peace process, violence and intimidation have not entirely disappeared. The response of social work agencies to violence, the need to define their role and the necessary extension to their protection role, combined to present a fluid and changeable scenario.

The second distinctive context was the long-standing operation of devolved government in Northern Ireland. Social policy and subsequently social work have had the status of key devolved matters within the system of legislative, executive and administrative devolution. Even during the replacement of legislative and executive devolution by Direct Rule from Westminster, a system of devolved administration remained in place. This allowed decisions to be made that organised the administration, planning and delivery of social work services in different ways from England, Scotland and Wales. The devolution of social policy in areas other than social security has produced policy divergence in social care, housing and education that has impacted on social work. Underpinning this divergence has been different social values and ideological commitments, at times challenging traditional social work values.

Two other unique features of social work practice are identified, which have rather lower profiles. Northern Ireland shares a land border with another jurisdiction and another EU country, the Republic of Ireland. This has had consequences for some aspects of social work delivery in terms of cross-border cooperation by social work agencies, delivering services to border regions and intergovernmental collaboration.

The most significant unique feature of social work arrangements is not closely related to any special characteristics of Northern Ireland society. Since the early 1970s there has been an integrated structure in place, in slightly different formats, for the delivery of social care with health, mainly with primary health care. This has developed with further changes in 2007/08 into a comprehensive integrated structure including all hospitals. This integrated structure is based on distinctive principles of delivery and governance. However, social work in Northern Ireland has had to work at developing the full potential and has faced issues of the hegemony of health within the integrated structure.

Northern Ireland has developed a large community sector, partly as a consequence of 'the Troubles' and this has at times pushed community development approaches to the fore in social work practice and partnership working. Some detailed consideration is necessary to judge the significance of community development in social work and its role in social work activities in supporting communities. Narratives on social work and social policy in relation to Northern Ireland have on occasions regarded the severe levels of disadvantage as almost unique or at least have sketched a background of poverty, unemployment, economic inactivity and low pay levels as significantly higher than in Great Britain. This profile of deprivation is also reflected in levels of mental illness, educational achievement, homelessness, child poverty and fuel poverty. It is possible to examine the degree of divergence within the UK and question if this adds up to uniqueness. Questions can be asked as to what extra pressure has been put on social work provision and in particular what responses have been devised by social work agencies to assist in preventing and alleviating poverty.

The focus of this book is on what is unique about social work in Northern Ireland, rather than the operation of social work where it is broadly similar to England, Scotland and Wales. It is the case that social work services are directed at similar vulnerable groups and issues in Northern Ireland: children and families, older people, disability, mental health, learning disability and, although to a lesser extent, ethnic groups, immigrants and asylum seekers. Also similar are the problems of social deprivation, child poverty, family breakdown, abuse, frailty, child protection, mental illness, addiction, rural deprivation and social polarisation. The existing methods of social work intervention also are similar: the use of casework and group work, managing risk and protection strategies, care assessment and management, supporting carers, use of direct payments, an enabling role, promoting community care, commissioning from the independent sector, and the increasing use of information technology.

A major question informing the analysis in this book is what lessons, if any, might be learnt from the distinctive experiences of social work in Northern Ireland. Such an exercise involves relating the Northern Ireland experience to debates and discourses on policy development and practice in cognate areas in England, Scotland and Wales. Thus the challenges and responses by social work to sectarianism, segregation, discrimination and diversity may be related to issues of anti-racism, anti-discrimination and anti-oppressive practice. Most significant for the possible transfer of ideas and practice is Northern Ireland's experience of the structural integration of health and social care, that is, a working example of breaking down the 'wall' between the NHS and social services. Northern Ireland's fully integrated system of primary and secondary health and social care can be compared with partnership working and collaborative arrangements in Great Britain. This can inform debates over the advantages or disadvantages of forms of integration and working together, the value of an emphasis on greater structural integration, the nature of the working of service integration and outcomes for users.

While the experience of social workers in dealing with violence and its aftermath may seem at first not so transferable, it has become much more so when placed in the context of emergency planning and the role of social work. Social work in the context of emergency planning has become more of a high-profile topic following both natural disasters and terrorist incidents in Britain. There is some evidence of experience from Northern Ireland influencing this form of emergency planning in Britain and the potential for more transferability is examined. Possible lessons from the Northern Ireland experience are also examined in relation to the profile of community development approaches in Northern Ireland and the influence of a strong vibrant community sector.

The question is also asked as to whether social work in Northern Ireland displays any innovations in dealing with deprivation and social exclusion. Local statutory or partnership projects, agency strategies and government programmes are assessed to identify any such initiatives. This analysis is also put in the context of wider social policies that form a framework for social work intervention. The political and policy impact on social work of a land border with the Republic of Ireland may not seem to have so many lessons for Great Britain, although there is increasing interest across Europe in cross-border cooperation in social work and social care. With devolution in the UK, issues have arisen concerning accessible social/residential care across internal borders, for example, the Welsh border.

The impact of devolution on social work in Northern Ireland, especially since 1999, is a subject from which lessons can be drawn relating to Scotland and Wales. The scope and nature of divergence in policy and provision can be examined and the underlying reasons for differences analysed. The extent of any policy copying, from or by Northern Ireland, in the social work and social care field can be identified and assessed. Each jurisdiction in the UK, England, Scotland, Wales and Northern Ireland, has initiated major and fundamental reviews of the role and function of social work. It is possible, therefore, to compare these reports and identify policy learning or the transfer of ideas that may influence future developments, as well as seeking confirmation of unique aspects of social work delivery in each country.

The book uses a wide range of available sources, nonetheless the overall amount of material on Northern Ireland is limited. Academic material is mainly in the form of journal articles supported by a small number of research reports. Articles in academic journals have tended to focus on aspects of mainstream practice in child protection and children's services. Major pieces of empirical research are rare and few relate to the main themes of this book.

The resources used include some multidisciplinary material and some of the themes addressed, particularly sectarianism and violence, have attracted the attention of psychologists, sociologists and health academics. A number of reports from research institutes, policy centres and research foundations are used, however whilst material on health and social care is growing, it is not extensive. Material from the only social work-led research institute in Northern Ireland, the Institute of Child Care Research at Queen's University Belfast, is used. Reports, evaluations and strategy documents from the Department of Health, Social Service and Public Safety and trusts and boards are used as appropriate. Again relatively little of this government material addresses some of the key themes explored. There is a dearth of books on social work in Northern Ireland, although the establishment of devolution has led to the inclusion of references to systems, policies and practice in Northern Ireland in UK books and in major reports relating to social work and social care. This is in sharp contrast to the vast array of books and sources covering the Northern Ireland conflict, some of these resources include relevant material on sectarianism and segregation. Consequently, one of the central aims of this book is to collate the available sources in a comprehensive analysis of key themes in social work.

The chapters are mainly organised to reflect the key themes that identify the uniqueness of social work in Northern Ireland. After an introductory chapter, Chapter Two covers the context of the development of the social work profession in Northern Ireland. It attempts to set its development in a political and social and administrative context. This includes reference to the establishment of Northern Ireland and the welfare state and mechanisms for the delivery of social services. This chapter also deals with the emergence of social work as a profession.

The next three chapters provide an analysis and exploration of the more unique context of social work delivery in Northern Ireland. Chapter Three deals with sectarianism, prejudice and the consequences of social polarisation, discrimination and issues of diversity and identity. It examines the serious and difficult dilemmas faced by social workers attempting to deliver services in particularly challenging and often dangerous circumstances.

Chapter Four examines the consequences of violence for social work practice including responses to civil emergencies. It looks at the role of social workers in emergency planning, immediate responses to conflict, the nature of continuing support in the aftermath of violence and civil disturbances. It also reviews their role in the provision of support for dealing with trauma.

Chapter Five turns to the more unique arrangement for the delivery of social work and social care in integrated structure with health and the NHS. It outlines the development of the integrated system in Northern Ireland including recent reconfigurations and relates this to current debates in Britain about collaboration and partnerships in health and social care. Following a review of how the system works in practice and the associated strengths and weaknesses, the key lessons of working through an integrated system are identified.

Chapter Six reviews the long-standing relationship between community development and social work. After a brief discussion of community development and its relationship with social work, it goes on to set this in the context of policy and strategy developments. Some examples of community social work are assessed to review the extent to which this approach has been used to empower local communities.

Chapter Seven assesses the significance of working in a region with a land border to another country. It begins with a review of the development of cross-border cooperation and moves on to assess the role and influence of the statutory and voluntary sectors in promoting collaboration. It examines in some detail the focus for joint working and the ways in which services have developed, and identifies the key drivers and obstacles to cross-border social work.

Chapter Eight discusses how relatively high levels of social and economic deprivation have formed the backdrop to social work practice in Northern Ireland. It examines the particular features of deprivation and inequality in the region including persistent and severe child poverty, high levels of economic inactivity, low pay and poor mental health. After a review of the evidence for social need it critiques the policy responses to these issues and goes on to examine specific social interventions and the role of social work in social policy formulation.

Chapter Nine addresses the key issue of devolution and its impact on the design and delivery of social care. It considers the organisational position of social work in the system of governance and the role of quangos in the delivery of services. Key social work agendas of personalisation and user involvement are assessed through the spectrum of the impact of devolution. This chapter ends by commenting on the extent of divergence in policies and initiatives following devolution between Scotland, Wales and Northern Ireland. A comparison is also made between the proposals emerging in the three devolved administrations and in England for the future development of social work. Finally, Chapter Ten concludes.

Note

[1] The term 'country' is mainly used to describe Scotland, Wales and Northern Ireland, rather than other possible terms such as territory, region, nation, jurisdiction or sub-national unit. The term 'United Kingdom' refers to all four countries and the term 'Great Britain' to England, Scotland and Wales. The term 'social care' has come to be used in place of social work and social services, but in this book it is used mainly to denote a wider range of social care services than social work practice. In parts of the text describing historical developments, the older terminology 'personal social services' and 'welfare services' is referred to.

TWO

Historical context

This chapter provides a brief introduction to the history of Northern Ireland and outlines how this influenced the development of social policy. It sets out the long-established nature of devolved government and parliament and its impact on the development of social policy and the welfare state. Devolution was underpinned by the influence of the political landscape in Northern Ireland on the development of personal social services. Prior to 1976 it was the responsibility of the devolved government to determine social workers' roles and tasks and it is necessary to assess the extent to which the growth of the profession was similar to the rest of the UK. The development of adult services, family and childcare services, mental health services, community care, and health and social care structures is outlined and explained in the historical context.

The creation of Northern Ireland

The Northern Ireland government and parliament was established by an Act of the Westminster parliament, the 1920 Government of Ireland Act. This Act established a system of legislative devolution that was unique in the United Kingdom. The Northern Ireland government and parliament were constitutionally subordinate to the UK government, but in reality they had a significant degree of autonomy and independent powers. The genesis of a government for Northern Ireland has been extensively assessed and reviewed in a number of authoritative studies (Rose, 1971; O'Leary and McGarry, 1993) and a broad outline of the developments is sufficient here. Crucially the Government of Ireland Act meant that neither Northern Unionists nor Nationalists had achieved their core objectives. Indeed, as Oliver (1978) noted, there was hostility and opposition to these developments across the political spectrum.

To the Protestants/Unionists, the new settlement represented a second best, a barely acceptable substitute for continued integration with Britain. To the Roman Catholics/Nationalists/Republicans, it represented such a bitter disappointment, such a setback of their aspirations for a united Ireland, that they could not find it in their hearts to give their loyalty to it. Following partition, the new Northern Ireland parliament was designed with an in-built Unionist majority, producing the now infamous boast of the Prime Minister, James Craig, that it was 'a Protestant Parliament and Protestant State' (Craig, 1934). These divisive constitutional arrangements caused permanent disaffection amongst the Nationalist/Republican population, which lasted for 50 years until the Stormont parliament was prorogued and Direct Rule from Westminster was instituted.

The precise powers of the parliament were not actually stated in the legislation but what were specified were the powers that it did not have. Thus legislation and policymaking on topics such as income tax, foreign policy, defence and national insurance were outside its remit. It had limited financial powers with Britain able to control about 88% of its revenue and 60% of expenditure (Lawrence, 1965). The revenue available to the Northern Ireland government came from two sources; the vast majority (about 90%) was money from taxation collected throughout the United Kingdom, and the remainder was from local taxation. Caul and Herron (1992, p 40) assert that the conclusions of a Treasury Committee of 1925 (the Colwyn Committee) were of 'great significance' to social policy decisions. The remit of this committee was to establish an appropriate and legitimate basis for domestic expenditure. It recommended that the financial contributions to Northern Ireland should be based on the difference between revenue collected and the actual and necessary expenditure. This should not involve spending to develop unique services or services that were better than those in other regions of Britain. Given that the standard of public services in Northern Ireland was substantially lower, this decision forced them to remain at an inferior or similar level. In the period up to 1931, old-age pensions and unemployment insurance accounted for much of government social expenditure. This Colwyn formula was abandoned after 1932 as to retain it would have meant that the British Exchequer would have been forced to contribute more to spending in this area. Rising pressures on the unemployment benefits system in the 1930s led to special arrangements to keep benefits at British rates. It was not until the inception of the welfare state in the 1940s that Northern Ireland's underdeveloped social services would be more strongly resourced and developed. This was mainly achieved through a series of financial agreements between 1946 and 1949 to ensure parity of taxation and major services including a social services agreement covering health and related social services and providing for a UK subvention if necessary (Birrell and Murie, 1980). Thus the introduction of the welfare state was underpinned by a general parity principle enabling Northern Ireland to aim at the same standard of social services as the rest of the UK.

State welfare from 1921 to 1948

At the outset of the Northern Ireland government, the Prime Minister, Sir James Craig, made clear the commitment of his government to a welfare policy that was closely modelled on the system in Great Britain (Buckland, 1981). This so-called principle of parity has had a lasting impact on policy and practice and still informs the existing system of welfare development (Birrell and Heenan, 2010). According to Ditch (1988) the concept of parity is simultaneously elusive and elastic and, as such, open to a number of interpretations. Birrell and Murie (1980) suggest that the term can be understood to mean absolute uniformity, where standards in Northern Ireland are identical to those in Great Britain; it could refer to similarity, but not duplication; or, finally, it could imply similar, which is broadly comparable but flexible enough to allow for divergence and adaption to local needs.

A number of explanations and justifications have been forwarded to explain the developments in the post-war period of this principle of parity between Northern Ireland and Great Britain. First, under the terms of the 1920 Government of Ireland Act taxes were levied across the UK by the British government, and as all regions paid the same rates of taxes, all should be entitled to the same rate of benefits. Second, the Northern Ireland government was under pressure to provide the same level of benefits as in Great Britain, in order to retain the support of the Protestant working classes, many of whom were members of British trade unions. Third, to diverge from the principle of parity could have serious implications for the province, where any additional spending would have to be funded by the devolved administration. Lawrence (1965) at the time contended that there was evidence to support the notion that the Northern Ireland government viewed parity as an opportunity to address the relatively low standards of living and services. As time went on further measures have been introduced to interpret the parity principle to permit Northern Ireland to make up a substantial leeway in services (NIO, 1974).

The application of this principle of parity, however, was associated with a number of other consequences. Buckland (1981) suggests that simply following welfare developments in Great Britain had the consequence of stifling debate about working conditions, pay and levels of unemployment. The approach did not take cognisance of the inherent differences between Northern Ireland and Great Britain, where issues were often similar yet different. Additionally, it has been suggested that powerful elements of the Northern Ireland cabinet and civil service were ideologically opposed to increasing state intervention and the further development of social services (Buckland, 1981; Ditch, 1988). The parity principle meant that they were unable to contain what they viewed as the alarming expansion and cost of state welfare. The final argument against parity was that Northern Ireland was a relatively small, poor region and to automatically expect similar standards to Great Britain was simply unrealistic.

The system for the relief of poverty that the first Northern Ireland government inherited resembled the system in existence in Britain. However, there were some crucial differences (Evason et al, 1976). In the first decade of the 20th century a raft of new social legislation had been introduced to improve living standards and enable people to avoid the Poor Law. Before partition some UK measures applied to Ireland and some did not. The 1897 Workman's Compensation Act was extended to Ireland. However both the 1906 Education (Provision of Meals) Act and the 1907 Education (Administrative Provisions) Act, which dealt with medical inspection and treatment of schoolchildren, applied only to England and Wales. Ireland was included in the 1908 Old Age Pensions Act and the 1909 Labour Exchanges and Trade Boards Act. The 1911 National Insurance Act covered Ireland, with health and insurance programmes administered by Irish insurance commissioners in Dublin, but medical benefits were not available to Irish contributors.

The new Northern Ireland government inherited a system of social provision that was an odd mix of the old and the new, although based on UK trends. The services introduced in the first decades of the 20th century sat alongside a system of poor relief that had changed very little since the 1840s. The Irish Poor Law of 1838, based on the 1834 Poor Law Amendment Act, was almost entirely intact. The Irish Poor Law was less flexible and limited in scope than its English counterpart, with an Act of Parliament required to deviate from its rigid structure. Whilst the Poor Law Unions provided some outdoor relief, this was generally begrudgingly given and the workhouse test was applied until the 1940s. Provision under the Poor Law was financed by local rates and administered by local authorities who were reluctant to increase demands on local rate-payers. Whilst some in the new Northern Ireland government of 1921 wanted to reform the Poor Law and align existing services with Britain, little progress in this area was actually achieved. Despite the fact that the Minister of Home Affairs referred to the 'very necessary reform of the poor law system' (Lawrence, 1965, p 38), and a Departmental Commission had recommended significant reforms including the abolition of the Boards of Guardians and the workhouse system, the Poor Law system remained until 1948.

In relation to the rest of the island, Northern Ireland was relatively prosperous due largely to its thriving shipbuilding, engineering, linen and tobacco industries. However, in comparison to the remainder of the United Kingdom, average income was much lower and unemployment was much more severe. The depression of the interwar years was particularly harsh in Northern Ireland largely due to the decline in traditional industries such as shipbuilding, textiles and agriculture. Darby and Williamson (1978) note that Northern Ireland had relied on agriculture, textiles and shipbuilding for over a century and it was unfortunate for them that all three experienced simultaneous depressions in the post-war years. In the years 1925, 1931 and 1938 almost one quarter of the insured population of Northern Ireland was out of work. This economic crisis, combined with the inheritance of long periods of neglect and mismanagement of services, resulted in alarmingly high levels of need and distress. Providing assistance to unemployed people was neither straightforward nor automatic, and was surrounded by dispute, controversy and occasional violence (Evason et al, 1976).

Consequently, by the end of the 1920s levels of social need were markedly higher than in Britain whilst state provision was relatively underdeveloped. Figures from the *Report on the Administration of Local Government Services, 1928/29* (HMSO, 1929) illustrated the levels of need in Northern Ireland. Over the period of the previous five years, indoor relief within the workhouse system had been given to 5,000 people and outdoor relief to 5,500. By 1929 legislation in Britain had abolished Boards of Guardians and their functions were taken over by local authorities who in turn appointed Public Assistance Committees to administer the Poor Law. In Northern Ireland, a combination of Unionist political ideology and financial considerations meant that Poor Law reform was not on the agenda and consequently provision for unemployed people began to lag behind Britain.

This lack of parity is highlighted by Evason et al (1976, p 27) in a comparison of benefit levels in the late 1920s: in Leeds a man and his wife and four children could obtain a maximum of 31 shillings per week, the comparative figure for a family in Belfast was 24 shillings. Evason et al (1976, p 28) provide a revealing account of how this inadequate and highly stigmatised system of relief led to a series of pitched battles between the police and those in receipt of outdoor relief. It is worth noting that at this point there was also violence in many cities in Britain – only in Belfast, however, did the conflict reach such a pitch. In 1932 approximately 2,000 relief workers went on strike and the subsequent Outdoor Relief Riots attracted support from both Catholic and Protestant workers. This upheaval is outlined in detail by Devlin (1981), who suggests that it led to improvements in the system of allowances.

At the end of the interwar period, the Poor Law remained a central element in welfare provision. In 1938, 4,912 persons resided in workhouses overseen by Boards of Guardians. The general mixed workhouse had endured with little change for over a century. In this landmark year over 14,000 people were receiving outdoor relief. The Poor Law Guardians in Belfast controlled the use of the Poor Law system to meet their own social and political philosophy and interests. They were fundamentally opposed to state intervention and refused to use the principle of parity to keep in line with developments in Great Britain. Their view was that increasing levels of social intervention were causing distress to taxpayers and acting as a disincentive to work. Devlin (1981, p 1) suggests that for the first two decades of its existence the Northern Ireland government used the system of outdoor relief as a tool for religious and social discrimination:

> The social policy of the Northern Ireland government at the outset was directed towards forcing Catholics and Labour supporters to emigrate or reduce the size of their families by economic deprivation.

Whilst the Poor Law was abolished in Great Britain in 1928, it was maintained in Northern Ireland until 1939. Unlike the situation in Britain, where its development was affected by increasing public pressure to achieve social justice and relieve hunger, poverty and despair, in Northern Ireland it was viewed as an important weapon of social control.

Voluntary action

By the beginning of the 20th century voluntary work had become a feature of Irish society. A range of organisations, groups and individuals aimed to address poverty and to varying degrees also hoped to regularise and normalise the poor by addressing waywardness and enforcing their moral standards. Social work as a profession with its own standards and methods had not yet emerged and this type of intervention was almost entirely within the sphere of voluntary and religious organisations. Both Catholic and Protestant Churches had an impressive range of services including industrial schools, residential care, housing associations and temperance groups (Skehill, 1999). According to an official register of Dublin's charities, by 1902 there were over 400 separate organisations. A defining feature of these organisations was their religious underpinning and denominational basis. By far the largest organisation was the Society of St Vincent de Paul, a Catholic group whose aim was to relieve poverty and distress through a variety of means, including cash donations, clothing and home visits. This society was established by merchants and professionals who undertook a variety of fund-raising activities (Daly, 1984). Non-denominational organisations were relatively unusual as the absence of any religious affiliation caused difficulties with patronage and general support. In their comparative study of the voluntary sector, Acheson et al (2004, p 25) comment on the significance of religious affiliation:

> The development of voluntary action in Ireland was shaped both by Protestant philanthropy, particularly in the north, and by the emergence and triumph of Catholic social action throughout the island.

A considerable part of the work of voluntary organisations in Ireland was motivated by a Christian crusading zeal, or reflected assumptions that justified being paternalistic to the deserving poor and judgemental of those deemed undeserving (Caul and Herron, 1992). Fierce competition between the two main Christian Churches at the time often meant that religious organisations were motivated as much by proselytising as philanthropy. Notwithstanding the fact that the Catholic and Protestant organisations shared similar objectives, the range and types of services they provided varied. Catholic organisations provided a wide range of services, including long-term residential care for children, whereas Protestant organisations tended to provide specialist services to particular groups (e.g. the Belfast Female Mission and the Belfast Women's Temperance Association) and were more concerned with general social reform, often linked to wider social issues such as anti-slavery (Luddy, 1995). During this period, Christian values and principles became embedded within voluntary social work and these values remained central to social work up to and including the 1960s (Skehill, 1999). Fund-raising and administering charity was a core focus of the religious organisations, with a strong emphasis being placed on ensuring that resources went to those who were considered 'deserving' and would benefit from assistance and support.

A mix of poor administration, a lack of coordination and the laissez-faire attitude of the Unionist government led to fragmented and underdeveloped statutory social services. This lack of state provision meant that the voluntary sector played a central role in welfare, indeed philanthropy was the main mechanism for poverty relief in the first two decades after partition. In the face of overwhelming poverty and distress in the depression of the 1930s, an umbrella association, the Belfast

Council for Social Welfare, was established to coordinate the work of various charitable organisations and distribute food and money to the most needy. The appalling conditions endured by sections of the population became apparent during the operation to evacuate people from Belfast following the Blitz in 1941. The reaction of the Moderator of the Presbyterian Church vividly illustrates the shocking extent of deprivation and squalor:

> I never saw the like of them before – wretched people, very undersized and underfed, down and out looking men and women.... Is it credible to us that there should be such people in a Christian country? (Cited in Acheson et al, 2004, p 35)

During the Second World War, voluntary organisations increased the number and range of their activities. In response to a raft of war regulations and the introduction of new welfare regulations, the Belfast Council for Voluntary Welfare developed a Poor Man's Lawyer Service. In a similar vein the Northern Ireland Council of Social Service established the Citizens Advice Bureau and provided a number of other voluntary services (Ditch, 1988).

Founded in London in 1869, the Charity Organization Society (COS) had an important impact on social work through its advocacy and codification of emerging methods. This, with its focus on the family, and on a scientific approach, provided a key foundation for the development of social work as a profession in Britain. The establishment of COS was largely a response to the lack of cooperation between the various charities and agencies in many parts of Britain and Ireland. This not only led to duplication, but also involved what was seen at the time as inappropriate and indiscriminate alms-giving. It was felt that insufficient attention was given to examining the claims and needs of potential clients and charity was simply addressing the symptoms rather than the causes of poverty. COS developed links with like-minded societies and helped to establish similar agencies in different parts of Britain. Its emphasis on organisation and upon investigation, when linked to notions such as the deserving and undeserving poor, and the significance of individual responsibility, ignited considerable debate. As Madeline Roof (1972, p 23) has commented, 'few societies have inspired such devotion; few have roused such bitter hostility'. The establishment of the Belfast COS in 1906 was largely the result of an initiative by the Belfast Christian Civic Union, which was founded in 1903 with the aim of enhancing the community by the furtherance of social reform and civic purity. This was a typical example of a Protestant voluntary group based on joint action between the clergy and the local business community, which aimed to promote social and moral reform.

The Belfast COS was not primarily a relief-giving organisation; similar to other Charity Organization Societies, its main purposes were to coordinate the work of others and reduce unnecessary waste and duplication. It did not advocate simply giving money to those in need, but saw its role as training and advising poor people on ways to restore their independence. Their work was largely with dependent groups within the population such as children, widows and older people. They were particularly concerned about the welfare of children who were undernourished and living in abject poverty. Despite their limited resources they campaigned tirelessly for improvements in social conditions. This work involved lobbying politicians, writing letters to the press and organising public lectures. The annual reports illustrate the nature and extent of their work and highlight the levels of deprivation and distress. In his account of their work, Macbeath (1957, p 10) notes they 'even tackled what we today call "problem families"'. According to him, these were families who had become so demoralised that they were unable to manage their finances.

In anticipation of the new social order that was promised after the First World War, in 1919 the society broadened its remit and changed its name to the Belfast Council of Social Welfare. It envisaged an ambitious programme of social welfare that would effectively address the high levels of deprivation. Its role would be to advise on and critique the proposed social legislation although ultimately it was over 20 years before this programme materialised. The interwar years were marked by a period of intense activity including:

- the development of a Mutual Register of Assistance to facilitate the coordination of voluntary activities;
- the introduction of a tax rebate scheme on charitable donations;
- a programme of aftercare for those discharged from hospital;
- the provision of free legal advice and subsequently legal aid;
- the development of a subsidised housing scheme for those on low incomes;
- a placement scheme for boys leaving Borstal Institutions.

Significantly in terms of the development of social work it advocated and championed the need for professional training and recognition. As part of a basic staff development course, a lecture series was organised on various aspects of social work. Guest speakers from relevant agencies such as the Unemployment Assistance Board reflected on appropriate approaches. Innovative and creative approaches to learning led to the Belfast Council of Social Welfare becoming a recognised centre of study for those outside Northern Ireland who wanted practical social work placement opportunities (Macbeath, 1957). It urged the Queen's University of Belfast to develop a training course for social workers and proposed that the University should provide the theoretical base while the Council would coordinate and supervise the practical aspects of the course. A scheme was introduced initially on a trial basis and then became an integral part of the School of Social Studies. During and after the Second World War the Council maintained a close working relationship with the public authorities, drawing their attention to areas of need. Acheson et al (2004) argue that the establishment of the Belfast Council of Social Welfare marked the end of Victorian philanthropy and signalled the beginning of a new relationship between voluntary organisations and the emerging welfare state. Caul and Herron (1992) suggest that there were glimmers of recognition appearing in the new probation and almoners services of the need for a trained approach to social work.

Beginning of a probation service

When Northern Ireland was established in 1921, there were relatively few probation officers in existence. It was not a recognised profession and individuals were appointed on a part-time basis by resident magistrates and paid on a per capita basis for each individual under their charge. Spending in this area was negligible and developments lagged behind the English system. In 1928, in recognition of the progress in Great Britain, the local ministry introduced a new set of probation rules that set down minimum standards for contact between the probationer and the probation officer. However, probation was a minimal service and had low priority for almost a decade. The 1935 Summary Jurisdiction and Criminal Justice Act (Northern Ireland) gave the Ministry of Home Affairs the responsibility for appointing probation officers; however, their appointment was not compulsory. Increasing frustration at the lack of provision and progress in this area led to the minister replicating policy developments in England and establishing a committee to examine the system of welfare for young people and the treatment of young offenders in 1938. This committee became known as the Lynn Committee after its chairman Sir Robert Lynn. This represented a milestone in the area and has been described as the most significant assessment of the role and nature of probation in three decades (Fulton and Webb, 2009).

Whilst the system in England had been subject to a series of ongoing reviews and assessments, in Northern Ireland this had not been deemed necessary or appropriate. The report produced by the Lynn Committee in 1938 revealed the extent to which the service had been neglected and was little used and called for a major programme of modernisation and reform. By 1938, there were just 10 probation officers employed in Northern Ireland and half of these were based in Belfast. Significantly, all 10 were employed on a part-time basis as probation was still not considered appropriate for full-time employment. The report advocated that probation should be seen as a statutory rather than a voluntary activity associated largely with religious organisations and missionaries. The report set out a strategy for the development of an expanded professional service within the arena of criminal justice, largely influenced by developments in the probation system in England (O'Mahony and Chapman, 2007). The key recommendations of the Lynn report were:

- the appointment of full-time probation officers;
- probation areas were to be established across Northern Ireland each with its own overseeing committee;
- probation officers should be present at all juvenile courts;
- an appropriate balance of male and female officers should be sought;

- the introduction of formal training; as many of the issues were common, probation officers should follow the social work training model;
- local authorities should subsidise this training programme.

According to Caul and Herron (1992), there is no doubt that if the recommendations of the report had been fully implemented the probation service of Northern Ireland would have been dramatically improved and become more akin to its English counterpart. Unfortunately, though, there was little appetite for change in the relevant government departments, which were focused on the war effort, and probation remained underdeveloped and left in abeyance. The question of probation reform was not addressed again until 1948. The 1950 Probation Act was the first major legislation since 1907 and laid the basis for the modern probation service. Probation remained separate from the developing social services and was later administered from 1982 by a single quango, the Probation Board for Northern Ireland, largely separating criminal justice and welfare issues (O'Mahony and Chapman, 2007, p 161). However, the rather contrary decision was made that probation officers would take a professional social work qualification.

The role of the almoner service

In 1938 the Royal Victoria Hospital in Belfast appointed the first qualified almoner to work in a Northern Ireland hospital. This development marked the beginning of a social services department in the hospital. The term 'almoner' is one that was used by hospital social workers until their amalgamation with the British Association of Social Workers in 1964. It can be traced back to the monastic origins of the larger London hospitals where the almoner was the person designated to look after the sick and destitute. Initially almoners were referred to as 'lady almoners', presumably a reference to the assumption that the post-holders would be female. Training was not available in Northern Ireland and was provided by the Institute of Almoners in Great Britain. Discussions about this appointment were protracted with some debate as to whether or not this was the best way to spend the money of the hospital. The role of the almoner was to ensure that all patients benefited fully from the treatment prescribed, to act as a link between the hospital and outside agencies, to organise aftercare for the patient, to assess patients' ability to pay for care, and to prevent abuse of the hospital system. The liaison role that they performed was invaluable when many individuals were suffering from chronic poverty and deprivation under the Poor Law regime (Caul and Herron, 1992).

The outbreak of the Second World War in 1939 greatly expanded the role of the almoners, who took on the role of liaising with military organisations and servicemen. In 1948, in line with other areas of the UK, a Regional Committee was established. Boyd (1988) suggests that this development had significant implications for this small professional grouping. First, it facilitated the setting up of a selection committee that could interview potential students of the Institute of

Almoners and thereby ensure standards were maintained. Second, representation of the Regional Committee on the parent body in London gave many staff the opportunity to develop their knowledge in a national context. Boyd (1988, p 29) notes that 'this inevitably, reinforced professional identity and standards in the years 1948–69'. By July 1948 there were 11 almoners based in Belfast and by July 1950 this had increased to 26. In 1964 the Institute of Almoners changed its name to the Institute of Medical Social Workers, as it was assumed that this would enable a greater understanding and awareness of their role.

Establishment of the welfare state 1945–50

Following the Second World War social policy legislation introduced in Northern Ireland broadly followed in the footsteps of the coalition and Labour governments in London. However, as Ditch (1988) highlights, whilst the Northern Ireland government introduced the National Health Service, National Insurance, National Assistance, education and a number of other welfare-related laws, it would be inaccurate to suggest that this was simply an exercise in 'legislative plagiarism' as they were adapted to take account of the particular circumstances in Northern Ireland. He argues that the Stormont government developed a rather unique system of 'differential universality', which had the double attraction of reflecting the advantages of being part of the British welfare state and highlighting the inferior nature of welfare in the Republic of Ireland. The Northern Ireland government did not adopt wholesale the system of welfare devised by Beveridge. Instead they took the opportunity to develop a system embued with a distinctly Unionist flavour, reflecting their core values of minimal state intervention, conservatism and the protection of personal freedoms. Fahey and McLaughlin (1999) contend that there were three perceptible amendments to the welfare state that had more external impacts on the system of personal social services:

• First, access and entitlement to cash benefits were more stringently controlled. Restrictions introduced into the system were largely designed to prevent the movement of people from the South to the North in order to claim under this preferential system. Consequently, a residential qualification of five years out of the last 10 was introduced to 'safeguard against infiltration from Eire' (Fahey and McLaughlin, 1999, p 128). Particular controversy centred around the newly proposed system of Family Allowances, Unionist politicians were concerned that this would not only disproportionately advantage Catholics who had larger families, but that it would also act as an incentive for them to have more children. To address this, the Bill in Northern Ireland had originally proposed giving fourth and subsequent children less than their counterparts in Great Britain, but this was not proceeded with.
• Second, the administration of health services relied on a number of unelected centralised public bodies. These quangos, as they are now known, were made up of appointees from a range of professions who were thereby afforded the

opportunity to influence the design and delivery of social services. Two key new health bodies with executive power and administrative responsibilities were established. The first of these was the Northern Ireland Hospitals Authority, which was made up of 36 members appointed by the minister and was responsible for the provision of hospital and ancillary services. Effectively, then, all existing hospitals were centralised under this new authority. The General Health Services Board was responsible for General Practitioner Services, Health Centres and health education. The Board, appointed by the minister, was made up of a number of professional representatives and lay people.

• Third, lower levels of expenditure on family services meant their redistributive effects were lessened.

The 1946 Public Health and Local Government (Administrative Provisions) Act (Northern Ireland) was crucial to the emergence of distinctive welfare (social work) bodies, as it established a new administrative structure to undertake the functions of the Boards of Guardians. County and County Borough Councils were compelled to provide welfare authorities acting through statutory welfare committees. A welfare officer was to be appointed in each area and each council area was to assume the responsibilities of the Boards of Guardians. This restructuring was as a direct consequence of a raft of post-war legislation that set out a comprehensive system of social services (Caul and Herron, 1992).

Legislation relating to income maintenance largely mirrored the changes introduced in Great Britain. Consequently, the 1946 National Insurance (Industrial Injuries) Act (Northern Ireland) and the 1946 National Insurance (Northern Ireland) Act were similar to provision in Great Britain. Existing legislation relating to outdoor relief was jettisoned by the 1948 National Assistance Act. The Assistance Board was replaced by the National Assistance Board for Northern Ireland, whose objective was to assist those who had insufficient resources. As in Great Britain, eligibility was divided into three main categories:

• those experiencing contingencies outside the scope of the insurance scheme, that is, one-parent families (other than widows);
• those who could not meet the conditions attached to insurance benefits;
• those whose benefits required supplementation.

This National Assistance Act (Northern Ireland) was not, however, as comprehensive as its Great Britain counterpart and did not deal with welfare services. These were instead included in the 1949 Welfare Services Act for Northern Ireland. This key piece of post-war legislation repealed previous legislation dealing with indoor relief. The preamble to the 1949 Welfare Services Act sets out its terms of reference: essentially it was to replace the Poor Law and it placed a statutory duty on welfare authorities to make provision for a range of people in need, including 'handicapped, sick and aged persons'. Its main purposes were 'to substitute for the existing poor law relating to workhouse accommodation and relief, provision requiring welfare authorities to provide residential and other accommodation for certain persons in need thereof'. This Act marked the end of the Poor Law and was built upon by the provisions of the 1954 Welfare Services Act (Northern Ireland), which detailed arrangements for domestic assistance.

Another piece of post-war legislation that dramatically impacted on the expansion of social work was the 1950 Children and Young Persons Act (Northern Ireland). Up until this point the care of children in need had been largely undertaken by voluntary organisations and the extent and nature of problems were relatively unknown. Statutory provision in Northern Ireland was relatively underdeveloped as it had been decided not to introduce an equivalent to the 1933 Children and Young Persons Act (England and Wales). Residential homes for children were usually provided by religious organisations and government had neither the power nor the inclination to intervene (Caul and Herron, 1992). In 1950 the local government welfare committees had to dismantle the Poor Law and workhouse system whilst simultaneously creating a regime and culture of care for vulnerable children (DHSSPS, 2003a). The responsibility for the legislation was given to the newly established six county council and two county borough council welfare authorities with initial steps centred on establishing children's homes and providing staff training. This 1950 Children and Young Persons Act set out the circumstances in which a child would be deemed in need of care and protection. These were either:

1. that he had no parents, or parents unfit to exercise care or not exercising proper care and was falling into bad association, or exposed to moral danger, or beyond control; or
2. that he had been or was likely to be the victim of one of the offences noted in the Act, that is, maltreatment or neglect.

In effect, then, the Act introduced a double test in terms of protection. As well as evidence that the child was at risk, the child had to have parents who were unable or unwilling to provide proper care. Also of particular interest was the direction of travel in terms of residential care for vulnerable children. Section 90 of the Act clearly stated that residential care was to be considered as a last resort only when other options had failed. This commitment to fostering rather than residential care was very much in keeping with the ethos of the 1946 Curtis Committee, which marked a move away from institutionalisation and towards placements in family settings. Significantly, another feature of this Act was the decision that welfare authorities were to appoint Children's Officers to undertake and oversee these new duties.

Whilst the provisions enshrined in this Act represented a major advance in care for children in Northern Ireland, it was subject to similar criticisms made about the corresponding Great Britain legislation. It was claimed that the Act was reactive rather than proactive and that social workers should have been empowered to undertake preventative work, rather than simply having a role when children came into care. A second issue of concern was the necessity to prove both that the child was placed at risk deliberately and that the parents were culpable. As Evason et al (1976, p 146) noted, the underlying message was that the needs of parents were paramount:

> The assumption embodied in these provisions was not that the interests of the child were the most important consideration but that the parents could not be deprived of their rights unless found guilty in some sense.

The 1968 Children and Young Persons Act was significant as it placed a stronger emphasis on the prevention of family breakdown and giving due regard to the welfare of the child. In January 1976, Sir Harold Black was appointed to chair a review of the legislation and services relating to the treatment and care of young people. This report, usually referred to as the Black Report (HMSO, 1979), was progressive as it stressed the need to take cognisance of the wishes of the child and advocated fostering over residential care (DHSSPS, 2000).

Mental health services

During the 1930s, mental health policy in Northern Ireland was largely in step with legislation in Great Britain. In 1937 there were 5,295 patients in the six mental health hospitals and the overwhelming majority of these had been certified. These hospitals were funded through the rates system, but this proved insufficient to meet need in this area of healthcare. The outcome was poorly funded generic services with very few specialised facilities. By the end of the interwar period the need for reform in this area was urgent. The 1948 Mental Health Act (Northern Ireland) provided a single comprehensive Act for the range of mental health services. It distinguished between the mentally ill and mentally subnormal and detailed appropriate actions. Under this legislation the newly established Northern Ireland Hospital Authority (NIHA) was charged with developing services that ranged from settlement or resettlement in the community to institutionalisation; although, as Caul and Herron (1992) note, the NIHA somewhat predictably focused provision on hospital-based institutional care. There has been some discussion in the existing literature about the extent to which the Act marked a new understanding of the concept of mental illness and a move away from the regressive attitudes associated with the Poor Law. As Evason et al (1976, p 86) noted: 'With regard to mental deficiency in Northern Ireland, the 1948 Act, taken as a whole, put Northern Ireland ahead of Britain in its provisions and the thinking behind them.'

Caul and Herron (1992, p 80) suggest that whilst the Act contained a number of progressive measures that made treatment more flexible and increased the options for temporary care, some of the treatment methods were described as 'primitive'. In line with the recommendations of the Report of the Mental Health Services Advisory Committee (HMSO, 1948) the terminology used in the Act also appeared to signal a less stigmatised attitude towards mental illness. The development of a special care service aimed at a comprehensive service for people with learning disabilities also had the effect of establishing segregated services including education (DHSSPS, 2003a, p 139). By the late 1950s, welfare authorities had established mental health social work services, although it would be later before social work teams were offering support to children with disabilities and their families.

The 1949 Welfare Services Act brought together for the first time social work services for older people, people with disabilities, people with mental health problems and children and families. The services became the responsibility of local government welfare authorities and in the immediate post-war period were not very different in terms of policy and structures to Great Britain. It has even been argued that the organisation of welfare services had adopted a more unified comprehensive structure than in Great Britain (Birrell and Murie, 1980, p 256). Whereas in England and Wales local authorities after 1950 had to set up separate children's services, Northern Ireland's administrative structure was unified with other personal social services.

Social work education

Social work education and training developed alongside the development of social work services and the growth of public-sector provision. In the post-war period, it was recognised that there was a need for properly trained staff to carry out the functions. By 1948, there were some limited signs of the emergence of professional social work with the appointment of probation officers and medical and psychiatric social workers. Progress thereafter was slow and uneven (Rea, 2008) with a shortage of professional social workers in local authorities.

In the 1950s one social work education and training course existed in Northern Ireland – a two-year diploma in social studies at Queen's University Belfast, which had the status of a basic qualification in social work. The course adopted a generic approach to training reflecting the welfare authorities' role (DHSSPS, 2003a, p 173). Similar generic social work training was adopted in Britain following the Seebohm Report in 1968.

The Younghusband Report in Great Britain recommended that two-year generic programmes, known as Certificates in Social Work, should be established at colleges of further education. In Northern Ireland the first such course was established in the Rupert Stanley College of Further Education in 1964. The creation of this new qualification meant that there were three distinct types of training available to those interested in a career in this area:

- a two-year Diploma in Social Studies, taken at university and accepted as the basic qualification in social work (available from Queen's University Belfast from 1965);

- a postgraduate masters training programme taken at the New University of Ulster; and
- the new two-year Certificate in Social Work.

Rather than clarifying the professional requirements for social work these developments somewhat confused the issue, and it has been argued that it actually devalued the profession, as the two-year Certificate in Social Work became recognised as equivalent to the postgraduate qualification (Caul and Herron, 1992). It was not until 1968 that appointees to the post of Social Welfare Officer were required to hold a professional social work qualification. By the late 1960s, the number of professionally qualified social workers began to increase rapidly. For example, in 1965 the Belfast Welfare Authority employed just one professionally qualified social worker, but by 1971 this had risen to 22 with an additional 14 staff training for the qualification. Such was the expansion rate in the late 1960s that many social workers were recruited from Dublin universities. More recently, the qualification requirement was extended to other statutory sector social work posts, including Education Welfare Officers.

Conclusion

The historical development of social work in Northern Ireland demonstrates a number of trends. The emergence of social work as a public service largely followed a similar pattern to Britain from origins in the voluntary sector and the post-war welfare state. Considerable leeway with Great Britain had to be made up given the political conservatism of pre-war governments to developing state welfare services. Its actual development was influenced by close links with the health sector and the development of the probation service. Post-war decisions took it in the direction of a unified personal social service within local government. This was accompanied by a generic approach to the role of social workers and their training.

The development of social work took place within the specific political system of devolved government, and a government controlled by the Ulster Unionist Party, which set a politically conservative ethos, as a background. This had some impact on social work practice, for example, the 1970 Chronically Sick and Disabled Persons Act was markedly less extensive than its English counterpart. However, there was a strong trend to follow British policy and legislation fairly closely, even if there was a time lag, for example, the 1968 Children and Young Persons Act mirrored the1963 Children and Young Persons Act in Britain. It is worth noting that social work policies and practices were not particularly responsive to specific 'Northern Ireland problems'. In contrast though, the development of probation in the 1970s and 1980s was strongly influenced by the ongoing Troubles. The reorganisation of local government in 1972 which resulted in the integration of health and social services represented the most notable departure from the British system of welfare.

THREE

Sectarianism and social work

Sectarianism has been identified as a unique factor influencing social work practice in Northern Ireland. Higgins and Brewer (2003) offer a discussion of the meaning of sectarianism, referring to behaviour, types of treatment and policies informed by religious differences leading to prejudiced attitudes, pejorative beliefs, discrimination and intimidation. In relation to social work, the term has been used in several different ways with different meanings, and these have not always been clearly articulated in academic, professional or government documentation and discussion. Thus it is possible to distinguish between several different meanings of sectarianism: (1) the expression of sectarian attitudes and hostility to a religious group or perceived members of a group; (2) discrimination against a religious group in the allocation of goods or services and subordination and power relations between religiously identifiable groups; (3) the identification of the state of Northern Ireland as sectarian; (4) the identification of sectarianism with segregation; (5) the identification of sectarianism with paramilitarism; (6) the prevalence of sectarian values; and (7) the linkage of sectarianism and anti-oppressive practice.

The impact of sectarian attitudes

In some ways the clearest definition of sectarianism is expressed as religious bigotry, meaning antagonism and hostility by members of one community in Northern Ireland towards the other. This moves beyond the narrowness of differences based on religious affiliation and perceived religious identity to alignment with national, cultural and neighbourhood identity. Sectarianism finds expression in different formats and can impact through individual attitudes and actions in relation to social work practice. The interpersonal relationship dimension to the practice of social work can be subject to sectarian influences and it is possible to distinguish a number of contexts for this:

1. *General sectarian views of clients/users.* Social workers may frequently encounter the expression of sectarian views, not directed at them personally, but in terms of antagonism, general negativity, prejudice, stereotyping, expressions of relative deprivation or in terms of fear and distrust. Such views can also be expressed more in terms of identity with one religion, culture or identity (Traynor, 1998).
2. *Sectarian hostility to social work staff.* A component of interpersonal relationships in Northern Ireland can be identifying or telling which community a person belongs to. This can often be an issue for clients/users and may create dilemmas if a social worker is perceived as coming from 'the other side'. Potentially

this can be such a dilemma that social workers may take action to hide their community identity (Traynor, 1998, p 38). Determining the identity of the social worker(s) may in some instances lead to discomfort or tension in the relationships or to extremes of outright hostility or abuse. A further context lies in the nature of the social work workforce, which has traditionally been predominantly Catholic and female. In one of the few pieces of research, Campbell and McCrystal (2005) found a high level of exposure of Catholic social workers to Troubles-related issues, but when asked to rank Troubles-related problems, sectarian harassment was ranked third overall, and was only ranked first by 6% of respondents. In the study the term covered organisational as well as individual sectarian harassment.

3. *Sectarian relationships between social workers in the workplace.* There is little evidence on this issue other than at the height of the Troubles when particularly violent incidents created the potential for tension, although this would have been common to most workplaces in Northern Ireland. This may also have encouraged the practice for work to continue without raising controversial, sectarian or political issues.

4. *The possible sectarian attitudes of social workers.* The large majority of social workers in Northern Ireland have been educated and socialised in a divided society so the question has been posed as to whether social work staff may also have acquired sectarian attitudes. Campbell and McCrystal (2005) and Campbell (2007) note the particular difficulties faced by social workers.

Sectarianism and discriminatory practices

A report from the Central Council for Education and Training in Social Work (CCETSW) in 1994 defined sectarianism as discrimination based on the grounds of religion (Gibson et al, 1994). The issue of religious discrimination was a major issue in Northern Ireland after the 1960s. In the case of social work this would have related to evidence concerning either discrimination in employment and/or in the allocation and delivery of services. In practice there have rarely been allegations of discrimination in social work employment or services. While it has been suggested that the reorganisation of social work in 1969–72 was to eradicate discriminatory biases in the existing local government system (Smyth and Campbell, 1996, p 82), this was not actually a reason or objective for setting up Health and Social Services Boards as quangos.

Social work representing a sectarian state

This is a perspective of social workers as agents of an illegitimate state and tends to refer to the perception of the nationalist community of the Northern Ireland state. Smyth and Campbell (1996, p 81) argue that the relationship between social work in Northern Ireland and sectarianism can best be explained by reference to the development of the state. Sectarianism is culturally reproduced within the context of the particular formation of the state, which creates and maintains conditions permissive of its reproduction. Garrett (1999) suggested that child protection and domestic violence tasks in social work in Northern Ireland had a distinctive characteristic because of the Catholic population not accepting the legitimacy of the state; although no empirical evidence is presented to support these assertions. Conceptually the idea of the Northern Ireland state is complex as it involves a devolved state and government and not a sovereign state. It has been argued that during the Troubles, when some communities felt alienated from the state, social workers, as agents of the state, were still able to go about their work in these communities and their role was accepted (Martin, 2008, p 7). The question of the legitimacy of the state has changed as well with the Good Friday Agreement and the Irish government's involvement in government structures in Northern Ireland. There is very little evidence for the view that statutory social services were historically seen as sectarian in the sense of lacking legitimacy.

Sectarianism as segregation

In this interpretation sectarianism is closely equated with a segregated society. Segregation impacts on social work in several ways. The most immediate impact is a consequence of residential segregation, particularly in disadvantaged areas. The degree of residential segregation grew in the 1970s after the outbreak of civil disturbances, but then rose more slowly in the 1980s (Doherty and Poole, 1997) and remained approximately at its 1991 level through to 2001, according to census analysis (Shuttleworth and Lloyd, 2009).

It is estimated that 35–40% of the population live in neighbourhoods divided along ethno-sectarian lines (Hughes et al, 2007), but in social housing provided by the Northern Ireland Housing Executive (NIHE) or housing associations, the degree of segregation is much higher. Using a measurement of having more than 10% Protestant or Catholic in an estate, just 29% were deemed to be integrated (Murtagh, 2001). Using a measurement of 20%, the figure drops to only 9% of estates integrated. Segregation also varies by geographic locality with Belfast, Derry and North Armagh having the highest rates. The most outward signs of segregation are most acute in areas of Belfast where some 40 peace walls exist as physical barriers in interface areas between Protestant and Catholic territories. Shirlow and Murtagh (2006) calculate that one third of politically motivated murders were committed within 250m of an interface. Despite the peace process the number of peace walls doubled in the 13 years between 1995 and 2008. The peace walls offer protection against attacks by the other side and promote feelings of safety for the local communities, but stand as monuments to the intensity of communal divisions.

There is a tendency for people in segregated areas to use only social care facilities such as day centres in their area and there is a chill factor deterring travel or use of services in other areas. A study of residents of interface areas found that 75% refused to use the closest facility because of the location, while 82% routinely travelled further to safer areas (Shirlow and Murtagh, 2006). On the other hand, in some locations facilities are used on a cross–community basis without difficulty and hospital location also does not normally produce major problems of access.

The actual consequences of segregation for social work provision have not really been researched. In some areas social workers are working in wholly Catholic or wholly Protestant areas. However, social workers and local offices may operate across segregated estates and areas. One significant consequence was the need to duplicate services because of segregation. An unpublished consultants study in 2007 estimated the cost of duplicating good facilities and services as totalling £1.5 million. The extent of segregation can also produce a dynamic to sustain sectarian attitudes, fears and antagonism given the lack of inter-group contact and integration (Jarman, 2005). A research study on health care found that the level of segregation did not help to explain variations in the use of acute and elderly services, but did explain variations in anxiety (French, 2009).

Although over 90% of pupils attend segregated schools, the implications of segregated education for social work are not so obvious. Northern Ireland has not developed a social work in schools strategy as in Scotland, and there is limited link–up between early years education and early years social care as in Britain. The *Every Child Matters* agenda and the creation of a children's trusts structure have not been copied. However, the main reasons for the divergence from policies in Great Britain are not related to segregated schools.

One other aspect of a segregated society relevant to social work provision is the nature of divisions in the voluntary sector and their relationships to the two main communities. A major research study (Acheson et al, 2007) found that the sector remained substantially structured along communal lines: 74% of organisations had management committees or boards of directors that were either wholly or mainly from one community. At the same time the voluntary and community sector has been the focus of major initiatives aimed at improving community relations and building bridges. Acheson et al (2007) reported that over 90% of respondents said their organisation provided opportunities for people to work together and to cooperate on common tasks. Many voluntary organisations provide services for all sections of the community, especially the larger ones, for example, Barnardo's, Save the Children, St Vincent de Paul and the Salvation Army, most of which would have mixed workforces. Acheson et al (2007, p 46) found either no major awareness or an avoidance of the implications for voluntary and community workers of the broader problem of ethnic and sectarian divisions in society, although the majority acknowledged their work was affected by communal divisions.

Some of the issues of residential segregation again impacted on the operation of community groups, for example, in the duplication of services/offices/ organisations. Community groups are likely to be based in a location that is clearly identifiable as occupied by one community although some aim at a neutral or shared space. At the same time activities of some groups, such as early years groups, may actually be based on church premises but draw cross-community support. Historically, in Northern Ireland, Churches have played a significant role in social work provision, although not as large a role as in the Republic of

Ireland. The major involvement has been in Church-run residential homes for children, with more limited provision for older people and some support for disadvantaged families.

Sectarianism and paramilitarism

Paramilitary organisations are able to exercise degrees of control over many local neighbourhoods, usually working-class social housing estates. This can arise in both communities and this is further complicated on occasions of change of paramilitary organisation in control within a local area, sometimes after local turf wars. Paramilitary activity relates to criminal and anti-social behaviour and consequently may involve more specialist areas of social work and the probation service. The effect on more general social work is more limited, but there can be issues of access and freedom to operate. Paramilitarism at times caused difficulties for social work practice on such estates. There were reports of social workers requiring police escorts and, at the height of the Troubles in some areas, army escorts as well.

It is also a reality that in many estates community associations are either controlled by or have an uneasy relationship with paramilitary groups (Acheson et al, 2007, p 63). Participation in politically motivated offences by paramilitaries was to have major consequences for the probation service. Probation officers were trained alongside social workers, gaining the same qualification, but the service was administered separately through a quango, since 1982, the Probation Board. In 1975 the National Association of Probation Officers developed a policy on politically motivated offenders that enabled probation officers to resist preparing court reports on people who had committed offences for political purposes and supervising them on statutory orders (Chapman, 1998). This was intended to preserve professional integrity, avoid political manipulation and establish neutrality and personal safety. This approach enabled prison welfare departments to operate and later form partnerships with local community groups. This stance has been criticised as meaning probation officers did not challenge sectarianism in the community or the criminal justice system (O'Mahony and Chapman, 2007, p 166).

Sectarian values

It is possible to identify values that pertain to the religious beliefs and cultural, social and ethical views of the two communities. These do form a context for the formulation and delivery of social care. In some respects these values differ between the two communities, although in other respects they may be in accord, yet differ from the dominant values in Great Britain. Thus a contrast has been drawn between the individualist values of Protestantism and the more communitarian approaches of Catholicism, which has meant comparatively fewer community development groups in the Protestant community (Acheson et al, 2007, p 27).

The British Abortion Act has not been extended to Northern Ireland, and abortion is regulated by 19th-century legislation that permits abortions in only very restricted circumstances. The uncertainties around the interpretation of abortion law have been the subject of much debate (Lee, 1995). There are fewer than 100 legal abortions performed each year, which means that women from the region seeking abortion have little option but to travel to Britain, where they cannot avail themselves of the NHS. Research on the experiences of women travelling for abortions has highlighted the stress, expense and the difficulties of accessing appropriate aftercare (Smyth, 2006). There is a strong anti-abortion ideology supported by all the main Churches and by the majority of political representatives. It is also the case that so confusing is the exact meaning of the 19th-century legislation that the Department of Health, Social Services and Public Safety has had difficulty drawing up policy guidelines. This can cause dilemmas about the advice that can be given by social workers. The acceptance of sectarian values also has an impact on fostering and adoption practices and has influenced the large proportion of children in care who have 'mixed', that is, cross-community, parents.

Agency approaches of neutrality and avoidance

Most social work agencies' responses to sectarianism or expressions of concern tend to take the form of assertions of a neutral/non-sectarian approach. This encompasses a non-confrontational approach and a non-political approach, as acting otherwise might cause risks to the client, the worker and the agency (Traynor, 1998, p 40). Thus, social workers largely found ways to ensure services were delivered in spite of the surrounding violence in some areas and overall political instability. Referring to children's services, McQuade (2001) identified a reluctance to acknowledge the prevalence of sectarianism or that a problem existed. An immediate reaction was the denial of sectarianism in agency attitudes or operations.

The other response has been seen as an emphasis on technological and managerial approaches. It has been suggested that, after 1972 under Direct Rule with a system of quangos, there was a technically competent approach, though one less likely to be helpful in addressing sectarianism (Pinkerton and Campbell, 2002). There has been an increased outsourcing of services such as domiciliary care to the independent sector, which may be less inclined to address training needs. Welfare voluntary organisations have also been seen as displaying a tendency to adopt an ideology of need that denies the relevance of communal divisions (Acheson et al, 2007, p 45). Agency managers and the government-appointed members of the Boards and Trusts (quangos) also tended to wish to avoid references to the influence of sectarianism, a response often defended as a 'neutral position'. The local branch of the British Association of Social Workers was also reluctant to focus strongly on such issues. The outcome can be seen as a denial at delivery level of the need for anti-sectarian practices.

Response of educators and trainers

The articulation of concerns about the impact of sectarianism on social work in Northern Ireland in the mid-1990s did lead to connections being made to the development of anti-racist, anti-discrimination and anti-oppressive practice agendas in Britain. At the time this emphasised disadvantage, discrimination and subordination. Clearly levels of widespread disadvantage could be identified in Northern Ireland. Definitions of sectarianism that were used in Northern Ireland frequently covered discrimination, but the application of subordination could imply a further dimension. Thus a system of subordination can be identified and challenging sectarianism in Northern Ireland was seen as relating to challenging sexism or racism.

The establishment of connections between anti-racist, anti-oppressive or anti-discrimination practice and anti-sectarianism led to a more important change in practice. As anti-racist and anti-oppressive training in the 1990s in social work in Great Britain developed, the call arose for this to be translated into anti-sectarian training for social workers in Northern Ireland (Smyth and Campbell, 1996). This stimulated a debate about sectarianism and social work training. Innovative, anti-sectarian training in social work unfolded in a context of a lack of guidance and research and unpredictable reactions from students (Smyth, 1994).

The CCETSW had been developing anti-racist and anti-discriminatory practice in Great Britain and its remit did include Northern Ireland. In 1999 it produced guidelines, *Getting off the Fence, Challenging Sectarianism in Personal Social Services: Standards of Good Practice* (CCETSW, 1999). This argued: that organisations should produce written policies on practices that challenged sectarianism; that organisations should have management structures and systems that promote practice to challenge sectarianism; that planning and commissioning should be free from sectarianism; that fair employment should be encouraged; that organisations should have an established identity that challenges sectarianism at the core of its values; and that staff should be trained and supported to understand and respect differences in culture and ideology. In relation to training, it was acknowledged that it had been slow to develop the guidelines and recommended further training to challenge sectarianism for staff at all levels in vocational, qualifying and post-qualifying training and through in-service training.

In 2001, after the establishment of a Northern Ireland Social Care Council (NISCC), a programme of radical reform for social work education and training was introduced. The overall framework specification identified six key roles for social workers: assessing needs and circumstances, planning and evaluating social work practice, supporting individuals, representing their needs, managing risk, managing their practice and demonstrating professional competence (NISCC, 2003). However, relatively little of the detailed material identified for knowledge and understanding refers to sectarianism or anti-oppressive practice or the consequences of the Northern Ireland conflict. The framework specification for the degree in social work did acknowledge that the impact of past and current violence, conflicts, and divisions in Northern Ireland society requires particular emphasis in the education and training of social work students.

Curriculum guidance entitled *The Northern Ireland Context* (NISCC, 2005) was produced, which had the aim of helping students understand the nature of social work services in a diverse society with reference to institutional discrimination including sectarianism, disempowerment and anti-oppressive practice. It noted that views about the conflict were contested and also aimed at preparing students to work with individuals in communities dealing with the consequences of conflict. However, unlike the commitment to an anti-sectarian perspective, it was noticeable that the approach was broadened to stress the importance of educators assisting students in examining issues from a range of perspectives, and stating that it was important not to claim certainty or longevity for any particular understanding. The curriculum guidance simply listed topics under the headings of historical and political, legal (meaning government), organisational (meaning policy, social, cultural and sociological contexts) and the psychological and personal context. This amounts to a somewhat idiosyncratic grouping of topics with little attention to social policy analysis, the impact of devolution, research and evaluation, or social care modernisation.

The specific guidance issued by the NISCC for social care workers, employers, practice learners and education providers has not particularly highlighted anti-sectarianism. In the codes of practice for social care workers and employers of social care workers there is only a very brief reference to 'processes and procedures to challenge and report dangerous, abusive, discriminatory or exploitative behaviour and practice' (NISCC, 2002). The standards for practice learning for the degree in social work contain statements that include a reference to course providers being 'committed to providing and respecting equal opportunities, human rights and anti-oppressive practice in all respects of practical learning' (NISCC, 2009). In practice, training for anti-sectarianism came to be redefined within the wider agenda of anti-discrimination and equality measures and good relations strategies.

Anti-discriminatory measures

Since the 1970s, a series of mainly legislative initiatives have been introduced in Northern Ireland to combat discrimination on religious and political grounds. These measures were not aimed specifically at social work or social care although they did have some impact. The establishment of the Northern Ireland Housing Executive saw the introduction of a single social housing points and selection scheme, new social house-building, and strategies to tackle unfitness and homelessness, although there was not a drive to end residential segregation in social housing.

Action to investigate individual allegations of discrimination in public employment rested with an ombudsman office, entitled the Commissioner for Complaints. The establishment of a separate Fair Employment Agency in 1976 meant that the Commissioner ceased to investigate allegations of religious or political discrimination. In practice very few cases involving social services had come to the attention of the Commissioner of Complaints. The Fair Employment Agency was a unique innovation in the UK set up to counter religious discrimination in both the public and private sector with wide-ranging powers of investigation, conciliation and enforcement. Individual investigations continued and the small number of cases relating to social services employment concerned clerical/manual posts rather than professional posts (Fair Employment Agency for Northern Ireland, 1989). This agency could also review patterns and trends in employment and, unlike the Commission for Racial Equality in Great Britain, did not have to have a belief that discrimination existed before holding an investigation (Osborne, 2007). The Western Health and Social Services Board was investigated in 1988, but the Fair Employment Agency was satisfied that both Protestants and Catholics had equal chances of successful job applications.

Fair employment was enhanced in 1989 with the establishment of a new body, the Fair Employment Commission. A key innovation was the maintenance of a register of all employers with more than 25 employees, reduced to 10 employees from 1992. The Fair Employment Commission could also review patterns and practices in employment and issue directives requiring employers to engage in affirmative action and also set goals and timetables. The Commission monitored employment in health and social care and by 1995 the composition of the health and social care sector was 49.8% Protestant and 41.5% Catholic. Since 1990 there had been an overall increase in the Roman Catholic share by 2% (Fair Employment Commission, 1995).

Following the employment initiatives, other initiatives were taken in relation to gender, disability and racial equality, largely based on British models. Just before the restoration of devolution, a new government White Paper (NIO, 1998) recommended a unified equality commission bringing together existing separate commissions dealing with fair employment, gender, disability and race, one argument being that a unified body would bring equality considerations more into the mainstream. These developments became part of the peace process and the Good Friday Agreement and a new Equality Commission for Northern Ireland (ECNI) came into operation in 2000, some seven years before the equality bodies in Britain were unified in the Equality and Human Rights Commission. The Northern Ireland Human Rights Commission was set up as a separate body from the Equality Commission.

In 1998 anti-discrimination measures in employment were extended to goods, services and facilities and monitoring regulations were extended to cover part-time workers. Empirical evidence showed that the overall position of Catholics in the labour market had improved substantially since the 1970s, especially in the public sector (Osborne, 2003). Direct discrimination had declined and workplaces were less sectarian. Pressure to strengthen and extend anti-discriminatory measures coincided with the political negotiations leading to the Good Friday Agreement and that was to contain a major initiative on equality of opportunity. Section 75 of the 1998 Northern Ireland Act required all public bodies to have regard to the need to promote equality of opportunity between nine categories: people of different religion, political opinion, racial group, age, marital status or sexual orientation; men and women generally; persons with a disability; and between persons with and without dependants. Public authorities are required to conduct equality impact assessments and construct an equality scheme, to be approved by the Equality Commission. They also have to produce equality impact assessments for significant new policies or changes in policy. The core of the new policy was to identify adverse impacts on the nine designated groups.

Initial assessments highlighted the potential of these innovative provisions as a significant development in anti-discriminatory practice (McCrudden, 2001) and as a contribution to promoting and mainstreaming equality of opportunity (Harvey, 2001). Section 75 requirements applied to all health and social care statutory bodies. The equality schemes produced by social care boards, trusts and other bodies mainly contain only a description of a process, while some general statements, such as targeting social care on the most vulnerable and needy, or ensuring decision-making is sensitive to local people and communities, are somewhat removed from the implementation of equality of opportunity. Equality impact assessments of social care policy and provision have tended to be narrow and descriptive, often only describing employment statistics by religion and gender and rarely using wider evidence or policy analysis. Some more relevant material was analysed at times, for example, evidence on higher or lower uptake of services by different groups. The overall approach in social care did not differ greatly from the public sector as a whole and, as Osborne (2003) has noted, the process was intensely bureaucratic rather than outcome-oriented, even diverting resources from front-line services. The whole approach was later described as diligent but unimaginative (Dickson and Osborne, 2007), and resulting in 'tick-box' practices (McLaughlin, 2007).

The ECNI commissioned a major review and evaluation of Section 75. The final report (ECNI, 2007) stated that the intention was to place equality of opportunity at the core of public policymaking and create profound and radical change in the implementation of policy. This review of Section 75 acknowledged that equality schemes were not outcome-oriented and the current focus had not addressed how inequalities could be reduced or removed. There were also comments that the impact of 'high-level policy' was not assessed. Section 75 has been successful in raising awareness of the equality agenda and the importance given to it. However, equality impact assessments were often limited and treated as an additional appendix rather than mainstreamed into the policy analysis. In practice almost the same statutory equality rules were introduced in England, Scotland and Wales, and Northern Ireland began to fall behind practice in the rest of the UK. Plans stalled on reaching agreement in the Executive and Assembly on a new single equality Bill while the proposals in Great Britain moved ahead. Equality impact assessments produced in Britain, for example on the Adult Social Care Bill, became much more comprehensive than in Northern Ireland, and were based on research and academic work. The ECNI has revised its guide to statutory duties and compliance frameworks to focus work more on auditing outcomes. The restructured emphasis of the Section 75 duty is clear in the definition in the guide: 'to make improvements in the screening of policies and shift the focus towards achieving measurable outcomes' (ECNI, 2010, p 5).

Post-1988: The good relations strategy

The third strand of anti-sectarianism since devolution is based on good relations or community relations. Section 75 of the 1998 Northern Ireland Act also required public bodies to 'have regard to the desirability of promoting good relations between persons of different religious belief, political opinion or racial group'. The legislation did not define 'good relations'. The ECNI, again, had the role of overseeing this duty and defined good relations rather generally as promoting 'respect, equity and trust and embrace diversity' (ECNI, 2006, p 9). The main non-governmental organisation responsible for promoting good relations, the Community Relations Council, has taken a stronger definition: 'good relations challenges sectarianism and racism, promotes equality, develops respect for diversity and raises awareness of the interdependence of the people and institutions within Northern Ireland' (Community Relations Council, 2004, p 7).

In 2006, the Equality Commission reviewed progress on the good relations duty and included detailed examples of practice from health and social care bodies in their documentation (ECNI, 2006). A number of bodies responsible for social care did report commitments to the principles of anti-sectarianism. The Eastern Health and Social Services Board, which covers Belfast, had a strategy to promote respect for diversity and challenge sectarianism and racism in both employment and services. Posters carrying the board's good relations strategy were designed for display at all Trust facilities. Within the Eastern Board, the North and West Belfast Trust was responsible for social care in the urban area with the most interfaces and history of sectarian violence. In 2003–04 it identified the need for the delivery of anti-racism, anti-sectarianism and cultural awareness training to staff, particularly front-line staff, and support for staff delivering services in areas of tension or that are unsafe (ECNI, 2006, p 64). Most of the examples of good practice in this review related to training and staff induction. The South and East Belfast Trust had developed practices to help staff deal with professional experiences, for example when a client wanted their social worker changed to one of the same religious persuasion.

Good relations practice was also seen as covering partnership working with groups in the community and voluntary organisations. The Probation Board included good relations as part of the criteria for eligibility to secure the Board's community development funding. One Trust reported an agreement with local residents on the contentious issue of the flying of flags on Trust facilities. However, some health and social care bodies acknowledged the complexities and challenges of the good relations issues and the difficulties associated with progressing the agenda (ECNI, 2006, p 59). The North and West Belfast Trust noted its continuing experience of major tensions across interfaces and also within communities at times. The Trust continued to state that sectarian issues were its main priority as they had a continuing impact on staff and methods of working.

Anti-racism

The ECNI review found, somewhat to its surprise, more reporting of race relations initiatives than work on religious belief or political opinion (ECNI, 2006, p 13). In 2003 a document *Racial Equality in Health and Social Care: Good Practice Guide* (ECNI, 2003) was published by the Equality Commission plus a further guide on *Embracing Diversity* (ECNI, 2005) aimed at helping staff who are the victims of racism. The race relations initiatives in social care consisted mainly of low-key activities, for example, interpreting services, multicultural handbooks, a helpline, an emergency multilingual guide, overseas staff in health and social care visiting schools, and a minority ethnic care handbook. Surprisingly, little of the activity in health and social care is based on research. Unusually, the Western Health Action Zone carried out a project that examined the experiences of black and minority ethnic people in accessing services. One subdivision of anti-racism work is more particular to Northern Ireland. The definition of racial groups in the legislation includes the Irish Traveller community. There have been a range of initiatives relating to the needs of Travellers including a Southern Area Action Plan for Travellers. Such work ranges from cultural awareness to early years and after-school provision, to mental health and care of young mothers. The Department of Health and Social Services and Public Safety (DHSSPS) specification of action for the implementation of a racial equality strategy and the elimination of racial inequality was heavily focused on Travellers (OFMDFM, 2006a). Interestingly, though, it has been claimed that despite the mainstreaming of Traveller equality issues in Northern Ireland, little has actually been delivered in terms of justice for Travellers (McVeigh, 2007).

How does one explain this focus on anti-racism? It is true that racism came late as an issue in Northern Ireland. A Race Relations Order was passed only in 1995 and the Commission for Racial Equality for Northern Ireland was established only in 1997, and there were no ethnic questions in the 1991 Census. Discussion and consideration of anti-racist practice among social work providers was very limited before the late 1990s (Yu, 1998). The following years saw a large influx of European migrants amounting to perhaps 40,000. There have, however, been major incidences of hate crime in Northern Ireland, including some cases given a high profile by the media. In 2005 the Northern Ireland Affairs Committee in the House of Commons had drawn attention to the increase in hate crime, up from 93 incidents in 1998 to 455 in 2004, and called the statutory response disjointed and the police clear-up rate low (Northern Ireland Affairs Committee, 2005). There has been continuing pressure to develop stronger anti-racist strategies. However, it can be suggested that the other reason for the focus on anti-racist strategies in social care good relations planning is that they are easier to find a consensus on and copy from existing practice in Great Britain than are anti-sectarian strategies.

Anti-oppressive practice

The principle of anti-oppressive social work practice has survived in Great Britain and often is used as an umbrella term, with a shift from anti-racist practice to anti-oppressive practice, and covers all forms of discrimination on grounds of gender, sexuality and disability, as well as race and religion (Laird, 2008). Thompson (2006) developed the idea that discrimination could occur at different levels, personal, cultural and structural, while Dominelli (2002) has expanded on the multiple oppressions that may affect an individual and sees anti-oppressive practice as a legitimate concern of social work. The anti-oppressive practice ideology has also extended to a number of areas, to discrimination on grounds of class or socio-economic divisions, to oppression on grounds of powerlessness, and exclusion and control by social workers. Alongside this there has been an emphasis on the values of social justice, rights and empowerment.

The anti-oppressive practice thesis has continued with much support, despite challenges from new agendas of user participation and personalisation. Miller (2008) has pointed out the dissonance between the prolonged ascendance of anti-oppressive discourse but the practical reality of a regulatory form of practice that is one of the major characteristics of social work in the UK. The majority of social workers and managers in Northern Ireland may be seen as not adopting a radical, critical or political approach. A similar lack of radicalism or silence on anti-oppressive practice also dominates decision-making on the boards of health and social care trusts. It has been argued (Miller, 2008) that anti-oppressive ideas were of their time and increasingly have been surpassed or subsumed by other agendas. In Northern Ireland at present the term 'anti-oppressive practice' is little used outside of social work education. To an extent, anti-discrimination approaches in social work in Northern Ireland have been absorbed into the Fair Employment and Equality (statutory duties) requirements of promoting equality of opportunity.

At the same time, much of the anti-sectarian agenda has been absorbed into the good relations strategies as promoted by: Section 75 of the 1998 Northern Ireland Act; the Government Good Relations Strategy of 2006 (which is due for updating); and guidance from the Northern Ireland Community Relations Strategy. In this context social work approaches can be summarised as follows:

- a legalistic approach to anti-discrimination practice and assessment of new policies and provision;
- a managerialist approach to anti-sectarianism and anti-discriminatory practice with a focus on strategies, top-down guidance and training and auditing of processes (Greer, 2004);
- a commitment to and use of a limited concept of equality, linked to Section 75 requirements, which ignore wider social inequalities and disadvantage;

- the lack of an evidence-based approach, with little research carried out on the impact of sectarianism, communal divisions or political conflict on social work or even the impact of Section 75 on social work provision;
- the lack of a commitment to principles of social justice in social work and social care documents and narratives produced by government departments and public bodies, which can be contrasted with approaches in Scotland and Wales;
- the limited range of good relations practice and training, including the notable lack of an overarching commitment to good relations, which is exemplified in the failure of the Northern Ireland Executive and Assembly to agree on a new good relations strategy between 2007 and 2010.

Conclusion

To a large extent, it has been left to small groups of academics, practitioners, trade unionists and politicians to continue to increase awareness of the issues of anti-sectarianism and anti-oppressive practice in social work. Does this mean that there is nothing to learn about the influence of sectarianism on social work from Northern Ireland's experience? The main lesson may lie in the importance of legislative frameworks and affirmative actions in tackling discrimination, most largely through the 'ethnic monitoring' of the workforce, including all public and private employers. In Great Britain when this issue was examined during the formulation of the Single Equality Bill such provisions were rejected without any detailed consideration of their success in Northern Ireland (Osborne, 2008).

Sectarianism in Northern Ireland can be seen as demonstrating a close relationship with other forms of prejudice on the basis of race, gender or disability, and thus anti-sectarian practice can be linked to anti-discriminatory practice and compared to such measures in Britain. Consequently, Northern Ireland practice can be examined for any particular insights that might be applicable in Great Britain. This is more relevant with the higher profile now given to issues of religious identity and discrimination on religious grounds in Great Britain. The absorption of anti-sectarianism into broader equality provision and good relations duties has provided a means of resolving the potential conflict between radical discourses of anti-oppressive practice and values, and more conservative and regulatory forms of social work practice.

FOUR

Violence and social work

For some 26 years (1969–95) Northern Ireland experienced high and intense levels of violence with bombing, shootings, riots and intimidation and community disturbances. In practice, despite the ceasefires by paramilitary organisations since 1995 and the reform of policing and withdrawal of the British army, there has been a continuing pattern of violence and intimidation at a less intense level. What is surprising has been the lack of studies of the role of social work in the aftermath of political and communal violence. Writing in the 1970s Darby and Williamson (1978, p 87) referred to a reluctance on the part of many social work staff to recognise the connection between violence and their work. Manktelow (2007, p 46) suggests that the needs of the victims of the Troubles were largely unmet for many years by the statutory social work services. Reasons included a pretence of 'normal' social care by agencies and limited options for individual social workers for intervention. Creating a perception of neutrality enabled access to clients in troubled neighbourhoods and reduced the risk to social workers. Furthermore, there was a lack of discussion of the issue in the strategies and plans of Boards and Trusts and a lack of research.

It can be noted that the Social Services Inspectorate review of social work research between 1998 and 2003 provided summaries of 53 of the main pieces of research, yet somewhat surprisingly none related to the impact of violence (SSI, 2004a). The Department of Health and Social Services' own series of research and evaluation between 1976 and 2004 produced 60 reports and, again, none addressed the impact of violence. Despite the significance for social work and social care of the political conflict the subject has been under-researched in the literature (Ramon et al, 2006). This chapter has been compiled using a range of available sources to create an overview of the impact of violence on social work practice. It looks at the main consequences of violence under five headings and also assesses wider lessons that can be learnt.

The nature of violence

The most obvious characteristic of the violence has been death and injuries through bombings and shootings during many years of spasmodic violence in the context of paramilitary campaigns of political violence, security forces responses/actions and inter-communal riots and disturbances. This violence has resulted in some 3,700 deaths since 1969 and some 43,000 injuries. Despite the ceasefires, there was still continuing sporadic violence, intimidation and tensions, and it has been calculated that in the subsequent 10 years since 1994 there were 215 politically motivated killings, 1,129 punishment attacks and 2,305 shooting incidents (Shirlow and Murtagh, 2006, p 52). A further study (Jarman, 2004) described a pattern of 6,581 sectarian incidents since 1996, including punishment attacks and intimidation with continuing damage to the social infrastructure and additional social problems. Little, however, was known about the mental health and social impact of the conflict and secondary consequences such as the impact on the development of children, particularly those with parents directly affected by the violence. Violent incidents are differentially concentrated in Northern Ireland with the consequence that social work practice was affected in some areas more than in others. Most violent deaths have been concentrated in Belfast. Other than Belfast, Newry and Mourne, Derry City, Armagh, Dungannon and Craigavon are the local council areas containing the highest number of deaths (Fay et al, 1999). Within Belfast, a detailed study of deaths of local residents between 1969 and 1999 found that over 60% of deaths were located in the north and west of the city (Smyth et al, 2001), an area covered until 2007 by one statutory health and social services trust. Studies on the location of deaths and violence also show a high correlation with the experiences of poverty (Morrissey and Smyth, 2002).

The Northern Ireland Troubles can also be identified with forms of violence other than bombings and shootings, particularly intimidation, whether of individuals, groups or small communities. This has resulted in displacement of families from their homes, and while normally generated by sectarianism, this can also be the result of feuding paramilitary groups within their 'own' communities. Population displacement of housing can bring with it issues of change of schools, childcare, access to social care services and financial support. The prevalence of violence also created a large area of justice-related work with increased numbers of offenders and the social consequences of large numbers of prisoners (Grounds and Jamieson, 2003).

What have been the effects of this violence on social work delivery? Two studies have sought to examine the views of social workers. The first is a study of the impact of the Troubles and the additional costs associated with delivering health and social care in north and west Belfast (Smyth et al, 2001), which is based on a number of focus group interviews with staff. The second study is of the impact of the Troubles on mental health social work and is based on a questionnaire completed by 101 social workers (Campbell and McCrystal, 2005).

The main effect of violence on everyday practice can be described under the following headings:

1. Creating special and unique needs
2. Adding a unique context to 'normal' social work services
3. The creation of special obstacles to delivering services
4. Placing pressure on staff workloads
5. Adverse stress, trauma-related risks and consequences.

The unique aspects of social work can be listed as dealing with bereavement and injuries caused by the Troubles, including multiple trauma regarding bereavement and rehabilitation for physical disabilities and mental stress. Smyth et al (2001, p 59) reported that the violence often permeated into counselling and work with those referred for other reasons, for example, family relationships, substance abuse or sexual abuse. A study by Dillenburger (1992) analysing the impact of violent bereavement on widows, found most had to rely on informal social support. There was also evidence of more children presenting with aggressive, violent and anti-social behaviour. It also appeared that the violence had contributed to the deepening of the social problems of drugs and alcoholism (Smyth et al, 2001, p 45). Williamson and Darby (1978) reported that a proportion of family breakdown could be directly attributed to the Troubles. In some localities most affected by violence or intimidation, it has been necessary to provide police or at times army protection for social workers, for example, when taking children into care. At other times, involvement of police was deliberately avoided in order not to make a difficult situation worse and place social services staff and police in danger. Fear of violence and intimidation and the segregation of localities have also provided the need in areas such as North and West Belfast to set up separate service provision, for example, day centres, thus providing a duplication of facilities, even within short distances of each other.

It is possible to list the impact of obstacles caused by violence on the operation and delivery of social work. The main obstacle was probably a very practical one, in the study by Campbell and McCrystal (2005, p 178) 'affected by traffic disruption' was the most frequently cited consequence caused by violent incidents, for example, in the form of roadblocks. This was cited by 62% of respondents as the first problem, second-ranked was 'affected by bombs', followed by 'sectarian harassment', 'disruption of statutory functions', 'crossing geographical areas', 'paramilitary activities' and 'shootings', although with relatively few high rankings. Williamson and Darby (1978, p 91) provided anecdotal accounts from the 1970s of damage to social workers' cars and the need for car identification discs. The mobility and responsiveness of staff can also be affected in areas at more volatile times after riots, feuding and parades. At times staff were not sent out in dangerous situations but Smyth et al (2001, p 86) noted that social workers throughout Northern Ireland were usually expected to operate as if the Troubles were not happening. Social workers often had to negotiate their access to and involvement in certain neighbourhoods and situations. Despite little official attention or discussion there was also the impact of a chill factor on social work and social care staff. Many social workers or newly qualified staff were reluctant, even fearful, to work in North and West Belfast, and there may even have been stigma attached to working in such areas. Apart from sectarianism, as previously discussed, there were other tensions between the personal and professional views of staff. It was often difficult for social workers to have sympathy for those they saw as responsible for the violence that was making their work more difficult. The incidence of stress and trauma caused to social work staff is discussed further later. There is little evidence on the proportion of social work caseloads attributable to the violence or exacerbated by the violence. One study in Derry estimated 10% of cases were Troubles related (Haverty, 1983).

Response to civil emergencies

Since 1969 social work agencies in Northern Ireland have found themselves faced with questions of how to respond to civil emergencies of violence, rioting, street disturbances, damage to property, intimidation of families and housing displacement. There was also disruption to normal services and the long-term aftermath of bombings, shootings and widespread disturbances. Three early events, the 1969 street disturbances, the 1971 disturbances following internment and the 1974 Ulster Workers Council strike, put pressure on social work agencies to intervene in helping with care, financial aid, evacuation and the relocation of people. It has been argued that the response of social services offices was generally slow, cautious and indecisive (Boyle, 1978). Community social workers in Belfast were reported as totally overwhelmed and medical social workers were drafted in from hospitals (Boyd, 1988). The suddenness and scale of events in 1969 may have caught agencies by surprise, yet when a civil emergency scenario happened again in August 1971, the organisation of emergency responses was not straightforward. Welfare officers were still sticking rigidly to 9–5 timetables with a reluctance to allocate resources without normal bureaucratic safeguards despite the civil emergency (Boyle, 1978, p 149). Locally based voluntary and community organisations often took over social welfare relief. It has also been suggested that the Belfast Welfare (Social Services) Department's response was poor, even compared to that of the adjacent County Antrim and County Down Welfare Authorities (Boyle, 1978, p 150).

The more widespread disruption accompanying the Ulster Workers Council political strike in 1974 again saw a lack of coordinated involvement by the health and social service Boards and Trusts. There were delays in activating emergency plans and social workers were allocated to relief centres, but often without adequate resources (Boyle, 1978, p 162). However, it has been noted that social workers were the only profession not to treat any part of Belfast as a no-go area (Boyd, 1988). In parts of West Belfast the social services staff were the only representatives of the state and often took referrals for other government agencies. At the same time attention had to be paid to dealing with disruption to 'normal' services, for example, day centres, luncheon clubs and domiciliary services. There was also the reaction by social work staff when they decided that they had no alternative but to cooperate with paramilitary groups who controlled access to areas and even for a time access to power supplies. There were clearly lessons to be learnt, in relation to how emergencies were to be defined and declared, the need for planning and training, the balance in such situations of relief work and normal work, the need for flexible responses, the need for cooperation with voluntary welfare organisations and community groups, the need for cooperation with other statutory services, and how to determine the exact contribution of social workers.

Following these three major incidents some social services departments began to prepare contingency plans for dealing with future emergencies. Subsequently the pattern of emergencies changed somewhat to an increase in bombings and shootings with more fatalities and injuries than in the previous civil disturbances; nevertheless riots and intimidation continued, albeit on a more localised basis.

The Northern Ireland Housing Executive (NIHE) largely took responsibility for emergency housing, which was one of the major consequences of violence and intimidation. The NIHE was responsible for emergency accommodation whether from the existing stock or temporary rented accommodation. Families made homeless by violent incidents or by serious intimidation are given 200 extra points in the NIHE selection scheme. If a person's house is destroyed in a terrorist or sectarian attack or if a household cannot live in their home because of the risk of an attack, evidence has to be produced from the police. Further points are awarded for homelessness or for primary social needs if a person has witnessed traumatic events in their home. The NIHE also introduced in 1973 a scheme for the purchase of evacuated dwellings, a strategy that has been in operation ever since. This is used to help owner-occupiers who have to leave their homes because of violence, intimidation or threats and who cannot sell their property. The NIHE purchases the evacuated dwelling for later sale or rent. The scheme has been used not just by civilians, but by police and prison officers and is dependent on police confirmation that it is unsafe, or there is a risk of death or injury in remaining in the house. With a large amount of damage to property the NIHE accepted responsibility for emergency repairs not only for social housing, but also for private housing, and also administered a home repairs assistance grant.

One of the surprising features of emergency planning through the 1970s and 1980s was the lack of central direction. The overall responsibility resided with a very small emergency planning branch in the Northern Ireland Office (Birrell, 1993, p 83). It was not until 1996 (actually after the ceasefires and the withdrawal of the army) that a review of emergency planning arrangements was carried out to bring major civil emergency arrangements into line with Great Britain (OFMDFM, 2009a). The focus was on the role of government departments and on major accidents and planning exercises including police, ambulance, fire and rescue, and hospitals. The previous position of individual agencies producing their own emergency incident plans continued and left flexibility for social workers to develop their own plans. Following the 2004 UK Civil Contingencies Act, a Northern Ireland Civil Contingencies Framework set out principles for emergency planning activity. In practice the physical and accident focus of the general emergency planning unit was to encourage and prompt social service disaster planning to develop with an emphasis on psychosocial responses. The health and social care delivery trusts or the health and social care commissioning body are not currently represented on the central emergency planning unit.

Social services continued to respond to emergencies related to the conflict with a loosely structured approach until the mid-1990s. It has been suggested that each incident was responded to on an ad hoc basis with no systematic evaluation in the aftermath, and lessons learnt from one incident were not always transferred to another scenario (McLaughlin and Kelly, 1998). No dedicated teams had been created to respond quickly and comprehensively to incidents.

One of the catalysts for change to this approach was the work of Marion Gibson, a principal social worker in Belfast who published a book on the theme of responding to disasters (Gibson, 1991). The book drew mainly not on emergencies in Northern Ireland, but on the experience of the Kegworth air crash when a team had gone from Northern Ireland to England to assist the bereaved and injured, many of whom were from Northern Ireland. Relatives arriving from Northern Ireland were met by a team of social workers. Gibson used a typology of staged intervention, a crisis stage, immediate post-crisis, short-term post-crisis and long-term post-crisis, and had a focus on psychosocial assistance for the injured and their relatives, the bereaved and children. This study went on to consider models for the delivery of a social service response based on these stages. This covered: the role of senior managers, the appointment of an emergency planning officer, staff training, involvement of the voluntary sector, the idea of a coordinating committee and a crisis counselling team (Gibson, 1991, p 118).

The lessons learnt from this analysis of the Kegworth disaster were used to design four crisis support teams within the Eastern Health and Social Services Board area (McLaughlin and Kelly, 1998, p 126). Staffing was primarily drawn from the physical health and disability programme of care. Each team had a coordinator to assess need initially and a protocol for liaison with voluntary groups was established. One team, the North and West Belfast crisis team, was to be involved in the Shankill Road bomb in October 1993 when 10 people died and 58 were injured. The team assisted 100 people following the bomb. Social services crisis teams also provided support following the intimidation of families. Assistance was initially on a practical and more multi-activity basis, but later developed on a basis of counselling. The lesson from this crisis intervention team was that in-depth assessment was critical to an effective response to ensure that services were targeted as appropriate and to offer people an informed choice over the type of support they received (McLaughlin and Kelly, 1998, p 125). The North and West Belfast crisis support team in subsequent years also sought to utilise the services and resources of local communities and organisations. The team offered both short-term and long-term support and saw its approach as based on well-established social work principles of empathy and empowerment, respect for the individual, and community development. A family trauma centre had operated in Belfast which, as well as family support, provided a consultation service for social workers seeking support for a client; the centre also provided training to other social service Trusts and agencies. Referrals could be made immediately after an incident had occurred.

All of Northern Ireland's delivery Trusts produced some form of emergency plan. These tended to reflect the integrated structure in covering both health and social services aspects in planned responses but often had a medical focus. Something of a tension did develop between social work and wider assistance approaches.

The social work helping intervention as developed by Gibson (1991), had staged processes of impact, immediate post-crisis, short-term and long-term post-crisis and a focus on social work psychosocial counselling intervention. In contrast, the Northern Ireland Office developed a concept of planned practical intervention, which consisted of a number of stages, including: physical impact, information, repair, social assistance stage – involving rehousing, finance and compensation – and social work counselling (Birrell, 2003). Local district council emergency plans also had a focus on practical assistance and monitoring the outcomes.

Mental health and trauma

The nature and extent of violent incidents and the threat of violence has been judged to have had an adverse influence on the mental health of the population, almost since the inception of the violence (Manktelow, 1998). In contrast to other social work-related issues, this is a topic that has been the subject of much research. Earlier studies have examined the impact of the Troubles on mental health (Kee et al, 1987; Prior, 1993). Muldoon et al (2003) reported 50% of respondents having some direct experience of the Troubles, with 22% of men having experience of a bomb, 26% of riots and 25% of intimidation. A further study by O'Reilly and Stevenson (2003) found that 21.3% of respondents reported that the Troubles had quite a bit of impact or a lot of impact on their lives. The authors concluded that the Troubles represented a significant and additional impact on the mental health of the Northern Ireland population. It has been suggested that the incidence of mental illness was not as high as might have been expected because of coping mechanisms that people developed (Cairns and Wilson, 1989). However, the Northern Ireland Health and Social Wellbeing Survey (DHSSPS, 2001) found an incidence of mental health problems of 24% among women and 17% among men. Such rates were over 20% higher than the rates in England and Scotland. The level of need for psychiatric care was identified as 25% higher than in England and the level of treatment by drug therapies for mental illness was 37–87% higher than in England (DHSSPS, 2005). The Belfast Health and Social Care Trust (2009a), whilst developing a strategy for the delivery of adult mental health services, referred to much higher levels of mental health difficulties among patients of GPs in North and West Belfast and quoted figures that 29% of male and 25% of female respondents were identified as suffering from borderline or severe psychiatric disorders. It has been asserted that it is the civil disturbances and political violence that account for these differences (DHSSPS, 2005). There was also increasing research evidence diagnosing post-traumatic stress disorder (PTSD) among those affected by the violence. Loughrey et al (1988) concluded that PTSD could be identified in the case records of victims of civil and terrorist violence. Fay et al (1999) found in a story of the cost of the Troubles that 30% of those who had been exposed directly to violence associated with the Troubles had symptoms approximating to PTSD. A psychological appraisal of the survivors of the Enniskillen Remembrance Day bombing in 1987 found that 50% had developed PTSD (Curran et al, 1990). In the aftermath of that bombing the local Sperrin Lakeland Health and Social Services Trust developed an approach based on trauma counselling, providing help to address the needs of those who had been psychologically traumatised.

The trauma-based approach was subsequently put into effect following the Omagh bombing in 1998, which resulted in the largest number of deaths and injuries in one single incident in Northern Ireland. The Sperrin Lakeland Health and Social Care Trust set up a community trauma and recovery team. The role and response of the team was identified as mainly:

- representing the Trust's response symbolically;
- spearheading the Trust's services;
- acting as an easy point of access for the community;
- providing initial responses, assessment and services;
- referencing and using appropriate conventional services and arrangements;
- compensating for inadequacies in existing support, if necessary with new services;
- coordinating the Trust's response with voluntary and other services;
- channelling media enquiries;
- participating with others in the tasks of community restoration; and
- bringing an end to the Trust's involvement (Bolton and Duffy, 1999).

The response to Omagh did draw on trauma analysis in relation to the ripple effect on the community, hierarchies of suffering and loss, and the trauma cycle. The impacts of the bombing identified reactions from 'normal' anxiety, mental health difficulties, intense inner feelings, alcohol, drugs, impaired relationships, impaired destructive social functioning and dysfunctional coping strategies. A review of the Trust's response did identify problems of communication with staff and the public and the need to review its emergency plan for greater clarity in the role of all agencies (Fee and Corrigan, 1999). This included arrangements for the continuation of care and follow-up, the handling of sensitive information, the suspension of routine social work, and the revision of the role of social workers to take responsibility for contact with relatives and determine responsibility for a casualty bureau. The review was used to restructure emergency plans and major incident plans, although the findings stressed that no two emergency incidents were the same and frameworks had to be adapted to particular circumstances. Belfast Trust has made further significant progress in the development of plans to cope with emergencies. By 2009/10 the Trust had a Community Emergency Response Team (CERT). This is comprised of 30 volunteers, the majority of whom are social workers. The CERT Co-ordinator and Senior Manager for Emergency Planning represents Belfast Trust on Belfast Resilience, a local forum looking at integrated emergency planning for the Belfast City Council area. The role of CERT is to provide back-up to emergency services; and practical and continued support to those affected by an incident and their relatives and friends.

The Team's intervention is short-term, with long-term intervention referred on to Trust colleagues and outside agencies as appropriate (Belfast Health and Social Care Trust, 2010b).

Social services responses

It was not until 1995 that the Department of Health, Social Services and Public Safety launched a project to develop services to meet the social and psychological needs of individuals affected by the conflict. Crisis support teams had been set up by social services in some parts of Northern Ireland. These provided an immediate and structured response to those affected by terrorist-related incidents, whether major or on a smaller scale. Crisis support teams were made up of social workers who could be called out to provide the initial response and then to assess the longer-term psychosocial needs of the people involved. This was a multi-professional response with social workers working alongside district nurses, health visitors, home helps as well as GPs and other medical staff (Gibson, 1996).

In 1998 the Social Services Inspectorate (SSI) produced a report on the range of services available to individuals who have suffered Troubles-related social and psychological trauma. *Living with the Trauma of the Troubles* aimed to further develop services to meet the social and psychological needs of individuals seriously affected by the civil unrest (SSI, 1998). It was anticipated that this report would form the basis of a charter for individuals affected by the conflict and set out the standards of service that an individual could expect. Major issues identified in the SSI report included public and agency awareness of services, the quality of services of voluntary groups and the need for training and accreditation in counselling. The approach of the review was based on a continuity of need through pre-trauma– short-term–mid-term–longer-term trauma. This spectrum was aligned to the role of agencies, to training and support, and to general guidelines to helping people with Troubles-related trauma. The main recommendation of *Living with the Trauma of the Troubles* was for the establishment of small advisory panels in each Health and Social Services Board area to improve coordination and liaison of services.

The emphasis on trauma developed further after the Omagh bombing and the SSI report with both Trust plans and more specialised strategies. All four Health and Social Services Boards established a Trauma Advisory Panel (TAP), which included representatives of voluntary organisations, whose role was to coordinate, promote and improve services to those affected by trauma. Each panel was chaired by a senior social work manager with a social worker appointed to the post of panel coordinator (Manktelow, 2007, p 38). TAPs acted mainly on a multi-agency basis and were concerned with:

- facilitating the coordination of health and social services for those affected by the violence of the Troubles;
- providing a forum for improved understanding of the identified and emerging needs and the development of methods for tackling them;

- enhancing the coherence of a network of partners working to promote and develop better services;
- assessing training needs and providing training for appropriate professionals and community groups; and
- promoting a better understanding of roles and relationships on the continuity of provision.

TAPs worked to identify the needs of victims, establish levels of provision, collect and share information, facilitate conferences, and promote best practice. Practical outcomes were directories of services, information packs, information leaflets and more specialist initiatives by individual panels, for example, long-term monitoring of needs, child bereavement and assisting intimidated families. However, TAPs functioned as mainly advisory boards and therefore tried to influence the development of Trust services. Some panels were able to expand their functions, for example, three trauma counsellors were appointed in the Southern Board area.

An evaluation of health and social services for victims of the conflict was carried out by consultants in 2003 (DHSSPS, 2003a). This identified concerns by consultees about recurrent funding, long-term funding and competition for funding, and also about gaps in coverage in south-western areas and the regional specialist services mainly used only by residents of the Belfast area. Examples of best practice were listed including long-term monitoring of trauma in children and attempts to reach the grass roots. The evaluation made recommendations related to the awareness of issues, needs and gaps in mainstream services for treating victims of conflict and the relatively small number of dedicated services provided by the Trusts for victims (DHSSPS, 2003a, p 34). It called for clarification of the responsible government department, for a regional centre of excellence, local outreach centres and for more research and evaluation. Although the remit was for an evaluation of health and social care, the focus of the report was almost exclusively on trauma, especially the role of the trauma advisory panels. Some initiatives involving the voluntary social care sector were included. One example was a child and family support service to victims of the conflict involving a Trust in partnership with Barnardo's. Overall the evaluation found that the voluntary/ community sector felt that communication could be improved across all those involved in the provision of services (DHSSPS, 2003a, p 48). A further study of services offered by voluntary and community groups (Dillenburger et al, 2007) noted an increase in voluntary victims groups since the 1994 ceasefire and found an increased reliance on these community services by people affected by violence rather than on in-depth professional social work and therapeutic help. Voluntary and community-based services covered self-help groups, befriending, respite care, youth work, advice and information, and narrative work as opposed to psychology-based skills including counselling. This study found servicing by voluntary and community groups varied in quality and often reflected available funding rather than an objective analysis of the needs of service users. However, the voluntary and community groups were able to relate closely to local people's experiences and it was recommended that social workers be encouraged to utilise these services.

The work of the Northern Area trauma advisory group included:

- the production of a *Dealing with Trauma* leaflet;
- a needs assessment of families intimidated and displaced as a result of the conflict;
- the production of multi-agency protocols for supporting families displaced as a result of trauma; and
- trauma-raising awareness roadshows (Northern Health and Social Care Trust, 2010).

The Belfast Health and Social Care Trust continues to operate a Trauma Resource Centre, despite the years that have passed since the main ceasefire. Research from the centre has confirmed a high level of trauma across the communities in North and West Belfast (Belfast Health and Social Care Trust, 2008). The centre treats what it diagnoses as traumatic stress disorders and related difficulties using a multidisciplinary approach and uses continuing research into Troubles-related experiences and on how individuals have been managing.

A major consequence of the Omagh bombing was the establishment of a specialist facility, the Northern Ireland Centre for Trauma and Transformation (NICTT). Based in Omagh, this was set up by a charitable trust in 2002 and is now mainly funded by government. The NICTT cares for people affected by incidents linked to the Northern Ireland Troubles, as well as developing and delivering accredited training and undertaking research and policy development, including disaster planning. The focus of the NICTT has been on trauma-focused cognitive therapy, which it sees as a treatment option that has not generally been available previously. A randomised controlled study of the NICTT's therapy programme concluded that cognitive therapy was an effective treatment for PTSD related to terrorism and other civil conflict (Duffy et al, 2007). The NICTT has also published further research (Ferry et al, 2008) confirming that PTSD and related disorders are still a specified need in the Northern Ireland population with approximately 50% of event types related to the Troubles. This study did include quantitative interviews as a follow-up into the experience of individuals who were linked to the civil conflict. The study concluded that there was a clear need for progress to be made in developing services with improved information support for primary and community care services and the development of specialist evidence-based trauma services. The long-term impact of trauma and multiple trauma has also been examined. Studies on the long-term impact of Bloody Sunday in 1972 has found evidence of transgenerational effects, and also that individuals indirectly exposed to a traumatic event can develop symptoms similar to PTSD (Hayes and Campbell, 2000; Shevlin and McGuigan, 2003). A further longitudinal study (McGuigan and Shevlin, 2010) found significant levels of psychological distress in response to an event that occurred 37 years previously, with those directly exposed to the event, or their family members, showing the highest levels.

Increasingly the development of trauma services and the importance accorded by them to cognitive behaviour therapy meant that within the statutory services the response was located within mental health. An SSI report (2004b) on the role of social work in mental health noted the ongoing impact of Troubles-related issues, violent behaviour, chronic stress and addictions on social work practice. A major review of mental health services in Northern Ireland, established in 2007, recognised the impact of the Troubles, accentuated by lower expenditure in Northern Ireland than Great Britain on mental health. The review, chaired by a professor of social work, noted that in many sectors of society there was still a thinly veiled undercurrent of violence and intimidation (Bamford, 2008). The review also referred to the development of PTSD services as piecemeal and patchy. However, the Bamford review and subsequent strategies endorsed developing PTSD services with early intervention after trauma, a single point of access and accurate referral, and this response was placed in a context of rebuilding mental health services.

Trauma and staff

The significance of trauma and PTSD approaches was further recognised by a growing recognition that in the aftermath of violent incidents, emergency services staff may be severely traumatised or suffer from what was sometimes called secondary traumatic stress disorder. In Northern Ireland large numbers of professionals sent in as helpers, including social workers, could be traumatised by major events, despite professional training and often considerable experience. The need for support for staff involved in the aftermath of violence was slow to be recognised, but by the 1990s two Health and Social Services Trusts had established counselling, debriefing sessions and stress management (McLaughlin and Kelly, 1998, p 129). Research also commenced on the issue. Luce et al (2002) carried out a survey of health and social care staff involved in the aftermath of the Omagh bombing. PTSD levels varied between different staff groups with the rate twice as high among social workers as among medical staff, but only slightly higher than nurses. The highest rate of all was found among home help/ domiciliary care workers. Those who witnessed the events or had previous emotional problems had the highest levels of symptoms and a high proportion still displayed symptoms 5–9 months later. The study did find that only a minority contacted professional agencies for support or help, whether for reasons of guilt, fear, stigma or confidentiality.

A study that included social workers involved in the aftermath of the Shankill Road bombing found that some 57% of the Shankill sample thought their mental health had been affected and some 58% of the sample reported that they had used support from their organisation (Gibson and Iwaniec, 2003). Social workers in the Shankill group all referred to the need to adapt their basic training to meet the needs of their involvement in traumatic events. Many, however, did feel overwhelmed and stressed by the wide range of work undertaken. Although they reported some training in addressing the impact of sectarianism, crisis debriefing and counselling, many were dependent on generic skills when dealing with complex Troubles-related problems (Ramon et al, 2006, p 446). There was general dissatisfaction with training addressing their emotional response to disasters and the lack of understanding on their return to normal work after their stressful experiences (Gibson and Iwaniec, 2003, p 864). In the aftermath of an attack on Musgrave Park Hospital in Belfast, it was reported that social workers felt that their morale had been shattered and their professionalism challenged, as a place of healing became a place of destruction (Gibson, 1996, p 88). Such research demonstrated a need for more training in stress management and coping mechanisms among staff dealing with the aftermath of violent incidents.

This, perhaps with a growing threat of litigation, led to the development of training programmes on PTSD. Marion Gibson, in a follow-up to her 1998 book (Gibson, 2006), was more specific in the context of training programmes for responders and the provision of critical incident stress debriefing. Such training became oriented to not just dealing with psychosocial impacts, but also with minimising the risks to begin with and seeking to enhance emergency workers' confidence and ability to cope with distressing events. Training would help personnel to recognise symptoms of traumatic stress in themselves and others. A service was launched, 'Staffcare', under the auspices of the South and East Belfast Health and Social Services Trust, to provide confidential counselling, critical incident stress management, training and consultancy to the statutory, private and voluntary sectors. The training was based on a modular programme to prepare people to cope with traumatic stress in the workplace (Gibson, 2006, p 199). The essence of this approach is to focus on trauma and to build support around this. It has, however, been suggested that this approach may be too medically oriented (Reynolds, 2006). Some controversy has surrounded the use of the term 'disorder' in PTSD for what may be seen as a normal distress. PTSD has been seen as a Western-based diagnosis that does not capture the essence of human responses to disastrous events in all parts of the world (Summerfield, 2000). However, the Centre for Trauma and Transformation, which has worked in Sarajevo and Nepal, suggests that in Northern Ireland, PTSD with cultural sensitivity is a very useful tool (Bolton, 2010).

The impact of the Northern Ireland experience

It is clear that it is the focus on psychosocial aspects of emergencies that has been the main contribution adopted from Northern Ireland practice, mainly through the books, writing and training input from Marion Gibson. The first major report of a Disasters Working Party set up in 1989 accepted the principle that social and psychosocial support following a disaster was best managed by the local social services or social work authority and contained a supporting document by Marion Gibson on training in preparation for providing a caring response to disasters (Disasters Working Party, 1991). By 2006 the Staffcare organisation based in Northern Ireland was undertaking projects and consultancy work throughout Great Britain, and training on the provision of a psychosocial response was being provided (Gibson, 2006). Many local authorities in Great Britain now have a civil emergency trauma support service with a range of social and psychosocial support services. The NICTT has also reached out to other countries through its training and education programmes, including work in Sarajevo, Bosnia, Sri Lanka and Nepal. The NICTT has also worked with the Emergency Planning College in England (Bolton, 2005). This work has a focus on the mental health consequences of disasters, although attention is paid to issues such as community infrastructure and resources, displacement and temporary accommodation.

Support for victims

The emphasis on trauma as a consequence of the Troubles coincided with the emergence of a new emphasis on support for victims and survivors of the Troubles in a wider setting. In 1997 Mo Mowlam, then Secretary of State for Northern Ireland, established a Commission for Victims and Survivors (Bloomfield, 1998) to look at possible ways to recognise the pain and suffering felt by victims of violence arising from the Troubles over the previous 30 years. The main years of the Troubles had seen few such initiatives dealing with care for victims and survivors. In subsequent deliberations the victims' agenda deviated in other directions and into politically controversial areas over the definition of victims, issues of truth and reconciliation, blame and guilt, physical memorials, financial compensation, and the appointment of commissioners as a voice of victims. However, the Bloomfield report did endorse the SSI report (1998) recommending more trauma services, accessible services and other practical social support. Following devolution, a Victims Unit was established as part of the Office of the First Minister and Deputy First Minister in 2000. This was a broad measure, going beyond social care to ensure that the needs of victims were addressed, based on an interdepartmental working group.

A report in 2009 was more focused on reconciliation and made a controversial recommendation to make a payment to the nearest relative of all the dead, but also called for improved health and social care services (Eames and Bradley, 2009). The Victims Unit within the Office of the First Minister and Deputy First Minister has continued to coordinate issues affecting victims of the conflict across the devolved administration. Also funded largely by government was the Northern Ireland Memorial Fund, which provides grant assistance for individuals who have lost family members, sustained injuries or are in need of care or are a carer. The fund has some 1,200 people on its books. A new government strategy set up a Commission for Victims and Survivors, made up of four victims commissioners, and proposed a forum and a new Victims and Survivors Service. The latter would provide a range of services including counselling and advice, and help with financial hardship, social isolation and exclusion. The intervention was aimed to improve the well-being of victims and survivors, although issues of truth and reconciliation were also referred to (OFMDFM, 2009b). The proposed service would, however, largely fund voluntary groups working with victims. The first work programme for the new Commission for Victims and Survivors (2009) referred to a comprehensive needs assessment, but it is not clear how far any support would be separately provided or enter mainstream caring provision.

Some organisations set up to focus on trauma have maintained a broader social care approach. WAVE is a voluntary organisation that supports anyone traumatised through the Troubles, including their carers. The organisation has some 600 new referrals per year and operates in five centres throughout Northern Ireland. Referrals have increased in recent years including some people traumatised up to 35 years ago (WAVE Trauma Centre, 2010). Psychotherapy and counselling, trauma training, peer support, and befriending services are offered, but also advice on social welfare matters, housing, advocacy, youth services and assistance with compensation claims.

New Westminster legislation in 2004, the UK Civil Contingencies Act, brought in new arrangements for responding to emergencies, specifically including major terrorist incidents. It imposed duties on local government services, emergency 'blue light' services, NHS bodies and other government agencies. The response was divided into three stages: preparedness, crisis management and recovery. The Act specified duties on emergency planning and also set up structures to improve coordination and cooperation. There is little evidence of any policy transfer or learning from the Northern Ireland experience in the large amount of documentation that has been generated in Great Britain. An examination of the Northern Ireland documentation reveals that there has been a reluctance to refer to conflict-related emergencies. When new emergency planning was drawn up in 1998, the year of the Omagh bombing, there were references to Northern Ireland being fortunate in that it had not had to face a major emergency. The need for a strategy was described as being due to 'a number of natural, industrial and transport disasters in Great Britain and the need to bring emergency planning arrangements into line with those available in the rest of the UK' (Central Emergency Planning Unit, 1998). The updated document in 2004 again made little reference to the conflict as the main source of emergencies, and in discussing the contribution of different organisations, makes almost no reference to the role of social services or social work (Central Emergency Planning Unit, 2004).

After 2004 the Central Emergency Planning Unit rather mirrored Great Britain, although the structural organisation of bodies was different. In England and Wales local resilience forums became the principle mechanism for multi-agency cooperation and the Civil Contingencies Group in Northern Ireland is a multi-agency forum analogous to the resilience forums. Guidance also mirrors the British documentation on the crisis stage aspects. The UK Cabinet Office has produced detailed guidance on meeting the needs of those affected by an emergency (Cabinet Office, 2010), including humanitarian assistance, centres for vulnerable people and roles and responsibilities in meeting immediate and longer-term needs. Social work services are ascribed a specific role in coordination, welfare responses, social and psychological support, and dealing with relatives; but again there is no reference to the Northern Ireland experience.

The Social Care Institute for Excellence has commissioned a study of the role of social care in the response to and recovery from emergency incidents. The report (Child et al, 2008) was based on a knowledge review and a practice survey that included six case studies of social care responses to emergency incidents including the Omagh bomb, but did not identify what particularly was learnt from the Northern Ireland experience. The report set out a range of social care activities, principles from social care involvement and recommendations/action plans. In practice it found some departments well prepared, but others less so.

The types of activities expected of social care were listed as:

- provision of basic emotional support;
- provision of information;
- establishing assistance centres;
- identification and assessment of needs;
- liaise with other support agencies;
- facilitation of meetings;
- facilitating access to education;
- provision of financial advice;
- supporting rehousing;
- provision of disaster funds;
- support for bereavement.;
- facilitation of memorial services.

Operational examples of all these activities can be illustrated from the Northern Ireland experience.

A number of principles can be extracted from the study, which Northern Ireland evidence supports:

1. The social care role can be divided between maintaining core services and tasks to service additional needs.
2. In emergencies, social care should be the lead agency in humanitarian assistance.
3. Social care should be part of the planning and preparation process.
4. Identification of vulnerable groups, older people, children, those with physical disabilities, learning disabilities and mental health problems.
5. The importance of early practical support.
6. The importance of multi-agency and partnership working.
7. Working with the voluntary and community sector, widening services and involving volunteers.
8. Social care has a role in the future recovery stage.

9. Social care has a role in strengthening resilience within communities through social networks and continuing engagement.

While the principles have been used in Northern Ireland, some have received greater priority than others. Principles 2, 3 and 9 produce fewer examples of implementation. Some principles of possible social work intervention have also been rather abandoned on the basis of experience and research findings, for example, early debriefing interventions (Manktelow, 2007, p 35). The report concluded that four higher-level themes emerged, which could be viewed as action points (Child et al, 2008):

1. clarification of the role of responders;
2. promoting effective management and communication within and across agencies;
3. training and support for staff for emergency preparation, response and recovery;
4. promoting strategies around ongoing support for recovery.

Conclusion

For a lengthy period throughout the 1970s and 1980s the response by social work agencies to violence was largely on an ad hoc basis, under-organised and underfunded. Social workers have had to react to the civil emergencies in Northern Ireland in four main ways:

1. developing tailored services to the needs of those involved, especially in the area of counselling and trauma support;
2. maintaining normal services in the context of emergency demands and physical disruption;
3. facing their own physical, psychological and ethical reactions to traumatic events and experiences, both directly and indirectly;
4. meeting the requirement to work closely in the aftermath of emergencies with other statutory and voluntary organisations.

The very limited amount of research, records, audits and evaluations of the contribution of social workers in responses to violence, has made policy transfer difficult. Northern Ireland's integrated structure of health and social care could have been used more to facilitate multidisciplinary teams. When more attention and resources were directed to the issue, the main focus developed in the direction of trauma services, followed by a focus on a victim strategy, which developed in more politicised ways. The experience of dealing with violent incidents and lessons on the role and contribution of social workers in Northern Ireland has not been fully analysed or widely used for the wider arena of emergency planning or training in either Northern Ireland or Great Britain. A possible reason relates to the concept of a disaster subculture where professionals, practitioners and the community have so adapted to emergencies that they have become used to seeing such events as routine and do not perceive responses as unusual or a crisis (Birrell, 1993, p 86).

It can also be suggested that the experience of emergency workers has been of value and use for social workers in small-scale routine work, for example, in relation to domestic violence. At the same time there were some unique Northern Ireland features that are not so transferrable, particular circumstances in emergency incidents or disturbances where professional staff offering assistance may come under attack as a spin-off from the unacceptability over a period of time of the police in certain areas, something also experienced at times by fire and ambulance crews. A general lesson from the Northern Ireland experience is that the social work contribution developed less in the physical and medical outcomes of violent incidents and less in certain aspects of social provision, such as emergency rehousing and social security assistance and compensation. Instead, there has been a particular focus on trauma and related consequences, which had been an overlooked aspect of provision. This trauma response was viewed as wider than simply health or psychiatric needs.

FIVE

The integration of health and social work

Northern Ireland has been an integral part of the National Health Service since its foundation. A Social Services Financial Agreement of 1949 between the devolved Northern Ireland government and the Westminster government required Northern Ireland to maintain the scale and standard of comprehensive health services in general conformity with the scale and standard of such services in Great Britain. This did not, however, rule out differences in the administrative structure or governance systems for the delivery of services. This was to become particularly significant when Northern Ireland went on to develop a structurally integrated system of health and social work services, which treated health and social care organisations as a single entity. Collaboration and integration between health and social care has become a topic of great interest to academics, policymakers, managers and practitioners in Great Britain over the last 10 years. Consequently the structurally integrated system in Northern Ireland provides an example from which many lessons can be drawn, in relation to its development, underpinning principles, management and operation, and the nature of the achievements of integration or difficulties encountered.

The development of integrated services

Northern Ireland has had an integrated structure of health and social services since 1972. The original decision owed more to a requirement to reorganise local government than any thought-out strategy on integration. Since 1948, personal social services had been organised in a system of comprehensive welfare departments as part of the existing local government structure, with six county council welfare authorities and two welfare departments in the county boroughs of Belfast and Londonderry, similar to the structures in Great Britain. In the late 1960s, the Northern Ireland government produced proposals for the reform of the existing local government structure and the final recommendation in 1969 proposed a single tier of 17 authorities and raised a question about the future administration of social services by county councils. Shortly afterwards the government published a Green Paper, *The Administrative Structure of the Health and Personal Social Services in Northern Ireland* (HMSO, 1969), which proposed the integration of health and personal social services under a structure of four area boards. The decision to integrate health and social services received remarkably little discussion in the Green Paper apart from brief references to the 'need for cooperation and joint planning becoming increasingly recognised' and 'the best framework for the continued development of personal social services is to be found in their coming into some form of partnership with health services' (HMSO, 1969, p 8).

The main reasons actually articulated in the Green Paper referred to administrative factors: that separate social work departments would have increased the number of bodies and the number of administrative and support staff. The process of consultation on these proposals was rather overtaken by a wider programme of administrative reform that followed the outbreak of civil disturbances (Birrell and Williamson, 1983). As part of the political reform programme a major review of local government took place and a final decision on health and personal social services was put on hold. The review body's report, the Macrory Report (HMSO, 1970), largely endorsed the Green Paper's proposals and legislation followed in 1972. At the time the restructuring received a rather cautious welcome from the social work profession. There was little objection to the removal of personal social services from local councils, although there was some concern about the likely effectiveness of separate social work committees and directors as a guarantee against domination by the health service. The Permanent Secretary of the Department of Health and Social Services speaking in 1971 identified the main advantages of the new system as: making possible comprehensive planning at every level; encompassing the totality of medical and social care; making possible a more rational grouping of professional resources and facilities; and removing an archaic structure of 47 bodies, which would improve medical and social care and ensure public participation (DHSS, 1972).

Originally, Boards with a district substructure were created. The 17 districts were considered to be the optimum size for the delivery of personal social services, however, as Caul and Herron (1992) note, the geographical form of the final administrative structure was dictated by the main hospital configuration. Thus, 17 districts were set up as subdivisions of four Health and Social Services Boards. The new structure was subject to an early review in 1978, which led the Department of Health and Social Services to modify the structures to enable the integrated services to be planned and managed more effectively. At operational level this resulted in the creation of a new substructure based on the concept of a unit of management, which could be based on an individual hospital, group of hospitals or a geographical area for community health and personal social services or client-care services for an area (McCoy, 1993, p 12). This reorganisation led to 24 units of management. These changes meant a move from fully integrated districts to specialist units of management for acute hospitals, psychiatric hospitals, community health and social services, or combined hospital and community units. The next major development followed the 'Working for Patients' NHS reforms in 1989, which saw major hospitals allowed to become Hospital Trusts, and Health and Social Service Boards reconstituted as management bodies with no local government representatives. The process of change continued in the 1990s with the emergence of the community care agenda and provider–purchaser split and a series of reforms published in the *People First* paper (DHSS, 1991). *People First* was Northern Ireland's version of the guidelines for community care in Great Britain published in the White Paper *Caring for People* (DH, 1989). Consequently, the four Boards' role changed to that of a purchaser/enabler. The providers, the units of management, acquired Trust status, which meant they managed staff and services on the ground and controlled their own budgets. A Health and Personal Social Services Order in 1994 facilitated the creation of Health and Community Trusts as well as Hospital Trusts. All the delivery Trusts had separate legal status from the Boards and there was no longer a managerial line between Boards and Trusts (Anderson, 1998).

The Board–Trust division reflected a purchaser–provider divide, but still with an integrated structure. Integrated health and social services were organised by four commissioning health and social services Boards, which geographically covered the whole of Northern Ireland, and by 18 Trusts. Of the delivering Trusts, 11 were community Health and Social Services Trusts, which were based on geographically defined areas, and seven were Hospital Trusts based largely on acute general hospitals. The role of the Health and Social Services Boards was to identify needs and priorities, develop new strategies and plan and commission services mainly from the Trusts. In their areas, Boards could issue detailed statements on how they expected their strategies to be implemented and could also issue information on quality standards. Otherwise the Trusts controlled their own budgets and were managerially independent of the Boards. All the health care and personal social services were commissioned in nine programmes of care, and the majority of these reflected the principle of integration, for example, services for elderly people, mental health services, services for people with physical disabilities and services for people with a learning disability. There was, therefore, a strong integrated approach built into the planning process at the level of the four Boards and all resource recommendations were made through programme commissioning teams, which were multidisciplinary. The Community Health and Social Services Trusts directly provided a comprehensive range of primary and community health services and social work services and some were responsible for a range of hospital services including acute district hospitals, local hospitals, specialist hospitals, mental hospitals and hospitals for people with learning disabilities. However, Trusts remained accountable to the Department of Health and Social Services in Northern Ireland for how they delivered services. Consequently the shape of integrated delivery rested with the Trusts. The continuing existence of seven separate Hospital Trusts did mean that Northern Ireland did not have a totally integrated system of health and social services. In 1998 two existing Trusts amalgamated – one a Hospital Trust including a large general district hospital and the other a surrounding Community Health and Social Services Trust.

The introduction of devolution marked a lengthy period of review, from 1999 to 2009, of the structure of health and social care. A major reorganisation of health was initiated and the major document *Developing Better Services* called for closer integration of primary, secondary and social care (DHSSPS, 2002a). Strategy documents produced by the relevant department contained a commitment to maintaining an integrated approach without barriers between the two parts of the system. Originally, the Northern Ireland Executive held the view that the reform of health and personal social services should be progressed only taking account of a major review of public administration that had already been initiated, but shortly afterwards the reorganisation of health and social care was subsumed within the wider Review of Public Administration (RPA). The RPA's further consultation document set out guiding principles for restructuring health and social services. It noted that the integrated system was one of the strengths of the health and personal social care system and any change in services should not work against the integrated approach (RPA, 2005). The proposal at this time was for the development of structures characterised not by the need to generate competition, but by the creation of partnerships between commissioning and delivery across a full range of integrated services, sensitive to local needs (RPA, 2005, p 64). The decisions announced in 2006, during Direct Rule by the then Northern Ireland Ministers, changed the principles to a separation of commissioning and provision to provide performance incentives (RPA, 2006). With the suspension of devolution in 2002, the UK government had taken on responsibility for the running of the RPA. This followed a review of the resourcing and efficient delivery of health and social care services that had criticised hospital productivity and recommended separation between providers and co-funders/commissioners to sharpen up incentives in the system, with a single pan-Northern Ireland commissioner (Appleby, 2005, p 12). There was still a commitment to integration and better joining up of the system. The commissioning system would have the advantage of a unique opportunity to commission social care alongside health services. By the time the Northern Ireland Executive was restored in 2007, the five new Delivery Trusts had been established and although the Health Minister reviewed the proposals, this led to only a few structural changes in the plans.

Each component of the final version of the new structures (see Table 5.1) had the integration of health and social care built into it, with:

1. a single new Health and Social Care Board, which replaced the four existing Boards, and would be responsible for commissioning health and social care and advised by five local commissioning groups;
2. five new fully integrated Health and Social Care Delivery Trusts, which would replace the 19 existing Trusts, including the seven separate Hospital Trusts, creating a fully integrated structure across primary, secondary and community care;
3. a single Patient and Client Council, replacing four previous councils, and covering health and social care;
4. a common business organisation, covering the integrated structures;
5. a single public health and well-being body.

These operated alongside a single Regulation and Improvement Authority, which also covered both health and social care. The only clear rationale presented for integration was a brief paragraph in the final consultation document on the proposal to establish five integrated Health and Social Care Trusts. The maintenance of the integrated system was seen as important in preserving and developing the advantages of combining medical and social models of analysis of people's needs (DHSSPS, 2006a). Integration was seen as more likely to stimulate opportunities for promoting health and well-being and develop richer care pathways, and was also valued as promoting parity of esteem between professionals.

Table 5.1: Structures for health and social care delivery

Pre-2007	New Structure
Department |	Department |
4 Health & Social Service Boards (Commissioning) |	1 Health & Social Care Board (Commissioning) |
11 Community Health & Social Service Trusts 7 Hospital Trusts 1 Ambulance Trust (Delivery) |	5 Health & Social Care Trusts 1 Ambulance Trust (Delivery) |
10 Special Service Bodies e.g. Mental Health Commission Health Estates Agency |	8 Special Bodies e.g. Public Health Agency Business Services Organisation |
4 Health & Social Services Councils (Public involvement)	1 Patient & Client Council (Public involvement)

The operation of integrated services

The main features of the actual operation and delivery of integrated services can be analysed under a number of headings. In general these features have been carried over from the 18 Trusts into the five reorganised Trusts. The main features of the operation of integration are categorised as:

- integrated programmes of care;
- integrated teams and working together;
- single employer and single budget;
- a one-stop shop approach;
- integrated management;
- professional forum.

Programmes of care and integrated teams

Integration in the delivery of services is mainly achieved in Northern Ireland through a programme of care approach at Trust level. This normally means identifying the programme and bringing together the resources under a focused management structure. At its most developed this encompasses a whole-systems approach to service delivery in the hospital and community. The internal structures and budget arrangements of Trusts facilitate integrated working, and the use of resources is not constrained by artificial boundaries between health and social care. The programmes of care follow a fairly similar pattern through all the Trusts including for older people, mental health, learning disability and physical disability. Some Trusts have a slightly different configuration, for example, separate community services programmes, while in some Trusts the Social Services Directorate overall may not include mental health. Programmes of care may then be delivered through a locality or sub-office arrangement. Childcare programmes tend to reflect less integration than adult social care as there are legal requirements that mean the programme and teams are often staffed exclusively by social workers. Thus, even within the integrated structure of Northern Ireland, the child protection area has a 'separateness' about it. Increasingly, it has been necessary to set up more detailed combinations across the traditional boundaries of different programmes of care (Griffiths et al, 2007).

The programme of care teams operate on a multidisciplinary basis. However, the degree of professional integration does vary between the programmes and the likely level of need. Mental health and learning disability are the most fully integrated professionally, although it appears that the multidisciplinary model is more extensive in mental health than learning disability and there are increasing examples of more specialist integrated teams, for example, child and adolescent mental health teams. Elderly care teams are more social work-based, but they or specialist subgroups may include nursing and therapists. This way of working is a general feature of the integrated system (Heenan and Birrell, 2006, p 54). The person responsible for coordinating assessment and care plans can be anyone who has a professional or social care qualification. Dornan (1999) found that 90% of professionals preferred to work in an integrated practice team and he found significant teamwork in operation. The devolution of integrated teams has continued with community mental health plans for older people, child and adolescent mental health teams, and integrated working involving hospital consultants providing treatment in community services, for example, with fracture rehabilitation teams.

Integrated programme of care teams usually work in the same office. Some Trusts do not insist on the same office, although teams are normally at least all in the same building and come together in team rooms. The shared office issue reflected the need to create systems that facilitate working together. Whilst some Trusts have made progress towards maintaining integrated files this was not fully operative for practical reasons. Integration may mean professionals taking responsibility for a range of tasks some of which would previously have been undertaken by colleagues in other professions, because of traditional job boundaries and work patterns.

Culture of working together

The integrated programme can be seen as encouraging the different mindset that is required for working together and for facilitating team-building and enthusiasm. Joined-up working leads to the identification of what is common between the professions and in elements of need for users and patients, or what is specialist and uni-professional and what is generic. Not everything has been done to remove professional staffing barriers; however, a number of Trusts have created a new grade of staff, albeit at a low level, a grade of health care assistants who would also help social workers, for example, in supporting families. Overall, though, professional boundaries have remained largely intact, other than for organisational purposes.

Single employer and budget

Even more important than inter-professional working as a distinctive feature of integration is the fact that all the professional staff are employed by the same organisation. The one employer organisation has the same goals and objectives and this clearly provides the context for close working relationships. Integrated trusts also avoid the issue of a 'lead' partner or pressure for professional domination by one partner. They also avoid one difficulty in partnership working of one partner giving up some responsibilities.

The integrated Trusts are funded from the same financial source in the same organisation. There is, therefore, a more dependable budget and the Trust has the power to allocate more financial resources to community care and away from institutional care. There is no need for negotiations between different health and social care agencies or for pooled budgets.

One-stop shop approach

Social services in Northern Ireland emphasised the advantages of a 'one-stop shop' or 'no wrong door' approach, that is, there is one front door for anybody who needs health and personal social services and clients can be appropriately dealt with or referred within the one organisation and possibly the one building. The one-stop shop/single door was a way of avoiding some still remaining perceptions of stigma attached to social work offices, particularly in encouraging some people at risk to attend. One initiative of integrated gateway teams meant that only one assessment was needed to access a range of services including child protection, family intervention and complex health needs. The single point of access and pathway into local services means older and vulnerable people do not have to move between organisations and this helps to ensure people do not slip through the net. More recent developments have seen the establishment in Belfast of Well-being and Treatment Centres as one-stop shops for health and social care provision.

Integrated management

In Northern Ireland's Health and Social Care Trusts it is common in all the programmes of care, with the exception of childcare, for the posts of programme manager or team leader to be open to those with a range of professional qualifications. Thus a social worker may lead a team involving nurses on a dementia team, or a nurse may lead a team including social workers on an older persons' team. There had originally been some expectation that, for example, nursing staff might have some reservations in having a social worker as an immediate line manager, but this has not proven to be a significant issue. Some Trusts have a policy that almost all services can be managed by someone from any professional background, while in others, integrated management was to be found more in mental health and physical and learning disability. A number of Trusts make a distinction between operational responsibilities and professional accountability, and a separate professional line of management is established to a senior manager. This requires clarity in deciding where professional accountability lies. A variation of this is that some allowance may be made for the requirements of professional development in recognition of the fact that staff have to be effective professionals to deliver an integrated multi-professional service. Thus there may be a professional group or forum, or the relevant Director/Head of Social Work may hold meetings with social work staff from an integrated team, but in an advisory professional role not in a management line of accountability. Thus it is accepted that individual professional competencies have to be maintained and enhanced and all staff have a right to professional supervision.

There can be some difficulties with integrated management, for example, health visitors may believe they are being disadvantaged by being in an integrated team with social workers, as the service may be totally social work-managed at the top. Each profession brings its own insights, practices and values, but traditional patterns can be deeply ingrained, and staff are more comfortable within their own disciplines. Management arrangements try to facilitate integrated multidisciplinary working. Inter-professional tensions can rise suddenly, perhaps triggered by any suggestion of change or reorganisation when people may go back into their professional box. It is also important for managers of a mix of services to treat disciplines as equals. Management posts down to the level of the first line manager can be held by the most appropriate professional, regardless of discipline (Taylor et al, 2010). The open management structure encouraged social workers to move across to management roles and to move on to directorships, for example, Directors of Planning in Trusts. One of the benefits of the integrated structure is that it opens up the pool of potential management talent. Having managers from any background means that what is being looked at is the ability of a person to deliver a function rather than a professional qualification (Heenan and Birrell, 2006).

Professional forum

It is widely recognised in Northern Ireland that even with integrated team structures and multidisciplinary working it is still necessary to allow staff to maintain their own professional identity in order to keep up their professional skills and look after the more technical issues of professional development. All the integrated trusts make provision for the different professions to meet as a separate professional group. The agenda for such forums covers training, professional governance, issues in professional experience for recognition purposes, professional advice, research issues and social work education. They can also provide peer support and current information on practice. It was seen as important within an integrated structure and multidisciplinary working to allow people to root themselves in their own identity and keep up their professional development so a professional line of management was kept open. Heenan and Birrell (2006, p 56) found that a professional social work forum was an essential prerequisite to the success of integrated working.

Internal assessment of integration

Northern Ireland has what has been described as one of the most structurally integrated and comprehensive modes of health and personal social services in Europe (McCoy, 1993). Despite its uniqueness and length of time in operation, comparatively little research and evaluation has been carried out, even within Northern Ireland. A report by a former Chief Inspector of Social Services discussed the benefits of the integrated system in general terms: access to responsive services through one point of access and an expedient pathway from the level of primary care to more complex and specialised care (McCoy, 1993). Campbell and Pinkerton (1997) suggested that the joined-up administration should result in more collaborative working. Anderson (1998) claimed that there was no doubt that the current system improved community care developments particularly in relation to hospital discharge, but it did not always guarantee integration at service delivery level. McLaughlin (1998) highlighted the benefits of the model, but asked whether real integration was undermined at that time by the existence of a number of acute Hospital Trusts. A former Trust director of social services stressed the positive aspects of integrated services and the importance of the recognition that no one profession has the ability to meet needs. He also, however, highlighted the absence of studies of comparative outcomes with the non-integrated services (Richards, 2000).

Empirical research on the integrated system is limited and spasmodic. Early research for the Royal Commission on the NHS (1979) found respondents taking the view that the system was not working as well as it should, but concluded that integration was inherently beneficial with improved conditions of care between hospital and the community and more effective planning and delivery of social services. Dornan (1999) carried out a small-scale study of integrated care teams working with older people and identified encouraging evidence of multidisciplinary working across the traditional health and social care divide. Challis et al (2006) carried out research on differences in care management for older people between Northern Ireland and England and found more evidence of integrated practice in Northern Ireland than England. All Trusts in Northern Ireland provided services to older people through specialist teams, while less than40% of English authorities had specialist older people's teams. More Northern Ireland Trusts reported having special community-based resources dedicated to the rehabilitation of older people. A higher proportion of Northern Ireland Trusts reported using social workers and occupational therapists in rehabilitation services and more involvement of health care staff in care planning and a more integrated approach to assessment. Overall this study suggested that the delivery of health and social care by a single organisation enabled a more integrated approach to meeting the needs of vulnerable older people through assessment and care management arrangements (Challis et al, 2006, p 344).

Some of the same research group conducted further research on a similar comparative basis into care management arrangements in mental health services (Reilly et al, 2007). This study concurred with the previous research, showing that structurally integrated Trusts in Northern Ireland were more conducive towards, although not sufficient to secure, integrated working. More Trusts in Northern Ireland had greater access to domiciliary services, daycare and residential care services to promote rehabilitation, and a higher proportion of them in Northern Ireland provided specialist care management. There was also more evidence of multidisciplinary working via more care managers in Northern Ireland being based in community mental health teams. However, Reilly et al (2007, p 240) noted an absence of more widespread multidisciplinary working and integrated assessment and care planning, which did not suggest a universal seamless delivery. Overall this work shows slightly more evidence of integrated practice in Northern Ireland mental health and social care, concurring with the previous study on old-age services.

A major independent review of health and social care services (Appleby, 2005) was undertaken for the government in 2005. This had a focus on financing, productivity and hospital services, as well as considering structures. Appleby suggested that the success of the integrated system in Northern Ireland varied, however he did highlight a number of examples of innovative practice in the area of community care. Qualitative research by Heenan and Birrell (2006), based on interviews with senior managers, found support for programmes of care as the key component of integrative working and the view that the integrated system was particularly well placed to meet increasingly complex needs, and encouraged a holistic approach with a shared vision and values. Although some inter-professional tension could surface and students still did their initial training separately, this research suggested that the integrated structures made integrated working more straightforward, but a culture of integration was equally important (Heenan and Birrell, 2006, p 63). A further analysis following the reorganisation into a totally integrated structure including hospitals (Heenan and Birrell, 2009) identified the continuing importance of integrated structures particularly in relation to beneficial outcomes for service users.

UK perceptions of the integrated structure

The issue of close collaboration and joint working has become a key issue in debates and policy development in Great Britain. This has focused on breaking down the barriers between delivery of social care by local authorities and the delivery of health services by NHS bodies. Dowling et al (2004) stated that it is difficult to find a contemporary policy document that is not based around partnerships, collaboration and joint working. The debate about future action tends to address three dimensions. The first dimension concerns structures, guidance and action plans based on the experiences of collaboration (Glendinning and Coleman, 2003, Glasby 2004). To promote joint working, sometimes called integrated working in Great Britain, the Department of Health has an integrated care network website to provide advice, guidance and support on bringing the NHS and local government together.

The second dimension is the experimentation or consideration of structural changes to promote integration. Following the publication of *The NHS Plan* (DH, 2000), which advocated stronger and deeper working together by health and social care agencies and called for fundamental changes, a new level of single multi-purpose Care Trusts was proposed for England. Legislation facilitated their establishment on a voluntary basis through local joint arrangements. In practice Care Trusts were NHS bodies and only 10, some with limited functions, were ever established. A Nuffield Trust Report (Rosen and Ham, 2008), based on lessons from evidence and experience of integrated care, advocated a system of clinical and service integration rather than organisational integration, while Glasby (2009) has put forward the case for a local government-led system of health care to overcome deficits around not only collaboration, but also commissioning and local democratic accountability. Scotland has moved towards a system of Community Health and Social Care Partnerships but there has been a tendency for the NHS to take the lead role (Evans and Forbes, 2009).

The third dimension has developed around the identification of the problems and limitations of integrated approaches. These analyses have stressed financial problems: the issue of common and cross-charging budgets (Freeman and Moore, 2008; Scottish Government, 2010); difficulties in setting up effective arrangements for seamless packages of care (Cooke et al, 2002); difficulty creating broad comprehensive integrated provision (Hudson, 2007); and joint staffing arrangements (Weeks, 2007). Wistow (2000) in reviewing *The NHS Plan* had also suggested that discontinuities of care cannot simply be overcome by structural integration.

Somewhat surprisingly, there has only been a very limited attempt to draw on the Northern Ireland experience of integrated care. Philpot (2001), for example, expressed dismay at the lack of research and analysis. Some comments that have been made have also been dismissive of any beneficial achievements. Hudson and Henwood (2002) argue that much of the integration between health and social care is more apparent than real, and that the system does not provide a solution to be emulated in managing health and social care integration. Field and Peck (2003) suggested that the system did not provide seamless joined-up service. These comments were, however, based on a brief government review of winter pressures (Heenan and Birrell, 2006, p 49). Studies by the Nuffield Trust on the integrated structure (Ham, 2009), and by the Department of Health on the evidence base for integrated care (DH, 2008), made no reference to Northern Ireland, yet both drew on American experiences.

The lessons from Northern Ireland

What lessons might be drawn in general from Northern Ireland experience in the context of the absence of major empirical studies? It is possible to comment on some of the key policy outcomes and improvements that might be expected from integrated working: hospital discharges, moves from institutional to community care, and innovative integrated initiatives whose introduction and development have been smoothed by the integrated system.

Hospital discharge policy

An efficient and speedy system of hospital discharge is seen as one of the real benefits of integration in Northern Ireland. Delays are cited in Britain (NHS, 2000, p 28) as a major example of rigid institutional boundaries, which can mean that the needs of the individual patient come a poor second to the needs of each individual agency. The escalation of the problem has led to the imposition of a drastic cross-charging system of fines to be paid by local authorities to health bodies to compensate for delayed discharges in acute care. The new fully integrated Trusts in Northern Ireland have reported significant reductions in delayed discharges. The Belfast Health and Social Care Trust noted that the 2007 restructuring had facilitated closer working relationships between colleagues in the same organisation (Belfast Health and Social Care Trust, 2008). The Northern Trust had been able to meet the target of efficient discharges from hospital within 48 hours for 90% of people. This can be attributed to the complete integration of care planning across the acute care–community care interface. If social workers, district nurses and hospital staff are working together in the one system then they are responsible for managing the process of moving patients in and out of hospital. The same group know the demands from people in the community and are fully aware of the pressures they are dealing with in the hospital. Some delays were possible because of the appropriateness of a place or service, but not because of resource difficulties or due to a gap in funding. Thus social workers in hospitals or discharge teams are the key people in a position to make speedy decisions when faced with the pressures of moving people out of hospital. Resources can be skewed from the same organisation to keep people out of the hospital system. There is also the flexibility to target more resources from residential care to domiciliary care, as the finance is all within one budget.

The full advantages of integration can be demonstrated when resources within and outside the hospital can be adjusted or redeployed. If the hospital is overheating in terms of not being able to get people out, waiting lists in the community can be adjusted to help people move out of hospital or there can be the flexibility, for example, to open a discharge ward and redeploy nurses from the community into the ward or to purchase a period of care in the community for patients. The integrated structure reduces the possibility of institutional divisions, and discharge policy is seen as everyone's problem, not a problem for either the hospital or social care. There is no need for a process of negotiation between the two sectors and it is accepted as in everyone's interest to clear hospital discharges quickly.

Northern Ireland had examples of separate Hospital Trusts before 2007. In these examples social work staff from the Social and Community Trusts normally worked in the hospital setting. This may suggest that a fully integrated structure may not be necessary to have a seamless discharge service and good working collaboration. However, there was still a difference with the structures in England and Scotland as even where there were separate Hospital Trusts, they were still operating with an integrated Board structure. Thus the Board could plan and commission an integrated discharge policy, which was delivered by cooperation between a Community and a Hospital Trust. Since 2007, a totally integrated structure, with its financial flexibility, has facilitated positive outcomes in tackling the problems of discharge delays, closures and resettlements (Heenan and Birrell, 2006, p 60). This can be compared to Great Britain where the experience on hospital discharge is mixed. Some local authorities had real problems with delayed discharges and problems in building capacity to prevent delayed discharges. In the worst scenarios, hospital discharge procedures were inadequate, driven by pressure for beds, the lack of available community health and social care services, and poor GP involvement in discharge arrangements. On the other hand, in some local authorities with social work teams based in hospitals, discharge worked relatively well with agreed discharge procedures, low rates of delayed transfers and the development of intermediate care services.

Moving from institutional to community care

One of the achievements of integration has been some success in facilitating the move from institutional to community care, particularly in the case of managing retraction in hospital provision. Integration made it easier in parts of Northern

Ireland to run down psychiatric and learning disability hospitals and to plan and prepare for discharging patients into the community. With only one Trust involved it has not proved necessary to hold joint planning meetings between different agencies. In these areas the key to resettlement was the ability to move resources around, all within the one budget, thus avoiding arguments about picking up the bill and the problem of transferring people from the health budget and onto social services. Thus as wards close the money saved can be put into the Trust to directly enable community services to be developed. The integrated structure meant that retraction, closures and resettlement could take place more quickly. There has been a reduction in the number of people in long-stay hospitals for learning disability, particularly with the support of learning disability teams. The integration of care enabled the South-Eastern Health and Social Care Trust to close a mental hospital that at one time had 800 patients. The final group to be resettled consisted of long-stay patients with complex needs transferring to new hostel accommodation (South-Eastern Health and Social Care Trust, 2008).

This might point to a major advantage of the Northern Ireland structure in promoting community care. However, it can be argued that Northern Ireland has not made the full progress that might be expected from the integrated structure. In 2000 Northern Ireland spent 58% of its total mental health budget on hospitals compared to England's 40% (DHSSPS, 2003b) and Northern Ireland still has five psychiatric hospitals. Prior (1993) noted that Northern Ireland had a much greater admission rate to psychiatric hospitals than England and suggested that although hospital beds at that time had been reduced, the increase in community-based services had not paralleled the decrease in hospital beds. In 2002 there were still 1,500 people in psychiatric hospitals, which may reflect a higher rate of mental illness in Northern Ireland. However, there is also evidence that the closure of adult acute psychiatric beds has not been as rapid as it should have been (Royal College of Psychiatrists, 2009). It can be argued that the integrated service should have produced expanded community provision and institutional closures earlier.

Integration and innovation

Integration has facilitated a range of intermediate care and rehabilitation schemes, for example, a scheme involving provision of bungalows to train patients discharged from hospital to be independent, and a primary care project to ensure that people do not go into hospital unnecessarily who can be supported at home with appropriate social, health or psychiatric help. There are a number of similar intermediate care schemes: crisis support teams and intensive domiciliary care schemes, and hospital and home schemes with multi-professional teams created out of both social and health care personnel. Homefirst Community Trust has reported a new community rehabilitation team to prevent admission to hospital and residential homes with a team consisting of a manager, physiotherapist, occupational therapist, social workers, speech and language therapist, community nurses, podiatrist, and support workers. Child and adolescent mental health teams were often quoted as examples of innovation, with a team of nurses, social workers, psychologists and psychiatrists who entered partnerships with local voluntary organisations. Other initiatives mentioned include trauma teams, addiction teams, an elderly person resource centre that had moved away from the traditional definition of personal social services provision, and a number of Traveller initiatives based on an integrated approach. The introduction of guidelines to good practice in dealing with domestic violence saw them applied to both the social work and health sectors. There are a number of initiatives in Northern Ireland that have been identified as reflecting more specifically the benefits of integration, catering for those with complex needs such as children and young people who are technologically dependent. One Board reported that five young people were being treated at home, which was more efficient than having them lying in an acute ward with all the funding going to the hospital. Instead there is a social carer providing the main inputs into their care with their families, with nurses and GPs coming in from time to time (Heenan and Birrell, 2006). There were similar cases where integration had facilitated a fluid transition from a health emphasis to a social care approach, for example, in recovery from brain injuries. A Trust reported a case of acquired brain injury where there had been a significant debate with medics who thought that the investments should all be made into services provided through medicine, but social services successfully argued the case for interaction and integration into the community with appropriate home care. Thus integration facilitated a health care approach being turned around into a social care approach or reaching the right balance. Treatment of the terminally ill in the community/at home with nurses and GPs coming in alongside social care was a further example. More people are surviving major trauma because of advances in medical techniques, but consequently have major needs for lifelong support. One Trust had recently established a brain injury integrated team.

Some of the most recent publications examining evidence in relation to devolution have paid particular attention to structures. The paper by Ramsey and Fulop (2008), published by the Department of Health, on the evidence base for integrated care listed eight lessons. It is worth noting that the five referring to structures are not especially supported by the Northern Ireland evidence:

- that successful integrated systems have grown organically;
- that integration that focuses mainly on bringing organisations together is unlikely to create improvements;
- that local contexts are supportive of integration;
- that initiatives need to be aware of local organisational cultural differences; and
- that there is a need for the right incentives, possible financial, to get staff to buy into the process.

The additional lessons of 'not assuming the achievement of economies of scale' and of 'patience' may be more valid and the last lesson of 'avoiding imbalance between acute and community services' is confirmed by Northern Ireland experience.

Nuffield Trust papers in 2008 and 2009, which also had a focus on structures (Rosen and Ham, 2008; Ham, 2009), again did not draw on the Northern Ireland experience, although they did suggest that the starting point of any discussion should be clinical and service integration rather than organisational integration. In contrast the Northern Ireland model demonstrates the value of a uniform imposed structure of integration. The question about whether the governance of integration requires the formation of a single organisational entity to fulfil the goals of integration or whether effective inter-organisational reporting and risk management can be developed was also raised. The subsequent discussion tended, however, to focus on partnership working, robust governance, accommodation, shared budgets, integrating information technology and improving relationships. Structure integration on the Northern Ireland model removes such issues being a major barrier. The Nuffield Trust paper in 2009 (Ham, 2009), which analysed examples of integrated working by Care Trusts and partnerships between Primary Care Trusts and local authorities, did raise a list of challenges that had to be overcome, including: the role of leadership, agendas not aligned, staff contracts, organisational protectionism, lack of an integration culture and the need to involve all NHS bodies including acute trusts and mental health provision. The Northern Ireland experience has some positive lessons for dealing with or overcoming such barriers and can also provide some evidence of problems and barriers that can emerge.

The problem of protecting social services

Integration raises the issue that in a merged structure there is a need to protect the social services sector from the demands of health. The experience of the last 30 years was that when they were alongside acute hospitals, social care services tended to get starved of resources because of the needs of the hospitals. It is easy to reduce community services, although it is not so easy to reduce hospital services. If there is a crisis in the acute sector, money may very easily get diverted and it is hard to achieve ring-fencing at Board or Trust level. This issue is highlighted by Heenan and Birrell (2009, p 9), who note that:

> A key dimension is the financial demands of the acute sector and its higher public profile with politicians and the media. The social care sector has repeatedly voiced concerns about the diversion of funding from them to shore up the acute sector.

The hegemony of the health agenda can be a persistent concern with organisational priorities reflecting this dominance. A report by Appleby (2005, p 89) had recommended in general ring-fencing of social services' budgets in Boards and Trusts. In areas with larger hospitals it may be more likely that community budgets would be used to clear deficits and so on, or to subsidise the acute sector. The acute services have a tendency to overspend while community services often remain within their budgets. Although, in practice, health interests tend to dominate in integrated Trusts, which included district hospitals and specialist hospitals for mental illness and learning disability, there was a view that by and large social services' budgets had been protected. Budgeting for a mix of health and social services in an integrated system means there is potential for some flexibility in resource allocation within a Trust, which can have advantages. As there is only one organisation, any financial problems can be viewed as the whole Trust's problem. A further view is that were Northern Ireland social services not in an integrated structure, they would not necessarily have got the same level of investment money for community, residential and domiciliary care. Social services may have at times benefited from extra levels of funding made available primarily for the health services.

Decisions can be made in integrated Trusts without having to engage in elaborate exchanges between different hierarchies, and a single hierarchy allows decisions to be made quickly. In integrated Trusts there has had to be an awareness that the bulk of service users are outside hospital, consequently the thrust of services had to be about community provision. Another concern is that performance targets set by the government department relate almost entirely to health, with very few relating to adult social care. Northern Ireland does not have a system of star ratings, which means that operational plans for social care are not clearly identifiable or recognised. There are also concerns that social care values and priorities are subsumed and/or not understood by a dominant health system and the social model–medical model conflict can arise. The focus on the integration of health and social care also sits alongside Northern Ireland not moving to implement the structural requirements of 'Every Child Matters' in England, which involved setting up integrated structures combining child protection, schools and early years provision. The management of social housing is also the responsibility of a separate administrative body from social care, meaning that initiatives such as Supporting People are located across separate housing and health and social care bodies and require collaborative working through partnership.

Conclusion

Northern Ireland does demonstrate a working model of integration of health and personal social services. This model has to be considered in the context that Northern Ireland, unlike Great Britain, has a structure that contains highly integrated elements. Integrated Trusts have three main characteristics: an agency with responsibilities for the delivery of comprehensive NHS health services and social care; internal structures that facilitate integrated working; and a culture of integrated multidisciplinary working. A key question is to what extent the level of integrated functioning is different from the pattern in Great Britain, which now has extensive examples of joint working and working together.

The most notable features of integration are that all professionals are employed by the same organisation, work alongside each other and formally have the same goals and objectives. With integrated planning and commissioning and programmes of care, integrated management for service delivery and teams of professionals working together, there is no need to operate partnerships between different organisations where each partner may have to negotiate giving something up. The facilitation of a seamless service at the point of access is important. Individuals move through a spectrum of care as they become more dependent and with integration they do not have to move between organisations and there are no arguments about who picks up the bill.

The integrated system has also brought together a professional energy and a commitment to a holistic approach and staff see themselves as colleagues not as someone working in a different scenario. In Northern Ireland the values of integration have been sustained through various forms of reorganisation. The structure has gone a long way to break down the traditional straightjackets of professional approaches and there have been fundamental changes in culture with professionals developing new definitions of team-working. Operationally major achievements can be identified in terms of having in place a smooth interface between acute and community services: the facilitation of strategic shifts from institutional to community care both financially and organisationally.

Notwithstanding some achievements in these areas, integration has not realised its full potential. There is still widespread recognition of difficulties that can arise in working together, that tensions can be caused by the resource demands of the acute sector, that there are still funding imbalances, and that social care resources can be stretched. It may be difficult to maintain social work values and welfare principles and there is a danger of being sucked into a different value base. A particular issue is that senior management at department and Board level outside Trusts may see themselves as primarily health officials, thus inhibiting integrated approaches and equality of esteem. Government, assembly, department and Board policy and strategy documents often pay scant attention to the potential of integration as a driver of improvement, well-being and modernisation.

SIX

Social work and community development

Introduction

In Northern Ireland, as in other areas of the UK, the relationship between community development and social work has a long history. In many ways they can be seen as having a similar value base with the promotion of participation, self-help and empowerment underlying policy and practice. While this all sounds fairly innocuous, in practice, however, the relationship between the two areas has proved controversial and complicated. Underlying tensions surrounding issues of identity, the relationship with the state and professionalism have contributed to long-running debates and competing perspectives. Some community development educators and practitioners are explicitly hostile to social work and concerned to distance community development from what they see as an allegedly conservative profession that is at odds with their radical non-conformist approach (Mowbray and Meekosha, 1990; Waddington, 1994; Kenny, 1999). On reflection, though, it is apparent that both community development and social work have conservative and radical components, and to draw this dichotomy is inaccurate.

Community development has proved notoriously difficult to define and the idea of community varies widely depending on the context of the discussion and debate. The approach can be found in various settings including social work, urban regeneration, health care and adult education. The underlying principle of community development is that people in local areas can be empowered to improve their own circumstances and this aligns to the fundamental values and principles of the social work profession. Community social work involves a recognition and understanding of the power structures and dynamics within an area and developing responses and initiatives that address the structural, systemic issues underlying social problems.

Mainstream social work has incorporated a structural and systemic perspective that holistically examines the relationship between individuals and broader social structures and community networks (O'Connor et al, 1998; Goldsworthy, 2002). Similarly, community development is based on the relationship between the community and broader social structures and networks. Many contemporary programmes such as neighbourhood renewal are based on working within our existing socio-political system rather than developing strategies to explicitly challenge social structures (Mendes, 2004; Mowbray, 2004). In the UK, the government has increased funding and support for community development projects and initiatives to address social exclusion and poverty. The emphasis on user consultation, participation and empowerment in these projects makes them ideally placed to address marginalisation. Locally based interventions have been given a key role in capacity-building and regenerating communities. New Labour recognised the value of using a bottom-up approach in a wide range of policy areas, and community development enjoyed something of a renaissance. It has been noted that the re-emergence of community development approaches within social work has witnessed a shift from being viewed as a radical approach to being accepted as a significant method of intervention (Heenan and Birrell, 2002; Heenan, 2004).

The work of community development tends to concentrate more on such communities of interest, and less on individuals (although the use of interpersonal skills are an essential aspect of practice). Some examples include residents of an urban or rural area, feminist community work, black and minority ethnic communities, carers, disabled people, and those experiencing mental health problems. Although it is important to recognise that these groups are not homogeneous and represent diverse interests, community development tends to be about helping people from similar and different backgrounds to achieve agreed goals. Community development has always been influenced by social, political and economic issues, and, as a result, competing definitions about its purpose have emerged in the UK context. For example, Popple (1995) has argued that there are two distinct strands to community development practice in Britain: the first espouses a form of benevolent paternalism, best represented in the work of some parts of the voluntary sector; the other, more radical version can be found in the work of some groups that tend to challenge the state and engage in community action as a way of addressing discrimination and social disadvantage. Whilst in Northern Ireland, historically, there have been some significant differences between community development and social work, it is indisputable that they have much in common. Both have played a key role in challenging sectarianism, inequalities and injustices, and both have taken the lead in promoting a more responsive society. In recent years there has been a re-emphasis on community development approaches in health and social care. This chapter sets out the relationship between the approaches and assesses the impact of the re-emphasis on community development perspectives in social work.

What is community development?

There are many views about what constitutes community development, which depend on circumstances, context and cultures. A comprehensive definition was provided by the Northern Ireland Community Development Review Group (NICDRG) (1991, p 2):

> Community development in Northern Ireland is a process, which embraces community action, community service, and other community

endeavours – whether geographical or issue based – with an emphasis towards the disadvantaged, impoverished and powerless within society. Its values include participation, empowerment and self-help. And while it is essentially about collective action, it helps to realise the potential of both individuals and groups within communities.

The concept of community development is about achieving social and political change and refers to a set of methods or ways of working with local groups to identify and tackle problems and develop appropriate evidence-based strategies. It aims to raise capacity by giving local people the skills and knowledge to address their own needs. It usually includes the following tenets.

Collective action

Community development is based on the idea of people in a locality acting together to formulate views and create change based on a community definition of issues. Fundamental to this principle is the notion that collective action can achieve more than individuals acting alone. Collective action can move along a spectrum from the simple expression of views to the provision of a service.

Active citizenship

Community development embraces the idea that the citizen can take action to influence public policy decisions and should be permitted access to channels to make their views heard. Citizens should be able to organise to make themselves heard on matters of major concern such as health and social problems. The process of involving members of local communities in working for change can impact on those individuals' capacity to act as citizens (Lister, 1997). Involvement in community and voluntary action has led to such groups being described as 'incubators of civic skills' (Verba et al, 1996); while community action in this sense can also be seen as contributing to a viable 'civil society' operating alongside government (Etzioni, 1993).

Empowerment

Community development embraces the ideas of empowerment through community groups achieving the capacity to influence policy and provision. There may be a prerequisite that groups develop self-competence, self-reliance and self-help skills. They may then exercise some effective intervention, say through activities to improve the community in which they live. Empowerment will also come through gaining knowledge and acquiring information, skills and expertise. Empowerment may also develop through the local community ownership of projects, whether through acquiring responsibility for planning or the actual delivery of services.

Participation and inclusion

Community development has a commitment to involve those who feel they have little power over their own lives as a means of facilitating participation by those who are in disadvantaged and isolated groups or localities. Community development, then, encourages involvement of the poor and socially excluded. Social exclusion not only impacts on individuals, but may also undermine and cut off whole communities from the wider society and surrounding economy. Participation in community and voluntary action has been increasingly described as a contribution to social capital through which participation enhances social inclusion, reduces alienation, strengthens consensus, and generates greater equality and social stability (Putnam, 2000). Thus community development fosters social capital, local networking, collaboration, trust, neighbourliness and engagement.

Partnership

Community development when established also has a commitment to joint working. This can operate at the level of collaboration between community groups to share knowledge and resources to their mutual advantage, but increasingly involves formal partnerships with the statutory sector, whether at local or central government level or with the voluntary or private sectors. In one of the few studies of community development in health and social services in Northern Ireland, a key finding to emerge from all the community development work described was the importance of multidisciplinary and inter-agency work (McShane and O'Neill, 1999).

Community social work

So what, then, is community social work? Is it simply social work based in a local community, rather than a hospital or a prison? The answer to this is a categorical 'no', with many commentators at pains to stress that community social work implies a different way of working, an approach that is about empowering people to use existing resources to change and improve their communities. It is working 'with' the community rather than 'for' the community. Rather than being something that has been bolted onto the end of traditional social work practice, it underpins the whole approach and informs policies and practice.

In their curriculum guidance for the degree in social work, O'Neill and Campbell (2005) list the main components of community social work as follows:

- Community social work embraces the functions of the whole social work agency and should not be ancillary to them.
- It is based on collaborative working within teams providing services and involves working cooperatively with formal and informal networks.

- It focuses on the nature and type of relationships between individuals, groups, organisations and the community.
- It acknowledges that the vast majority of care is undertaken by informal carers and this contribution is not well recognised, nor acknowledged.
- It is proactive rather than reactive, and actively works to ensure communities have adequate resources.
- It is often informed by needs analysis and partnership working.

Unlike traditional social work methods, which are based on individual needs and casework, this approach looks at the person in the context of their wider community. It adopts a holistic approach that aims to develop the capacity of the individual and their communities. Rather than reacting to a crisis and intervening as a last resort, social workers work to ensure people are continuously supported. Key objectives are, therefore, to create and sustain partnerships and networks and employ a range of methods that reflect the needs of the community.

There has been some resistance to this way of working because social work has traditionally been managed hierarchically with clear lines of control. Community social workers do not fit easily into this pattern and can be viewed as a threat to conventional management systems. Additionally, such an approach can lead to a conflict of interest between the needs of a community group and the objectives of a social work department. In periods of financial cuts and retrenchment in the public sector, it is often projects based in the community that are sacrificed first, as they are considered less essential.

History of social work and community development

The history and relationship between community development and social work in Northern Ireland has been markedly different from that in the rest of the UK. An overview of the turbulent history of the two traditions in Britain is provided by Clarke (1996). He claims that social work and community development have had an almost non-existent working relationship due to three key strands of history and tradition. First, following the attack on social work by Barbara Wootton, the profession sought a way to redefine and reinvent itself by embracing centralisation and case-centred professionalism as the way forward. Bureaucracy, hierarchy and corporate strategic planning did not fit well with the decentralised, autonomous community development approach. Second, when it became clear that the welfare state was not a panacea that could eliminate all want, class again became a key issue, and it was not clear where social work stood in relation to class problems. Finally, community development workers were reluctant to become associated with what they viewed as elitism. They preferred a hands-on approach to poverty and deprivation, which contrasted sharply with the approach of their newly professionalised colleagues in social work.

As long ago as the 1950s, Eileen Younghusband argued for a 'closer working partnership' between social work and community development. She maintained that the use of community development could help in 'enlarging the horizon of social work'. Her contention was developed and resulted in the *Report of the Working Party on Social Services in the Local Authority Health and Welfare Services* (Younghusband, 1959). This report marked a turning point in the emergence of community development as a distinct entity and signalled the official acceptance of community development in Great Britain. It was strongly influenced by the North American division of social work into casework, group work and community organisation. The latter was described as primarily aimed at helping people within a local community to identify social needs, to consider the most effective ways of meeting these and to set about doing so, insofar as their available resources permitted. The main thrust of the argument was that community work should be one of social work's three methods alongside group work and casework. Following this the terms 'community work' and 'community development' became popular and were often used interchangeably. The term 'community development' was adopted by those who were working in local projects or initiatives where the focus was on self-help and anti-poverty.

The academic debate about the relationship between social work and community development had little impact on practice in Northern Ireland (McCready, 2001). Social workers did not engage in the debate and remained at an intellectual and geographical distance. However, when they were forced to deal with the consequences of violence and intimidation, the social work agencies acknowledged that their priorities had to change dramatically. In this period of social unrest, community development was recognised as a tool for dealing with changing social work priorities. A key issue in continuing and expanding this approach was that social workers had their comprehension of the concept of community development and its relevance to existing modes of social work practice challenged. The social work agencies and the profession held fairly rigid ideas about the nature of social work intervention and were reluctant to embrace change. Not surprisingly the beginning of the Troubles in Northern Ireland led to a huge change in demand for the personal social services. Between 1966 and 1974, the number of social workers more than doubled (Williamson and Darby, 1978). When the Seebohm Report (HMSO, 1968) suggested that emerging social services should contain a commitment to community development, Northern Ireland with its strong tradition of voluntary and community work, appeared ideally placed to respond to this proposal. The report stressed the need for social services to be informed by their location and be cognisant of the needs of the local population. McCready (2001) contends that this report was a landmark in British social work as it advocated working with communities and preventing problems, rather than simply reacting to issues by dealing with cases as they emerged.

Whilst in Britain the community development approach achieved pre-eminence with the launch of the Community Development Programme in 1969, which was the first large-scale action-research initiative funded by central government. In Northern Ireland the escalating violence and social disorder largely prevented a large-scale shift towards community development. This approach within public services remained marginal and was largely confined to voluntary groups. Other reasons for the relegation of community development to the periphery and resistance to its adoption were listed by O'Neill and Douglas (1999, p 10) as follows:

- the concentration on focusing on what the 1972 Health and Personal Social Services Order identified as 'persons in need' rather than taking a broader, community-based perspective;
- budgetary constraints diverted resources from promotional/preventative activity such as community work, into more acute individual/family-focused activities;
- the 'democratic deficit', which left Northern Ireland government departments relatively free from local influence and accountability, militated against more open and democratic methods of service delivery (such as community development);
- the tendency in government thinking, in some UK and Northern Ireland administrations, to promote the notion of individual pathology and personal responsibility again militated against more collective approaches to human problems and needs; and
- the continued growth of a bureaucratic structure for delivering personal social services, which led Caul and Herron (1992, p 167) to bemoan: 'It is one of the very sad features of social work in Northern Ireland that ossified, complex organizations have been allowed to displace the original goals of professional social workers with a totally unjustifiable detachment from local communities'.

Robson (2000) has suggested that community action in Northern Ireland can be divided into two distinct phases. The key feature of the first period is the absence of state involvement. This period in the 1950s and 1960s witnessed the emergence of local initiatives such as credit unions and housing associations. The second phase in the aftermath of the civil rights movement was marked by a new relationship between community groups and the state. By the beginning of the 1970s, largely as a response to social unrest, a vibrant community and voluntary sector had begun to emerge. It has been estimated that by 1974 some 500 community groups were in existence, with the origins of many groups lying in the violence that began in 1967 (Griffiths, 1975). According to Frazer (1981, p 14):

> The early 1970s saw a tremendous growth in community activity and new, dynamic and progressive forms of voluntary effort in Northern Ireland. Pressures for social change came from a range of different sources inspired by a variety of motives, including compassion for victims of misfortune, anger at injustices and fear of unrest.

This work was supported by the statutory Community Relations Commission, which was set up in 1969 'to foster harmonious relations throughout the community'(McCready, 2001, p 31) and a community development approach was adopted to achieve this. While the community development activity within local areas provided a focus for welfare rights, housing issues and redevelopment, much of this work was within nationalist communities. It was largely a response to a state-within-a-state mentality, where the minority Catholic community felt marginalised and excluded. Indeed, as McCready (2001, p 40) noted, within Protestant communities the Community Relations Commission became known as the Catholic Relations Commission. Under the 1969 Social Needs Act (Northern Ireland), the Ministry of Community Relations provided capital grants to local community groups for the building of community centres in urban areas of social need. In effect this funding was concentrated in areas that engaged in disorder and rioting, leading those who were not engaged in this type of activity to feel neglected. Government reforms were seen as appeasing the Catholic community at the expense of Protestants. An unspoken objective of the Community Relations Commission was to create bridges between the two communities by mobilising campaigns around common social and economic issues. This overly simplistic view of the complexity of the conflict in Northern Ireland was ultimately to lead to its demise (Gaffikin and Morrissey, 1990).

The decision by the Moyle Report (1975) to promote community development through district councils, fundamentally altered the nature of this work and marked a new phase of development. The community and voluntary sector became more institutionalised and many local activists refused to become involved with what they viewed as a state-dominated profession. Under the direction of district councils the emphasis in community work was on the provision of resources and facilities rather than empowering local communities. In recognition that local councils were unlikely to expend significant effort promoting community development, the government set up the Community Worker Research Project, which was designed to employ individuals to undertake and evaluate a range of supported community projects. Additionally, a Northern Ireland Voluntary Trust (NIVT) was established as an independent charitable trust designed to empower local communities to bring about positive change. In many ways these measures prevented the development of further links between health and social services and community development. Social work and community development were seen as two distinct spheres with two distinct methods of working. It was some time before there was a renewed emphasis on social work and community development and their methods and approaches were viewed as inextricably linked.

By the early 1970s the crises in Northern Ireland led to the local government at Stormont being prorogued and the reintroduction of Direct Rule from Westminster. As local government had been the focus of many of the allegations of discrimination and sectarianism, powers were stripped from them and placed with a number of democratically unaccountable, well-resourced quangos, which included integrated Health and Social Service Boards. Whilst the 1970s was a period of intense violence and prolonged social unrest, the era heralded a coming of age for social work. The profession expanded rapidly with unprecedented access to resources and influence and was transformed from a relatively small area of operation to a flourishing professional activity. However, this expansion and success was not without its costs, as social work could be viewed as detached and removed from the communities it served. Social work became remedial rather than developmental and focused on individuals rather than their communities. The disintegration of community development approaches within these Health and Social Services Boards can be viewed as evidence of these changing priorities (McShane and O'Neill, 1999). This period has been referred to as the technocratic expansion of social work by Pinkerton and Campbell, who go on to note (2002, p 729):

> As with the rest of the UK, in the 1980s efficiency and effectiveness became the watchwords of an ascendant technocratic professional ideology, reflected in management practice and training.

A further impetus for a closer working relationship between social work and community development was the publication of the Barclay Report (Barclay, 1982). This report recommended that social services agencies and their employees should move beyond the casework role and become more involved in community-based approaches to meeting need. This implied a closer and more direct relationship with community groups. For instance this could involve a local carers group or volunteer bureau initiative in supporting a vulnerable client. New skills were needed to carry out community needs assessment and the initiation and development of new groups or community organisations to meet identified need. Significantly, this report advocated a rethinking of the relationship between service providers and users. It also favoured a wider remit for social workers, which included counselling and social care planning. It proposed that social workers should take a partnership approach with the community and advocated the practice of community social work (Barclay, 1982, p xvii):

> By community social work we mean formal social work which, starting from problems affecting individuals or groups and the responsibilities and resources of social work departments and voluntary organisations, seeks to tap into, support, enable and underpin the local networks of formal and informal relationships which constitutes a basic definition of community.

In this context, community social work means devolving power to local communities and working with individuals who have detailed knowledge of the local area. It recommended that close working relationships be developed between those delivering the services and the citizens in receipt of them. Community social work required a patch-based approach where the social worker had a detailed knowledge of a small area and could draw on local resources and knowledge. Overall, it was suggested that this would require a particular set of skills and knowledge. To facilitate these developments, resources would have to be devolved to local level. This view was contested by Pinker in a minority report, who contended that the model of client-centred social work was fit for purpose and that social work should be selective rather than universal, reactive rather than preventive. In his view social workers should not be engaged in wider community issues as this was not their job. The minority report proved more popular with social services departments and the Conservative government at the time, and, as a result, social work tended to become more polarised and specialised over the years (O'Neill and Campbell, 2005).

Following the publication of the Griffiths Report (Griffiths, 1998), the community care agenda emerged as a dominant theme in health and social care. Although the Griffiths Report did not extend to Northern Ireland, it was very much in keeping with the Regional Strategy for the Northern Ireland Health and Social Services 1987–92. The Regional Strategy stressed the need for an empathic implementation of community care policies. It set out the need to develop comprehensive community-based services with a corresponding reduction in the dependence on institutional places. Boards were required to develop effective programmes to enable patients to be cared for in the community. These policy changes meant an increasing need for multidisciplinary community teams led by or including social workers to have responsibility for coordinating this movement and ensuring people had the appropriate support to remain in their homes. The focus for health and social care was firmly in the community with packages of care tailored to meet individual needs. According to McCready (2001), at this juncture the lack of a mature community development skill base within the service negated the potential of an empowering practice approach to social work taking hold in Northern Ireland.

In 1993 the Northern Ireland administration, for the first time, put in place a clear strategic policy framework to support the expansion of community development. This document, *Strategy for the Support of the Voluntary Sector and for Community Development in Northern Ireland* (DHSS, 1993), represented clear support and recognition of the work of community groups. It acknowledged that community development approaches were already implicit in a number of key government programmes and policies, but that a greater commitment to this work was required throughout the statutory sector. In many ways this policy was viewed as bringing community development in from the cold and endorsing the approach as a way of working. The government accepted the need to improve and enhance the efficiency and effectiveness of existing commitments to community development. A new emphasis on community development was to be achieved by establishing a Voluntary Activity Unit in the Department of Health and Social Services. As McCready (2001, p 92) noted, the establishment of this new unit represented a significant commitment to community development within the senior echelons of government and although 'it may have been a long time coming it was welcome'.

Shortly after coming to power in 1997, the Labour government restated a general commitment to community development approaches as a way to ensuring equality, empowerment and partnership working in social policy. A compact between government and the voluntary and community sector in Northern Ireland – *Partnership for Equality* (NIO, 1998) – confirmed the ongoing commitment to this work and stated that there were a number of shared principles that would inform the working of the government with these other sectors. It noted:

> The shared principles state that government and the sector support community development processes as an important way of enabling people to contribute to issues which affect their lives and communities in which they live, and of ensuring bottom-up rather than top-down policies and programmes in both the statutory and voluntary sectors, on the basis of empowerment, inclusion, equity, partnership and collective action. (NIO, 1998, p 13)

Policy developments since the 1990s

In the years that followed there was little evidence to suggest that social workers radically changed their practice towards this community-based perspective. Nonetheless, policymakers, through a range of initiatives, have increasingly emphasised the need for agencies and their workers to consult and be more connected to localities and communities. In particular the arrangement of services for adults was seen as benefitting from a community social work approach that could also assist service users in articulating their needs (SSI, 2002). According to Barr et al (1996, p 12):

> The principles of community development apply to community care, both in terms of collective empowerment of care users and carers ... and in relation to the role that people in neighbourhoods might play in supporting community care.

Since the early 1990s there has been a rediscovery of community development approaches by policymakers in Northern Ireland. A raft of government initiatives and policies have emerged that have encouraged and facilitated community social work approaches. As a response to high levels of deprivation, the Direct Rule Conservative government launched the Targeting Social Need (TSN) programme in 1991, to secure greater equality of opportunity and equity in Northern Ireland. Its objective was to achieve a more permanent and structured elimination of community differentials. This new policy contained a formal recognition by the government that the community had a role to play in tackling inequalities and improving social conditions in disadvantaged areas. This initiative was re-launched by the Labour government as the New TSN programme, which aimed to identify people and areas in greatest need and ensure that policies were effective in helping them (OFMDFM, 1998).

Simultaneously, changes in health and social care strengthened community development in the social work profession. The reorganisation of health and personal social services in 1991 aimed to move services from a traditionally bureaucratic model to one that embraced the purchaser–provider divide, and also policies that paradoxically appeared to emphasise greater dialogue with service users and communities. In 1993 a Department of Health and Social Services document, *Strategy for the Support of the Voluntary Sector* (DHSS, 1993), recognised perhaps for the first time the value of a community development approach. In the forward to the report, the minister welcomes the inclusion of 'a clear statement of the importance which we attach to the work of community groups and the process of community development' (DHSS, 1993, p 1). This community development approach was described as the means to assist the statutory and voluntary sectors with the ability to reach those in need. The government's *Regional Strategy for Health and Social Wellbeing 1997–2002* (DHSS, 1997a) acknowledged that community development had an important role to play in providing positive health and social well-being. It noted that this should involve supporting local communities to identify the health and social concerns of the greatest importance to them and helping them to devise and implement solutions. This Regional Strategy was updated and amended to reflect the priorities of the New Labour government in a document entitled *Well into 2000* (DHSS, 1997b).

More significantly, in 1999 the government published a report, *Mainstreaming Community Development in Health and Personal Social Services* (DHSSPS, 1999b), in which the government declared its desire to see community development extended, strengthened, promoted throughout Northern Ireland and mainstreamed in all health and social services agencies. At the more general level of social work activity it has been acknowledged by central government that a community development approach can be used by social workers and other helping professions to address poverty and social exclusion. A series of initiatives, including the Active Communities Initiative (1999), New Targeting Social Need (1998) and the Children Order (1997), have encouraged people to adopt a self-help approach and 'discover their own resources which empower them to become active citizens in society which in turn creates communal life' (DHSSPS, 1999b, p 12). Healthy Living Centres were launched in Northern Ireland in 2002 and there are now 19 across Northern Ireland, which provide a wide range of services to disadvantaged communities by focusing on wider determinants of health and health inequalities such as socio-economic issues and access to services. Their success is largely dependent on community engagement and ownership as they are viewed as a resource in the community for the community. The activities and programmes are informed by local area needs profiling and the aim is to enable people to improve both their own health and their community's health and well-being. An evaluation of Healthy Living Centres noted that they should be considered a model of good practice as their proactive user-centred approach represented value for money (DHSSPS, 2008a).

A further important influence on social work education training and practice during the last decade has been the debate about the significance of anti-oppressive practice (AOP) (NISCC, 2003). It can be argued that, in using community social work and development approaches, social workers can actively address structural oppression. If service users are to participate fully in society then a community development and empowerment process is required to address their rights, responsibilities, difficulties and disadvantages. Social workers and their agencies are now required to listen to the voice of the service user, and enable them to express their concerns. This may involve an increased role for communities where social workers are expected to promote participation and partnership.

In addition there have been a number of international drivers that have implied the need for community-based approaches in dealing with the conflict in Northern Ireland. For example, European Union, North American and cross-border funding has focused on the role of the community and voluntary sectors to find ways of promoting positive social change and tackling disadvantage, exclusion, racism and sectarianism. The community development movement in general in Northern Ireland has continued to expand, facilitated by the availability of extensive funding, largely from European Union sources. The community infrastructure is particularly strong in the areas of youth work, rural development, women's issues and urban regeneration. In the last decade community development has been reinvented and is depicted as having the potential to play a key role in welfare intervention policies. At the core of this resurgence is the belief that if social intervention of any form is to have a chance of success it must take account of the views and opinions of the communities in which the intervention is taking place. It is widely accepted that strategies that have been imposed on reluctant communities are doomed to failure.

At a national level, since coming to power in 1997 the Labour government emphasised the importance of policies that address social exclusion at a neighbourhood level. In the last decade there has been an expansion of locally based interventions in communities and an increase in paid community development workers. In *The Community Development Challenge* (DCLG, 2006), it was noted that government, in theory at least, has moved away from trying to tackle inequalities on a top-down basis, and acknowledged the importance of a bottom-up approach. This means that community development theories and language are becoming increasingly used, as managers and policymakers wrestle with the complexity of drawing people into the decisions that affect them. But there is as yet no correspondingly clear strategy for community development, and funding and deployment continue on the piecemeal, semi-invisible pattern established in the preceding decades. This publication also stressed the importance the government attached to this approach. It was suggested that all public agencies should contribute to the empowerment of communities by supporting community development. The New Deal for Communities Programme (1998), which focused on a multi-agency approach to tackling disadvantage within the most deprived neighbourhoods, again stressed the importance of community engagement.

Community-oriented services

In their book, McShane and O'Neill (1999) describe the introduction of a community development approach in health and social services within the then Banbridge Health and Social Services Trust. They concluded that following the *Mainstreaming Community Development* document (DHSSPS, 1999b), community development in health care was at an early stage. Yet it was worth noting that most of the Boards and Trusts did not have a published community development policy. There was a lack of focus to this approach and training needs in this area were not being addressed. Many community work projects with a health and social care focus were precarious, with issues around sustainability and funding. Despite the rhetoric they remained peripheral to mainstream health and social services. Bringing together professional health–care workers and those based within the community can involve conflicting priorities and values, but these issues can be acknowledged and overcome. Of particular concern were the areas of Northern Ireland with a weak community infrastructure, which had limited capacity for this type of working. Resources were required to ensure that these communities did not become further marginalised.

In his chapter, O'Neill (1999) highlighted the need to move away from a traditional bureaucratic model of service delivery to one that emphasised greater dialogue between the statutory services and local groups and communities. He reviewed the work of a community work team, which included three community workers who were all professionally qualified social workers. This team, located in a social work department, aimed to develop and maintain positive working relationships between the statutory and community sectors. Furthermore it aimed to identify and help meet local needs. He concluded that this method of working enabled the team to make a powerful contribution towards empowering local people. The work increased their potential, self-confidence and willingness to become engaged. These team members worked on a patch basis, as advocated by Barclay (1982), and had developed specialist knowledge and skills. The ability of a community development approach to achieve the team's desired outcomes was noted (O'Neill, 1999, p 67):

> Community development has an increasingly important role to play within health and social services. The author would contend that the value bases of community development and health care, social care and social work have broad similarities, and that the principles of partnership, engagement and empowerment with people can happen by using community development approaches.

A review of knowledge and adaptation of community development methods among health professionals (Teahen et al, 2002) highlighted a lack of understanding and information. Over 28% of subjects, including social workers, said they were unfamiliar with the concept of community development, 39% described their knowledge as adequate, and 4% as good. Questions on training required by professionals suggested that the majority required training in methods and techniques, values and principles, definition and clarification of professional roles, and knowledge of practice elsewhere. It concluded that there was a lack of national and international research into the community development awareness and training needs of social workers. Such a high level of unfamiliarity with the principles of community development amongst professionals suggests that it is not afforded a high priority. Community development is generally considered to be a core component of social work practice, but discourse and education are often relegated to the margins (Mendes, 2008).

Within the social work profession there is real concern that the financial constraints, statutory duties and procedural requirements have squeezed out more creative, proactive approaches. The government's stated commitment to community development is viewed with scepticism, with engagement with local communities largely viewed as window-dressing rather than a fundamental shift in values and methods. While community development does underpin the practice of some social work teams, this is the exception rather than the rule. Also, although there can be no disputing the advantages associated with neighbourhood community-based social work, practically it can prove difficult as social workers are increasingly charged with managing risk and fulfilling bureaucratic requirements. The demands of an increasingly risk-averse profession due to legal requirements mean that there is often little space for innovative approaches (Heenan, 2004).

The rhetoric of recent government policies, with their emphasis on partnerships, user involvement and the big society, at first glance appear sympathetic to the objectives of community-based social work, but the reality is somewhat different. In Northern Ireland the model of practice within health and social care means services are delivered to specific client groups rather than on an area basis. Services are fragmented by client group. Financial issues are the top priority; with services being reactive rather than proactive, and needs coming second to targets and budgets. Local autonomy is discouraged with an emphasis on conformity; professional discretion and creativity are viewed as too risky.

In Northern Ireland, as in other parts of the United Kingdom, social work has become increasingly bureaucratic with a proliferation of record-keeping requirements. Whilst there has been a raft of policy developments that emphasise user empowerment, capacity-building and human rights, the extent to which they have actually facilitated the move towards a community-oriented system of social work is debatable. Health and social care policy now overtly requires services to be more flexible, responsive and people-centred. Greater support is being offered to enable people to live their lives independently, including technologically assisted methods of care, which have already made an impact on the workforce. Increasingly user-led services, such as direct payments legislation and the independent living budgets, are designed to give individuals more choice and control over the nature of the service provided. To date, uptake of this option has been extremely low in Northern Ireland. This may be partly a reflection of the fact that the 'choice and freedom' associated with individuals taking responsibility for the design of their own care package can be viewed by service users as an additional burden.

Following the Review of Public Administration (RPA), organisational and managerial arrangements in health and social care were rationalised and streamlined. From 1 April 2007, 18 trusts were merged into five Health and Social Care Trusts, each managing its own staff and services on the ground and controlling its own social work provision. The extent to which community development approaches have been adopted both within and across these Trusts is variable and uneven.

In 2009 the Northern Trust produced a five-year strategy outlining how community development would be incorporated into their work. In the introduction they noted that community development was designated a core responsibility and that the Trust had a key role to play in ensuring that the design and delivery of services was in the context of ensuring wider, positive community change. Whilst the beginning of this document stresses that community development methods mean that services should be delivered in a way that takes account of community resources and circumstances and seeks ways to ensure that these resources can be utilised in the most appropriate manner, it goes on to stress that long-term community development approaches can mean needs being prevented rather than just tackled. Interestingly, though, within the report the concept of community development is considered synonymous and confused with user participation, with a focus on health care interventions.

Social action and the ability to address the social and economic condition of communities are not referred to. Interestingly, despite all the policies, strategies and documents that have advocated the adaptation of community development methods of working, the report identifies 13 barriers to successful implementation and the embedding of community development including the financial position, lack of training, need for champions and resistance to power sharing. Implicitly there is an acknowledgement that earlier commitments from health and social care providers to mainstream this approach had failed to materialise. Almost a decade ago, it was pledged that this method would be no longer 'bolted on', but would be at the core of every aspect of the Trust's work, as it could not be an add-on or an afterthought, but, instead, a core component of work. Whilst the report and its reiteration of the significance of community development is to be welcomed, its focus in part on user involvement does not address how social services can move away from a technocratic approach to regenerating deprived areas.

The Southern Health and Social Care Trust inherited a strong commitment to the process of community development. This legacy continues to influence their agenda with community development identified as a core element in the promotion of health and well-being. This commitment is reflected in their corporate priorities and strategic plans. Since its inception the Trust has actively supported community development across the programmes of care and has sought to ensure that community development principles underpin all aspects of their work. The Trust developed relationships with community groups and networks to ensure effective engagement and involvement. Mindful of the criticisms regarding a lack of training in this way of working the Trust has worked in partnership with the local rural college to design, develop and facilitate the delivery of a three-year Community Development Training course at three levels: Basic Awareness, Information for Managers and Specialist Community Development training. This training has been devised in conjunction with staff from the voluntary and community sectors and is subject to ongoing evaluation. Building knowledge and skills in this area is viewed as fundamental to addressing the health and social needs of the service users. Community development is described as an integral part of the work of the Trust directorates. Additionally these processes are governed by a service-level agreement with key partners, which ensures the work can be monitored and evaluated. Mainstreaming community development is a key objective and all staff are supported by the Trust's new Promoting Wellbeing Department. This method of working has led directly to a number of initiatives aimed at improving quality of life, for example, the Older People's Mental Health Forum. Support is also provided for clubs and networks to facilitate social activities for older citizens in the community, including a programme of training to develop improved physical activity and mobility for older people, particularly those with disabilities.

Conclusion

What, then, does this history mean in terms of the social work profession and community development in Northern Ireland? There has been a long tradition of social work and social work agencies working in collaboration with the voluntary and community sector on a huge range of community projects that challenged disadvantage, poverty and discrimination. The renewed emphasis on community action, user participation and capacity-building affords social work the opportunity to play a more meaningful role in promoting community development. It has been argued that the climate in which they now work underscores the need for them to adopt this approach (Barron and Taylor, 2010). It is essential that social workers have the skills and knowledge to assist individuals and communities who suffer from multiple disadvantages.

The relevance of community social work is clear in Northern Ireland with its large community and voluntary sector. Social workers need to be aware of the wider politics of their role and be given the skills and knowledge to enable the communities they serve to face existing and new challenges. Advocating on behalf of others has traditionally been one of the strengths of social work, people, whether as individuals, groups or communities, look to social workers to speak up for them and ensure that their views are heard. As inequalities have widened and deepened in the last decade, the role of social workers has become even more vital in ensuring communities are empowered and resilient. Close connections to the community is the way to ensure that interventions are effective and resources used in the most efficient manner, and for this to happen social work must be community-oriented (Mantle and Backwith, 2010). In a speech launching the reviews of the roles and tasks of social workers, in Northern Ireland, Chief Inspector of Social Services Paul Martin (2008) stated that it was time to reclaim the traditional roles and tasks of social work, such as advocacy and community development, and establish them as core social work activities.

SEVEN

Cross-border social work

The island of Ireland has a total population of just over 6.5 million people separated by an internal border stretching over 450 km. This means that social workers in Northern Ireland are unique in the UK in having at times to work across a land frontier. It is broadly accepted that the creation of the border in 1922 divided the island into two inward-looking and centralised states whose institutions and political culture have developed back-to-back, but along different trajectories. This has distorted economic and social development and is surrounded by suspicion and fear. For many years, the two governments on the island would not have considered each other's perspectives in the course of their daily work, planning or service provision – although located a mere 160 km apart. In both jurisdictions systems of health and social care developed with little if any reference to their close neighbours. Unsurprisingly, then, there are significant differences in policy, structures, coverage and funding. Each system is led by separate structures and legislation and shaped by different experience and drivers. The Irish border region is characterised by peripherality and lower levels of economic activity, and these are exacerbated by being at a distance from centres of decision making. These factors were further compounded by the impact of over 30 years of violence and conflict. The problems associated with this remote region were further intensified by the actual existence of the border, which acted as an obstacle to the development and implementation of solutions.

The Republic of Ireland provides a mix of public and private health care, with patients having to pay for some treatments provided free of charge north of the border. For example, there are charges for GP appointments although around a third of the population are entitled to free health care (income-related or aged over 70 years). Approximately half of the population in the South are privately insured. By contrast, Northern Ireland operates an NHS universal public coverage health care system with just over 10% of the population also having private health insurance. Social care provision is less comprehensively developed in the Republic of Ireland and there are also differences in eligibility and payment regimes. At the same time, there are also many similarities, particularly in that social care is administratively integrated with health care in the two jurisdictions. In both North and South the health sector commands the largest allocation of public-sector funding and is the single largest employer. Both jurisdictions are facing similar challenges, such as ageing populations, child protection issues, increasing levels of disability and mental ill-health, gaps in community care, and Traveller and immigrant needs. Additionally, each system must deal with the higher expectations of citizens and resolve persistent inequities in access and in social conditions among different groups. Statistics point to the important health challenges on the island, including: increasing levels of child sexual abuse, literacy problems, rising obesity levels, particularly in children, and increasing levels of poverty and inequality. According to the Centre for Cross Border Studies (2008), the island of Ireland has one of the most unequal societies in Western Europe, for example, Travellers live on average 15 years less than those in the settled population. Poverty and deprivation are endemic in the island with almost one third of all children living in poverty. Not surprisingly these social and economic conditions coupled with a border raise particular challenges for social workers, whose work may have a cross-border dimension.

This chapter reviews the extent and nature of cross-border social work in Ireland. After a short background section on the evolution of cross-border cooperation, it identifies the main areas of cross-border provision of personal social services. It is argued that this cross-border cooperation in social work has not been developed systematically and is largely funding-led and dependent on the skills, knowledge and commitment of a small number of individuals who have driven cross-border projects. Whilst there is a clear rationale for this method of working, and its value in a post-conflict society cannot be disputed, in many respects it exists in a conceptual vacuum and is vulnerable to funding difficulties and short-termism. The mutual benefits of collaborative working are obvious and can be seen as a vital part of cementing peace and reconciliation. Notwithstanding a strong desire for close cooperation, cross-border social work has not been embedded into the routine business of health Boards and Trusts, consequently the impetus for collaboration is constantly undermined.

Context

Recent political developments involving the Republic of Ireland, Northern Ireland and Great Britain have given a major impetus to cooperation across the border in aspects of social and economic well-being. However, to date, academic research has focused on economic cooperation (O'Dowd and Corrigan, 1995; Tannam, 1999), health (Clarke and Jamison, 2001; Jamison et al, 2001), education (Burgess et al, 1998; Pollock, 2000), tourism (O'Maolain, 2000) and local government (Birrell, 1999a). Assessing cooperation in the area of social work has been largely neglected and there is a dearth of analysis of the nature, scope, form and value of cross-border cooperation in social work provision. The economic implications of cooperation have dominated the political agenda, so this lack of emphasis on civil society and well-being is hardly surprising. In their most recent scoping study of North–South cooperation commissioned by both governments, the focus was on economic cooperation, inward investment, trade and enterprise. A separate chapter, devoted to infrastructure, outlined how £68 billion would be spent by 2017. Here was no reference to social work, social policy, community development or voluntary networks, and none of the money was earmarked for community infrastructure (Harvey, 2010).

Background to cooperation

The Irish border came into existence in1921 identifying the six Northern Irish counties of Antrim, Armagh, Down, Derry, Tyrone and Fermanagh as Northern Ireland forming a region of the United Kingdom and the remaining 26 counties eventually becoming the separate state of the Republic of Ireland. This frontier, of approximately 450 km, divided communities, natural hinterlands and much of the existing infrastructure of roads, railways and waterways. Since the creation of the border governments in the two political entities, Northern Ireland and the Republic of Ireland have pursued different paths of policy and legislation. Welfare agendas and systems of social security, education, health and housing have diverged with no common goals. The two states developed with little regard to the potential for cooperation in border areas and individuals were forced to look solely to their own jurisdictions for support and assistance. The outbreak of the most recent civil disturbances commonly referred to as 'the Troubles' in 1968 altered the shape and nature of communities living along the border.

Violence and intimidation in border areas led to huge increases in security there. Government policy in Northern Ireland focused on control and consequently much of the border area was heavily fortified and containment of the conflict took precedence over economic or social considerations (Quinlivan, 1999). In Northern Ireland the police and army closed roads with the consequence of towns and villages being cut off from their natural hinterlands.

The impact of the conflict in Northern Ireland on cross-border cooperation was commented on by Tannam (1999, p 4), who noted:

> The border that separates Northern Ireland from the Republic of Ireland reflects the deep division between different communities within and outside Northern Ireland on the constitutional status of Northern Ireland. This division means that cross-border cooperation has been extremely limited and even economic cooperation has been politicised.

Similar to many internal European Union borders, the Irish border region displays many of the disadvantages associated with peripherality from economic and political decision-making. In this case, uniquely, this isolation is combined with the difficulties associated with rural society, notably, poor infrastructure, high transport costs, lack of employment opportunities, poverty and deprivation, and is further compounded by the consequences of over 30 years of violence. Unsurprisingly, therefore, the Irish border region exhibits many of the characteristics of social and economic deprivation (CAWT, 2002). There is little doubt that the existence of the border has exacerbated many of the problems associated with isolated areas and has prevented solutions to these problems being pursued. Quinlivan (1999) has argued that the Irish border has physically, economically, socially, culturally and psychologically isolated communities. Historically there has been a lack of social capital on both sides of the border, as the voluntary and community sectors are relatively underdeveloped and ineffective. Local government has been described as inept as it lacks resources and dynamic leadership (McCall and Williamson, 2000), and on both sides of the border, it has no direct responsibility for the delivery of personal social services.

Development of collaboration

In the last 20 years, the historic, social, economic and political factors that obstructed and restricted cross-border and inter-group contact have altered radically. Cross-border cooperation had existed before the recent political initiatives, but was not extensive in the area of social policy. The current context for North–South cooperation on the island of Ireland, in this as in other areas, is grounded in a series of international and intergovernmental agreements. A British–Irish government summit in 1980 had led to a report surveying the existing areas of cooperation and providing a more structured framework for intergovernmental contact, but cooperation at the time was largely confined to two broad spheres: first, economic issues (including energy matters, tourism and transport), and second, the encouragement of mutual understanding, which covered youth affairs, community relations and higher education. The Anglo-Irish Agreement of 1985 gave a further political boost to cross-border cooperation, which was seen as embracing economic, social and cultural matters, particularly the social development of deprived areas. Following the 1985 Agreement an illustrative list of matters for cross-border social and economic cooperation was published (Hadden and Boyle, 1989). One of the 11 categories listed was health and social security matters, but there was again no explicit reference to personal social services or social work. Yet, at the same time a number of cross-border ministerial meetings held under the auspices of these structures had exchanged information on wider social issues, such as drug abuse and AIDS.

Further political initiatives in Ireland in the 1990s developed with North–South cross-border relationships as an important strand alongside relationships within Northern Ireland and the East–West, Britain–Ireland, relationship. A framework document (HMSO, 1995), in setting out the way ahead, gave a rationale for cooperation in terms of: a common interest in a given matter; the mutual advantage of addressing a matter together; and the avoidance of duplication. The framework document did identify a number of areas of potential future harmonisation and the health matters included were: co-operative ventures in medical, paramedical and nursing training; cross-border provision of hospital services; and major emergency/accident planning. However, again, there were no specific references to personal social services.

The eventual agreement between the political parties in Northern Ireland in 1998 (the Good Friday Agreement) contained major provisions for North–South cooperation and provided the greatest impetus for cross-border cooperation since the beginning of the conflict. Under this Agreement, the new devolved power structure put in place in Northern Ireland embodied a formal commitment to work towards specific objectives in relation to cross-border cooperation in health. A North–South Ministerial Council (NSMC) was set up with a secretariat and oversaw six new cross-border implementation bodies to develop consultation, cooperation and action (Coakley, 2001). The functions of the implementation bodies relate mainly to infrastructural matters. In addition to this, five special areas of cooperation were identified including health and education (where children with special needs were designated as a special subcategory). Common health and social care policies and approaches are agreed within the framework of the NSMC, but implemented separately in each jurisdiction. Specific areas of cooperation, mainly in health, were identified as follows: accident and emergency planning, major emergency planning, procurement of high-technology equipment, cancer research and health promotion. Despite the disruptions to the devolution arrangements in Northern Ireland, the Irish and British governments, and the European Union (EU), continued to encourage cross-border cooperation and initiatives, although in the context of a policy of 'no surprises' (Coakley et al, 2007). Since devolution was restored, cross-border cooperation has continued albeit at a low level.

The broader rationale for inter-regional cooperation has been outlined in a number of EU documents and strategies and academic studies. Increasingly the EU provides the backdrop and context for cross-border cooperation. Their extensive funding initiatives, particularly those relating to social and economic topics, have had a significant impact on the sustainability of border areas.

The combination of the changing political climate in Ireland, the successful expansion of European integration and an increasing convergence between Britain and Ireland in social policy in the 1980s and 1990s appeared to create the ideal conditions to ensure that cross-border working in the personal social services would be firmly integrated and embedded into the delivery of social care. However, the reality is that cross-border initiatives remain sporadic, and extensive resources, time and energy are devoted to following short-term pilot projects with limited funding.

Identifying cross-border cooperation in the social services

In both Northern Ireland and the Republic of Ireland the delivery of health and personal social services has been based on an integrated structure. In Northern Ireland, Health and Social Service Boards and Trusts deliver an integrated service mainly through programmes of care, for example, for family and child care services, older people, and mental health. In the Republic of Ireland social work is also integrated structurally, initially it was controlled by the Health Boards but is now part of the single Health Service Executive. Thus, some cooperative projects developed under the heading of health involve quite substantial personal social services components. There is also a structural similarity in that the probation service is administered separately from social services.

Classification of cross-border cooperation

A typology of cross–country provision of social services in Europe was developed by Maucher and Rotzinger (2002). An in-depth review of 24 cross-border projects was used to assess the extent to which this model could explain developments in social work in Ireland (Heenan and Birrell, 2005). The model set out five main dimensions of provision as follows:

1. Cross-border supply: a supplier of social services located within country A signs a contract on service provision with a social institution in country B enabling him to make his service available to his target group in country B.
2. Consumption abroad: clients with a permanent residence in country A travel to country B in order to obtain social services (with possible reimbursement of at least partial costs by the country of residence).
3. Commercial presence of a provider in country A in the territory of country B.
4. Delivery of social services in country C by non-nationals of country C, either as employees of a voluntary organisation or on the black market.
5. Trans-border social work through central authorities (working in the context of national or international treaties); a model mainly applied to the area of family law and the related social services.

Heenan and Birrell (2005) concluded that cross-border social work in Ireland did not fit with this typology, which might be more reflective of cross-border health provision. They suggested an alternative classification, which categorised cross-border working into four different areas. These were as follows.

Cooperation between statutory services

Actual purchase of social care across the border is limited, although a specialist example can be found in learning disability provision (Birrell, 1999b). Under the NSMC, cross-border cooperation has taken place in the areas of health and social care. Cross-border cooperation in the area of child protection was brought into sharp focus by the case of a Catholic priest, Father Brendan Smyth. In 1990, when an allegation was made against this priest to a social worker in Belfast, he was charged and released on bail and subsequently returned to the Republic of Ireland, where he ignored requests to return to Northern Ireland for trial. The case highlighted the inadequacies of the system and sparked intense media and public scrutiny of the processes in place to deal with such issues. There were calls for harmonisation of the cross-border processes dealing with allegations of child abuse and sex offences. Since this time, cooperation has been continuing on child protection issues including the establishment of an innovative North–South child protection hub website in 2010. There will also be a draft joint protocol dealing with children in care and those on the child protection register who move between jurisdictions and a joint communications strategy (NSMC,

2010). Much of the work on child protection has been undertaken by a specific cross-border intergovernmental child protection group. There has also been a joint taskforce on Traveller education.

Even after the Republic of Ireland introduced a register of sex offenders in 2001 a number of cases arose, both about tracking sex offenders who crossed the border and the legal basis for possible action against them for breaching the terms and conditions of bail set in the other jurisdiction. The National Society for the Prevention of Cruelty to Children and the Irish Society for the Prevention of Cruelty to Children have noted that there is still a lack of mechanisms to tackle the issue of child abuse on an all-Ireland basis, for example, there are no mechanisms for organisations in the Irish Republic to access the Northern Ireland Department of Health and Social Services and Public Safety's Pre-Employment Consultancy Register (PECS), and it has been suggested that the vetting process in the South needs to be strengthened by appropriate legislation (McNamara, 2001). The systems on both sides of the border to vet those applying to work with children have developed in very different ways and new arrangements to extend and strengthen cross-border vetting arrangements are required. The Irish Society for the Prevention of Cruelty to Children (ISPCC) has highlighted these problems in a high-profile media campaign. Following the Soham murders the government in the UK enacted the 2006 Safeguarding Vulnerable Groups Act with a subsequent equivalent Northern Ireland Order. This legislation bolstered the powers of the Independent Safeguarding Authority (ISA) and extended the regulations into additional spheres of activity with children. Following the introduction of these more stringent regulations there were fears that the Republic of Ireland might be regarded as a safe haven for high-risk sex offenders, given that Irish laws on vetting have been described as dangerously weak (McKay, 2009). In 2006 the Irish and British governments signed an agreement on the sharing of information on sex offenders. A funding agreement was made in 2008 between the Police Service of Northern Ireland (PSNI) and the Garda on the sharing of information in relation to the investigating and monitoring of sex offenders on both sides of the border. The Republic still does not have the equivalent of the UK-wide multi-agency procedure for the assessment and management of sex offenders, which constitutes a significant barrier to harmonisation. North–South deliberations on mechanisms for harmonisation have received priority attention (McKay, 2009, p 77) and the issue of safeguarding children is a high-priority agenda item for the NSMC. A further high-profile initiative between the two governments has been the Middleton Centre for Autism, established in 2007 to promote the development of services for children and young people with autistic spectrum disorders. A relatively more low-key development has been the production of an All-Ireland Suicide Prevention Plan.

The main vehicle for statutory cooperation across the border pre-dates intergovernmental cooperation agreements. Co-operation and Working Together (CAWT) began as a major cross-border cooperation project between two Health Boards in the Republic of Ireland and two Health and Social Service Boards in Northern Ireland. CAWT has led the development of cross-border health work since the early 1990s, establishing extensive cross-border networks and implementing 78 EU-funded pilot projects in areas such as cognitive therapy, suicide behaviour, sex offenders, fostering care, health impact assessment training and emergency planning.

This joint venture consists of a high-level management board, a secretariat and a central resource unit. Within the field of health and social care, there was a realisation that the health and social well-being of the border communities could be enhanced by identifying and exploiting opportunities for working together (Jamison et al, 2001). The aim of the initiative was to promote improved planning and cost-effectiveness, avoid duplication and ensure that services were not developed in isolation. Originally the main focus of CAWT was on providing a forum through which senior management from the member statutory Boards could work together on charting future developments in mutually beneficial areas rather than on actual cross-border provision. Clarke (2007) has referred to the need for analysis of the difficulties associated with introducing cross-border projects to areas where none existed.

The majority of the CAWT projects have been in the health sector, but there are a number of projects that fall more under the heading of personal social services. The overall aim of the initiative is cooperation to improve the health and social well-being of the resident population. The objectives are to explore the possibilities for working together in the planning and provision of services, and to assist the border counties to deal with the particular difficulties associated with isolation. A Family and Child Care subgroup has organised projects on the protection of children with a disability, parenting initiatives in communities and a preventative community youth project. A Learning Disability subgroup has been looking at carer approaches to the support of persons with learning disabilities and the protection of vulnerable adults from abuse. Other social care projects have been in the area of drug awareness and young men and mental health.

CAWT has been the subject of numerous evaluations and Clarke and Jamison (2001) highlighted the significant positive outcomes from collaboration including:

- enhanced service delivery for those living in border areas;
- increased cross-border patient movement;
- networks of service providers with a shared sense of purpose;
- joint appointments to ensure resources and expert knowledge are shared;
- training and good practice days organised to share good practice.

Reports also highlighted the need for mainstreaming the projects through embedding and consolidating cross-border work in individual Boards' and Trusts' strategic and service delivery plans. Cross-border work is still largely viewed as something that can be added on, rather than at the heart of health and social care. Clarke (2007) has also suggested that there was a need to progress from building relationships between professionals on both sides of the border towards the formulation and implementation of a clear set of performance indicators that are based on tangible benefits for both countries.

In 2009 CAWT secured £24 million from the EU INTERREG IVA programme for 12 strategic, large-scale cross-border health and social care projects, which are due to be completed by 2013. A number of these projects are in the area of social care and will involve social workers from both North and South, for example, one project aims to provide ambient assisted living and develop support for older people living in their own homes. This will involve assessing needs and providing tailored packages of care involving telehealth, telecare and automated living. Identifying and disseminating good practice in community support will be a key feature of this initiative. Another is focused on supporting people with disabilities and facilitating choice and flexibility, which will enable service users to take control over their own lives. The primary aim is to work with communities to ensure greater participation and inclusion of disabled people. Of particular relevance to social work is the three-year cross-border mobility workforce project. One of the three aspects to this project is social worker education and mobility, which involves the development of a comprehensive resource to support cross-border collaboration and mobility among social work staff. The objective is to enhance the mobility of social work professionals between the two jurisdictions and facilitate their ability to deal with service users who need access to services in the other jurisdiction.

Although, on the one hand, CAWT has played an important role in creating a focal point for cross-border work, on the other hand, it has distanced cross-border health care from mainstream health-care strategies (Clarke and Jamison, 2001). Aside from special projects such as CAWT, cooperative working between the statutory social service organisations across the border is extremely limited and largely confined collaboration to individual cases that have a cross-border dimension.

Partnerships between statutory and voluntary agencies

More popular are projects involving a partnership between the statutory and the voluntary sector to work across the border. In the latter half of the 1990s, strategies for addressing the social and economic malaise in the Irish border region were focused on the active engagement of local community and voluntary groups. The European Union (EU) aimed to facilitate this mobilisation at a community level through a number of Community Initiative funding programmes. The two main cross-border programmes were INTERREG (an initiative dealing with cross-border, transnational and inter-regional cooperation), introduced in 1989, and the Special Support Programme for Peace and Reconciliation (SSPPR), introduced in 1995 following the Republican and Loyalist paramilitary ceasefires. Examples of projects include: 'Shared Frontiers', which was a mental health consortium of statutory and voluntary bodies that has involved professional carers and users of services in undertaking an assessment of needs; the Cross Border Rural Childcare project, which was a large partnership network funded by INTERREG; and the Cross Border Elderly Needs project, which developed out of an evaluation to identify potential cross-border working on a multi-agency basis. In their assessment of social partnerships involving the voluntary sector, McCall and Williamson (2000) contend that the EU peace and reconciliation initiative has promoted increased voluntary- and community-sector involvement with statutory bodies through partnerships to tackle social inclusion.

Cooperation between voluntary bodies

The largest category of forms of cooperation involves direct cooperation between voluntary bodies with no statutory input. This reflects the lack of mainstreaming of cross-border cooperation in social services, and the availability of special project funding, which is accessed mainly by the voluntary non-governmental sector. Some voluntary linkages operate on a localised basis. The Dergfinn Partnership was a project that covered a 'natural' geographical area divided by the border, and focused on training for carers and a range of projects for disadvantaged groups. Others bring together existing groups or networks on each side of the border. The Cross Border Childminding Alliance is a linkage between the Northern Ireland Childminding Alliance and the Childminding Association of Ireland, which created a forum to exchange ideas and improve training and facilities in adjoining border counties. Its main aim is to raise the profile of childcare to attain higher standards for the benefit of all children, North and South. It also identifies areas with a lack of childminding provision and targets them accordingly for registration and training. Voluntary cross-border work, however, does tend to be concentrated along the border, for example, Partnership Care West is a charitable organisation that operates a cross-border community development family support project in the Derry and Donegal area. This project aims to identify and respond to areas of unmet need within the social care sector in the North West. Developing innovative responses to need has been a feature of the charity's work. Voluntary and community groups' successful engagement in projects can be facilitated by more flexible approaches as it does not have to be state-centred or hampered by statutory differences (O'Dowd and McCall, 2007).

All-Ireland voluntary bodies

It can also be noted that there are some voluntary social services agencies that actively operate on an all-Ireland basis (Powell and Guerin, 1997). Agencies such as St Vincent de Paul have an all-Ireland remit, but in practice their work may be organised separately to meet the requirements of each separate jurisdiction in areas such as social security benefits and childcare provision. STEER mental health, a voluntary group that provides a range of services to those with mental ill health, including a listening ear, advocacy and counselling, started life in Northern Ireland, but has expanded its activities into the Republic of Ireland. Whilst this has enabled them to develop their services and disseminate good practice, their work is hampered by a lack of core funding and the constant need to chase pots of money (Heenan, 2009a).

The nature and focus of cooperative projects

In their review of the extent and nature of cross-border social work projects, Heenan and Birrell (2005) categorised the initiatives according to client groups. The majority of projects, five, were focused on disability and were largely innovative in nature in relation to the prevention of physical abuse, restorative labour and befriending schemes. Early years childcare had four highly structured projects, which were quite extensive in scope with a strong cross-border ethos. Family care had three projects, but with only one mainstream family support project involving caseworkers. Four projects can be categorised as mental health and a further four projects give support for people with learning disabilities. The number of learning disability projects may reflect the comparative lack of service provision in this area in the Republic of Ireland. The role and contribution of carers was an issue that was common to many of these projects with particular emphasis on strategies, which provided training and support. Of the remaining projects, two related to older people and one to homelessness. Projects can also be divided into the following themes.

As a response to the absence of baseline data and a general lack of knowledge, a number of cross-border projects undertook comprehensive needs assessments. The Parenting Initiative completed a mapping exercise of provision involving the statutory, voluntary and community sectors to help identify areas for the delivery of the project. The Cross Border Childminding Alliance started with a survey to collect statistical information on the quality of provision in designated areas, and the qualifications of childminders, and had sought to identify areas of need and gaps in provision through a survey of parents and childcare organisations. The Cross Border Rural Childcare project had carried out a comprehensive research survey on the needs for childcare in six border counties. As well as an analysis of childcare provision, it involved local communities and parents in the identification of needs and priorities. Some projects have consisted mainly of a research survey. The Cross Border Elderly Needs project involved a survey in rural border areas to obtain information on health details, access to services, levels of satisfaction with services and feelings of insecurity, isolation and loneliness. The Shared Frontiers project on mental health had reviewed existing provision and undertook a needs assessment based on the views of carers, users and community mental health teams. There has also been a special cross-border research project on homelessness based on an analysis of the scale and nature of homelessness and an evaluation of provision based on a multiagency approach.

A further feature shared by many cross-border projects was the exchange of information about provision and practice across the border. A major purpose of the Cross Border Childminding Alliance was to exchange ideas and disseminate knowledge. The Challenge project on learning disability aimed to promote examples of good practice within both border communities. The Parenting Initiative built on the experiences of Boards across the border and used this knowledge to set up schemes based on the best practice identified. The Rural Child Care project also sought to disseminate information on models of good childcare practice in rural areas. Heenan and Birrell (2005) noted that, in practice, knowledge transfer was somewhat one-sided as many services were more developed in the North. In relation to some projects it was also recognised that there may be some benefit to users/clients who live on opposite sides of the border coming together to share and learn from each other in regard to issues, interests and experiences that are common to them. The transfer of knowledge had led to joint training initiatives. A project on 'protecting children with a disability' developed training and teaching resources for carers and adolescents. Six of the main projects studied had set up cross-border training programmes to meet needs and develop relevant skills. A number of projects had designed training workshops and practical seminars, while others had produced guidance and teaching material based on their experiences. Some projects have attracted large-scale community participation, for example, 45 community and voluntary groups have participated in a cross-border plan for social inclusion launched in 2006 by the Cross Border Women's Health Network. The main aim of this venture was to ensure that planning to address social inclusion in the border regions should be person-centred rather than simply a separate planning exercise by both jurisdictions.

A notable feature of the dominance of special projects and the involvement of the voluntary sector was the extent to which innovative services occur, for example, projects in arts and drama for those with learning disability, and in restorative labour, that is, facilitating cross-border training, education and employment opportunities for individuals who are marginalised. The Cross Border Rural Childcare project focused on promoting innovative approaches. Many such initiatives have filled a gap across the border, with a new service where none previously existed. An Extra Care Domiciliary Dementia Night Help service started in the North and has moved to develop across the border in partnership with voluntary bodies. The Challenge Project has provided a service for people with learning disabilities where practically no services existed.

The number of schemes that can be identified as delivering a cross-border service is quite small. A number fit into the categories of new or innovative services perhaps where cross-border working has facilitated a sufficient population group to justify the service, for example, a cross-border day centre in the South Tyrone/North Monaghan area for those with a learning disability, a cross-border after-school club for disabled young people, and the provision of a cross-border sign language course. These are examples of a service in a location where users come from both sides of the border. The alternative is a service operating across the border. Partnership Care West has a team of family support workers to work across the border assisting families in cases with household management and childcare. In this project the statutory bodies on each side of the border had franchised various services including domiciliary care. The 'purchaser' model across the border, which has been growing in the area of health care, is mostly underdeveloped in the case of personal social services. Dergfinn Partnership is one of the largest examples of cross-border working. It has an emphasis on the training of carers, but has encouraged self-help groups for carers and the disadvantaged, and has provided a range of cross-border services in a specific 'natural' geographical locality that the border happens to cross. Some projects have identified the danger of running projects in isolation on each side of the border and, for example, the Lifestart project encourages actual cross-border contact between parents and children who participate in the scheme through the efforts of a cross-border development worker.

For a number of the cross-border initiatives, lobbying for funding or highlighting the extent of social exclusion, marginalisation and poverty are core objectives. The Cross Border Childminding Alliance has a strong commitment to lobby to improve services and facilities in adjoining border counties and identify areas with a distinct lack of child-minding provision. The Cross Border Rural Childcare project also seeks to raise the awareness of special needs of children in rural areas. The Challenge project on learning disability has the stated intention of creating an effective lobbying group for the development of services within their own areas. Most funded cross-border activity in social care is required to have a reconciliation dimension, and research has suggested that the voluntary sector's promotion of cross-border cooperation can make a significant contribution to building peace (O'Dowd and McCall, 2007, p 145).

The funding of cross-border work

A major facilitating factor in cross-border cooperation has been the availability of special funding for this process, particularly from the European Union. The EU Special Support Programme for Peace and Reconciliation is unique to Ireland and has several sub-themes, which are specifically cross-border within its overall commitment to promote reconciliation and social inclusion. The cross-border measure on reconciliation has particularly promoted cooperation between voluntary bodies. The initiative that funds cooperation between statutory bodies has been used to fund cooperation in health and social services. A number of other EU initiatives have been significant. INTERREG is a programme to assist border areas overcome problems of peripherality and deprivation, and while many eligible projects cover public initiatives, some cover more social aspects. There are other sources of funding, two of which are of particular note. The International Fund for Ireland (IFI) was established in 1986 with contributions from the United States, the EU, Canada, Australia and New Zealand. The main component of the IFI is a disadvantaged areas initiative and generally the IFI has operated to improve infrastructure and create employment in Northern Ireland with a number of the projects being cross-border. Co-operation Ireland is more focused on cross-border cooperation and is a voluntary body funded by the British and Irish governments, the EU and corporate supporters. Its main programmes promote contact and cooperation between youth, schools and community-based groups through a variety of reciprocal exchanges.

There is, thus, quite a degree of fragmentation of sources of funding, and social services agencies and groups may depend on a 'cocktail' of funding from different sources to run cross-border projects. There is little doubt that cross-border cooperation has developed in certain directions because it is 'funding-driven'. The availability of this patchwork of funding has determined the nature and scope of cross-border collaboration. Funding requirements have set the guidelines for the subject matter of projects, the management of projects and the monitoring of projects, as well as determining the resources for cross-border work. Special project funding also serves to maintain cross-border developments as additional to the normal functioning of councils. Mainstream funding from government and statutory social services Boards and Trusts is very limited and does not move much beyond support for the CAWT initiative. In the period 1996–2001 CAWT secured funding of £5.56 million from EU sources and the four Health Boards contributed £440,000 (CAWT, 2002).

Compatibility of professional qualifications in social work

Although social work in Northern Ireland and the Republic share a common history and legacy, divergences in professional social work education have stifled collaborative activity. Cross-border projects in personal social services do not appear to have a major input from professional social workers who are employed mainly in the statutory sector. There has been an issue about the recognition of the Northern Ireland professional social work qualification (similar to the United Kingdom) in the Republic of Ireland (Campbell and Christie, 2005). Differences between the Diploma in Social Work (in Northern Ireland) and the National Qualification in Social Work (in the Republic) have impacted on cross-border employment opportunities for social workers. There have been attempts to resolve such difficulties with the Northern Ireland Central Council for Education and Training in Social Work and the National Social Work Qualifications Board in the Republic agreeing to a comparative report on social work qualifications in Northern Ireland and the Republic of Ireland (National Social Work Qualifications Board, 2001). This exercise included an investigation into curriculum content and professional competence. The report noted that social work practice in the border counties raised particular issues for the mobility of workers between the two jurisdictions and identified the need for cultural sensitivity when dealing with service users on either side of the border.

Until 1993, social work education programmes in both jurisdictions were accredited by a British body, the Central Council in Education and Training in Social Work (CCETSW), with identical standards and requirements for professional accreditation. The withdrawal of CCETSW from the Republic of Ireland and the subsequent establishment of the National Social Work Qualifications Board as the Irish accreditation body of social work have led to somewhat different development paths in the two parts of the island. Notwithstanding the fact that there are many similarities between the separate systems in terms of core values, skills and competences, there are still 'substantial epistemological and organisational differences' between the two education systems (CCETSW and NSWQB, 1998). For example, Wilson et al (2009, p 632) note that a 'major difference' is that the Republic of Ireland did not adopt the competence-based approach to standards in social work that was the norm in Northern Ireland and other parts of the UK. In October 2001 the situation changed again when a radical reform for social work education and training in Northern Ireland was announced. Since 1999, social work in Northern Ireland has become a devolved matter and social work education is overseen by the Northern Ireland Social Care Council (NISCC). The Northern Ireland framework specification for the degree in social work jointly published by the Department of Health and Social Services and Public Safety (DHSSPS) and the NISCC sets out a single comprehensive set of learning outcomes for the honours degree in social work. This new degree programme, commenced in September 2004, prepares students to work in Northern Ireland and elsewhere in the United Kingdom, but not in the Republic of Ireland. It is, however, hoped that ongoing work by CAWT on cross-border mobility may address some of the issues associated with professions wanting to cross borders.

Obstacles to cooperation

As cross-border work is comparatively limited it is necessary to comment on a number of factors that may be barriers to cooperation and obstacles that prevent further cooperation. Historically, there are some significant differences in policies on social policy and social care. While Northern Ireland has largely taken social services policies as developed in Great Britain, although within an integrated framework, the welfare system in the Republic of Ireland has developed somewhat differently. While this difference has even been described as a separate model of welfare, for example, identified as Catholic Corporatism by McLaughlin (1993), there has been a tendency over the years to look to Britain as a reference point for new schemes, even if modified (Curry, 1980). Notwithstanding a degree of convergence, significant policy differences remain and the comprehensive range of community care services in the North is not really mirrored in the Republic of Ireland, where aspects of the Northern Ireland social security system do not harmonise easily. The St Vincent de Paul organisation has to operate separately in both regions because of policy differences such as the distinctive nature of the social fund as an assistance measure in Northern Ireland.

It has already been noted that there are not extensive differences in the overall administrative structures in the two jurisdictions, although the Board–Trust division in Northern Ireland at decision-making level is not reflected in the single Board structure in the Republic of Ireland, and different funding and management arrangements for social care can cause difficulties. One integrated cross-border project had to be shelved after differences in the police vetting systems and remuneration systems between the North and the Republic were deemed to be insurmountable (Clarke and Jamison, 2001). It also appears that statistical information relating to social need is not as readily available or user-friendly in the Republic of Ireland as in Northern Ireland. There are also a number of other legal obstacles to cross-border working in terms of differences in health and safety legislation, the licensing of products, conditions of employment and pay scales.

Cross-border cooperation in Ireland remains a politically sensitive area and although Unionist politicians are relatively sympathetic to the practical benefits of cooperation, attitudes can be volatile. Potential users of cross-border provision may be reluctant to use the service for reasons of a political, religious or cultural nature or due to a perceived threat to their personal safety. Initial negative perceptions and attitudes usually dissipate after practical cooperation and sharing has begun, but the implementation of cross-border projects requires sensitivity. A study of all Irish peace programme projects concluded that a major hindrance to cooperative working was the difficulty in overcoming the fear of working with groups from across the border and a lack of mutual understanding between these groups (Co-operation Ireland, 1999).

Conclusion

Despite the political arrangements, new North–South institutions and the peace process, statutory cooperation in the area of social care is largely ad hoc and extremely limited. To date much of the cross-border work in the personal social services has been located in the voluntary sector and dependent on a small number of committed individuals who work in diverse areas, but are committed to improving cooperation. These range from people at the highest level of management in Health Trusts to people working on the ground in deprived communities. In many cases, advances in this policy area have largely been due to the personal dynamism that has generated trust and facilitated interaction. The availability of special EU funding has acted as a catalyst for cooperation, but projects are often short term and vulnerable to a sudden loss of finance.

An overall structure for cross-border cooperation has been put in place at intergovernmental level, but there is a need for cross-border work to be seen as a core part of Health Boards' and Trusts' strategies rather than an afterthought bolted onto the end of existing policies. At present cross-border social work is not seen as integral, but rather as a special interest area, and is likely to remain marginal unless it is mainstreamed. This cross-border working in the area of social care is relevant to much practice across the European Union, but its applicability to other regions of the UK is somewhat restricted; although it is important to note that since the devolution settlement of 1999, working across borders has come into sharper focus in the UK, particularly in relation to the border between

England and Wales and the accessing and funding of social care between the two jurisdictions.

Considerable expertise has been built up regarding the operational requirements of cross-border working and it is essential that this knowledge is disseminated. Cross-border social work lacks an overall coherence, many projects are insecure, short term and vulnerable to a loss of funding. Cross-border cooperation would be strengthened by a coordinated strategy provided by the Health Boards and resourced from dedicated cross-border funds, rather than relying on a patchwork of funding. The absence of mainstreaming and continuity threatens the continued development of cooperation. In the absence of an overarching strategic framework development in this area has been ad hoc and uneven. Cross-border relationships in Ireland do not fit into existing theoretical perspectives and it is difficult to identify an approach that could provide a valid explanation of their nature (Tannam, 1999). To date a significant proportion of existing examples of collaboration are short-term solutions to immediate problems and are not underpinned by a strategic framework. They are not part of the routine business of Health and Social Care Trusts and largely remain an afterthought. Funding has acted as a catalyst for the development of personal social service projects and has shaped their nature and form. Furthermore, the application for EU funding is a complicated, expensive business that requires expertise and resources. Small community organisations often lack the expert knowledge to compete and this unequal playing field causes friction and discontent. It is concluded that cross-border social work programmes will remain marginal and insignificant until they are mainstreamed rather than bolted on as an afterthought to existing programmes. While it should be acknowledged that EU funding has enabled creative collaborative work to be undertaken, to some extent it has also been a double-edged sword that has allowed both governments to divest themselves of responsibility for some aspects of provision.

Cross-border community social work has the potential to address disadvantage and help rebuild communities decimated by conflict and economic neglect. Future projects need to mainstream and institutionalise cooperation and establish a database for good practice and a forum for disseminating outcomes. It has been suggested that the political context is the single most important factor affecting the nature and extent of cross-border cooperation. The fragile political settlement in Northern Ireland has stifled and hindered developments (Pollock, 2009; Harvey, 2010). There is no formal vehicle for developing and coordinating cross-border policy and, in the absence of this, there appears to be an inability to act in a coherent coordinated way. Cross-border social work has the potential to address many of the issues faced by those in disadvantaged, often remote, communities and produce efficiencies in delivery, but in order to reach its full potential it requires a long-term commitment from both governments.

EIGHT

Poverty and social work

In Northern Ireland, as in other parts of the UK, poverty is a defining feature of the lives of the majority of social work users. The relationship between poverty and social work has a long history, with charity, alms-giving, philanthropy and voluntary activity features of the origins of the profession. Social workers intervene in the lives of some of the most impoverished and socially excluded people in society. Unlike other aspects of state provision such as education and health, social work tends to be largely concerned with working with those who are marginalised and vulnerable. Commenting on this aspect of social work, Smale et al (2000) noted that those who use social services continue overwhelmingly to be poor and disadvantaged. In comparative studies of poverty and disadvantage across the UK, Northern Ireland has traditionally languished at the bottom of the tables with the worst rates of social deprivation and exclusion. As a region, it is marked by higher concentrations of poor people in a number of areas of pronounced deprivation. A range of indicators confirm that social work practice takes place against a rather bleak and challenging backdrop of high levels of social need coupled with persistent and severe disadvantage. This chapter begins with an overview of the extent and nature of poverty and disadvantage in Northern Ireland and then reviews the policy initiatives designed to tackle these issues. Finally the implications of this context for social work practice are assessed.

Poverty in Northern Ireland

Despite the fact that local and regional statistics and indicators such as unemployment rates, income levels and mortality rates have invariably confirmed that Northern Ireland is the most deprived or one of the most deprived regions of the UK, there is a dearth of empirical research and reliable information on the nature and extent of poverty. Unlike other regions of the UK, Northern Ireland has no tradition of publishing household income data to allow comparisons with other regions, and such data were not included in the Family Resources Survey until 2003 nor in the Households Below Average Incomes series until 2004. Commenting on this, an ESRC report (2005) noted that one irony of poverty in Northern Ireland was the poverty of research and reliable statistics. The first ever large-scale survey of poverty and social exclusion in Northern Ireland, *Bare Necessities*, was undertaken in 2002–03 (Hillyard et al, 2003). Until this study there was no detailed data on poverty, reliable information was difficult to obtain and consequently rigorous analysis of need was virtually impossible (Dignam, 2003).

The findings in *Bare Necessities* were based around two measures, low income and being unable to afford items that most people regarded as necessities. After extensive consultation the study came up with 29 basic necessities and these were then used as indicators of disadvantage in a survey of almost 2,000 households. The key findings of the study highlighted a deeply fractured society where income was unevenly distributed:

- 37.4% of Northern Ireland children were growing up in poor households;
- 67% of lone parents were in poverty;
- 29% of women, but only 25% of men, were in poor households;
- 56% of households containing one or more disabled people were in poverty;
- Catholics were 1.4 times as likely as Protestants to live in poor households;
- the richest 40% of households together possessed 67% of the total household income; and
- the poorest 40% of households had 17% of total household income.

This study concluded that rates of poverty were higher in Northern Ireland than in either the Republic of Ireland or Great Britain. Overall measures revealed that in Northern Ireland 30.6% of people were in poor households compared to 28.2% in the Republic of Ireland and 25% in Great Britain. The authors of the survey described Northern Ireland as one of the most unequal societies in the developed world.

The Joseph Rowntree Foundation has also produced a number of detailed reports designed to monitor poverty and social exclusion in Northern Ireland. These studies draw on a wide range of existing sources, including government statistics and Health Trust data. The information used is considered to be the most robust and reliable available (Kenway et al, 2006). In 2006, their first report revealed that, on a range of indictors, Northern Ireland compared unfavourably with all of the nine English regions, as well as Scotland and Wales. These indicators include income poverty, benefit receipt, workless households, homelessness, child health, childcare, levels of mental ill health and fuel poverty. This work also highlighted the inequalities that existed within Northern Ireland, with significantly higher levels of disadvantage in western districts. In terms of costs, two particular areas, childcare and fuel, were singled out for attention. The subjects where Northern Ireland stood out compared to Great Britain were:

- high numbers receiving out-of-work benefits;
- high numbers of disabled people;
- the extent of low pay among full-time employees;
- high numbers without paid work;
- a very high fuel poverty rate;
- a rise in numbers presenting as homeless; and
- a high proportion of 16-year-olds failing to reach basic education standards.

However, the Northern Ireland rates were around the Great Britain average in relation to certain items. These included:

- the overall income poverty rate;
- the child poverty rate;
- the pensioner income poverty rate; and
- the income poverty rate among disabled working-age adults.

These statistics were updated in a further monitoring round in 2009 (Joseph Rowntree Foundation, 2009), which concluded that the overall picture had remained more or less static. However, it was surmised that proposed changes to the welfare system designed to move people off incapacity benefits and on to the actively seeking work register would have a disproportionate impact in the region, given the relatively high levels of dependency on disability benefits.

Child poverty

An ESRC report (2005, p 2) on income distribution in Northern Ireland provides a particularly damning assessment of child poverty when it notes 'that nowhere in the UK is child poverty more entrenched, reaches greater depths, or in many places is more concentrated'.

Until the mid–1990s there had been a lack of reliable statistics and information on the nature and depth of child poverty; consequently, analysis tended to be limited and largely descriptive. Prior to the publication of *Britain's Poorest Children* (Adelman et al, 2003) child poverty was generally calculated solely on household income. The most severely poor were children residing in households in the lowest deciles. Adelman and her colleagues contended that this was a flawed system of measurement that did not take account of the nature of poverty. They investigated poverty using three measures: low level of household income, child deprivation and parental deprivation. They concluded that a more effective system of measuring severe child poverty would use all three indicators. The approach was adopted by Monteith and McLaughlin (2004) in research commissioned by Save the Children, and they found that roughly the same proportion of children in Northern Ireland and Great Britain were living in severe poverty: 10% in 2004/05 and 8% in 2005/06, but increasing to 10% in Northern Ireland in 2007/08. Significantly, though, half of all children in Northern Ireland were considered poor using at least one measure compared to 45% of children in Great Britain. The research also revealed that whilst the same proportion of children were in severe poverty, children in Northern Ireland were much more likely to go without three meals a day. A further Save the Children study, Monteith et al (2008), compared types of child poverty (see Table 8.1). The data in this study allow comparison of poverty type among children.

A key underlying factor in severe poverty was the number of children living in households wholly dependent on social security benefits for income. Statistics for Northern Ireland from the Department of Social Development (DSD) revealed that 32% of children live in these households compared to 19% in Great Britain.

Almost three quarters of children in persistent and severe poverty reside in lone-parent households.

Table 8.1: Poverty type among children (2008)

	Northern Ireland (%)	Great Britain (%)
No poverty	52	68
Short-term poverty	27	22
Persistent poverty	22	9

Source: Monteith et al (2008)

The entrenched and persistent nature of child poverty was again confirmed in a Joseph Rowntree-sponsored report on poverty in 2009 (Horgan and Monteith, 2009). It referred to the data from the first longitudinal analysis of four years of the Northern Ireland Household Panel Survey (NIHPS), which revealed that at some stage in this four-year period 48% of children were living in poverty (before housing costs) and 21% were in persistent poverty, that is, in poverty for at least three of the four years. Therefore, the proportion of children in Northern Ireland who were poor at some point (48%) was considerably higher than the comparable figure for Great Britain (38%). Even more alarming, the rate of persistent poverty in Northern Ireland (21%) was over twice that of Great Britain (9%). Consequently, over half of children in Northern Ireland are likely to experience poverty at some point in their lives, while a fifth will spend a considerable period of their childhood in poverty. On the other hand, when using the after housing costs measure, the Northern Ireland position is not as bad as that of either England or Wales (NIA, 2008a). This research study identified the geographic spread of child poverty, with the worst areas for child poverty being Derry, Larne, Newry, Mourne, Limavady and Ards (all over 30% on both measures) (NIA, 2008a, p 9). A further Northern Ireland Assembly (NIA) report focused on the causes of and the difficulties in tackling severe and persistent childhood poverty in Northern Ireland (NIA, 2008b). It noted that there was no official UK measure for severe childhood poverty and much of the work in defining the issue and developing monitoring mechanisms has emanated from the voluntary sector. A number of short- and long-term actions to alleviate the problem are listed, but no commitment is given to adopting any of these.

A report on severe child poverty by Save the Children (2010) highlights the lack of progress in reducing levels across the UK. As Table 8.2 illustrates, there has been little change in levels reported in Northern Ireland and Scotland, although the numbers in Wales have actually increased, as has the UK average. Despite Northern Ireland not being in the worst position, Save the Children (2010, p 2) has called for the Northern Ireland government to focus its efforts on the poorest children.

Table 8.2: Severe child poverty

	2006 (%)	2008 (%)
Northern Ireland	9.7	10
Scotland	9.2	9
Wales	13.4	15
UK	10.2	13

Source: Save the Children (2010)

The 2010 Child Poverty Act was enacted in March 2010 and requires the production by March 2011 of a UK-wide strategy setting out the measures the Secretary of State proposes to take to meet the targets set out in the Act. The aim to end child poverty by 2020 has been maintained by the Coalition government but it has not been highlighted as a priority area.

Childcare

The availability of childcare is a core component of any child poverty strategy and the lack of childcare facilities, affordable childcare and safe and secure play areas in Northern Ireland has been repeatedly highlighted in studies of early years provision (OFMDFM, 2008; Horgan and Monteith, 2009). Detailed comparative research on the availability of childcare in the UK and the Republic of Ireland gave a damning assessment of provision in Northern Ireland, describing it as 'woefully inadequate' (NIA, 2008c, p 1). It also noted great variation across the country, with rural areas poorly served, and lone-parent families and families with a disabled child particularly disadvantaged. The chronic lack of provision was further compounded by a mismatch between the needs of parents and existing services. In England and Wales, the 2006 Childcare Act created a statutory duty on local authorities to meet the local demand for childcare, but there is no corresponding duty in Northern Ireland. Childcare in Northern Ireland is not only relatively scarce, but, outside of London, is also the most expensive in the UK (Horgan and Monteith, 2009).

Worklessness and unemployment

Poverty is especially related to employment status and the higher rates of poverty in Northern Ireland are partly explained by the relatively high levels of unemployment and worklessness. Relatively high levels of economic inactivity have been a feature of the labour market in Northern Ireland. This phenomenon has not been spread evenly across the province, but has been concentrated in a number of severely deprived wards, particularly in Derry, Strabane, Belfast and Limavady. In their series on monitoring poverty and social exclusion, the Joseph Rowntree Foundation (2009) examines the proportion of working-age adults not in paid work in Great Britain and Northern Ireland from 1996. The proportion of working-age adults not working was invariably higher in Great Britain than in Northern Ireland. From 2000 the proportion of workless adults in Northern Ireland fell to a low point of 30% in 2007. This improvement has, however, been short-lived and the levels of worklessness have risen more sharply in this region since the beginning of the recession, increasing to 34%.

The workless population is not homogeneous and can be divided into three parts (see Table 8.3). The Joseph Rowntree Foundation study compared the Northern Ireland and Great Britain figures, and the employment rate in Northern Ireland is now the highest among UK regions.

Table 8.3: Comparison of worklessness (2009)

	Northern Ireland (%)	Great Britain (%)
Unemployed	3	5
Inactive but wanting to work	4	6
Inactive but not wanting to work	23	15

Source: Joseph Rowntree Foundation (2009)

While there are small comparative differences in the first two categories, it is the third category of 'inactive but not wanting to work' that is markedly different in Northern Ireland. In 2008 this group accounted for a much bigger proportion of the working-age population in Great Britain than in Northern Ireland. The Labour Force Survey from January to March 2010 reveals that the proportion in Northern Ireland who did not want to work due to sickness or disability was 31% compared to 21% in the UK. The proportion of the working-age population in Northern Ireland in receipt of Disability Living Allowance (DLA) has risen by a quarter over the last decade and the rate is twice that for Great Britain (Joseph Rowntree Foundation, 2009). Statistics from the Department of Social Development reveal that over 60% of those in receipt of benefits were sick or disabled. Additionally, 79% of the sick and disabled claimants had been on benefit for at least two years. Disabled people are typically among the very poorest in society. They often experience poverty more intensely and have limited opportunities to move out of poverty. The link between disability and poverty appears intractable with policies and reforms making little discernible difference to labour-market outcomes. Poor mental health is a serious challenge in Northern Ireland with almost half of all claimants of out-of-work disability benefits having mental or behavioural conditions. This is more than twice the size of the next largest group, namely those with musculoskeletal disorders (Joseph Rowntree Foundation, 2009).

Low pay

Poverty among those in employment is a long-standing issue of concern. UK government employment and welfare policies have been underpinned by the belief that work is the surest and most effective route out of poverty. Their 'making work pay' strategy, a combination of minimum wage regulation and means-tested, in-work relief, aimed to demonstrate the financial consequences of different employment options and help to make benefit regimes more transparent. The persistence of low pay in Northern Ireland has been identified as a key factor in terms of inequality and deprivation, where it is estimated that 20% of people live in low-income households (Joseph Rowntree Foundation, 2009). Regionally, within the UK, Northern Ireland does not have the highest rates of low pay; however, its pay structure is marked by inequality with considerable differences in wage levels. Earnings for those in the lower deciles of the labour market are relatively low, while conversely earnings for those at the top end are considerably higher than other regions of the UK. Circumventing in-work poverty in Northern Ireland is a difficult proposition as the prevalence of employment that does not provide an adequate income to support a family has worsened (Kenway et al, 2006). Research by Barnardo's found that poverty was the reality for many working families, with 47% of the children experiencing poverty living in a household with at least one working parent (Barnardo's, 2007). A further feature of the labour market is the relatively high dependence on public-sector employment. Although this is not traditionally associated with a high risk of low pay, it still accounts for a quarter of all those in low pay (Horgan, 2005; Horgan and Monteith, 2009). The overwhelming majority of public-sector workers are women and many of them work in either education or health and social care.

Mental health

Northern Ireland has a higher incidence of mental health problems than the rest of the UK. A range of measures and indicators can be used to confirm that Northern Ireland has strikingly high levels of mental illness, which may be partly explained by the impact of the prolonged conflict and enduring poverty. One in six people in Northern Ireland will suffer from a medically identified mental illness at any one time and extensive research indicates that the history of sectarian violence in Northern Ireland continues to have a serious impact on the mental health of individuals (Kelleher, 2003; O'Reilly and Stephenson, 2003; Kapur and Campbell, 2004). It has been estimated that the incidence of mental ill health in Northern Ireland is 25% higher than in England and mental ill health affects one in every four citizens (DHSSPS, 2005). In 2006, the proportion of people in receipt of DLA for mental health reasons was 2.9% of the total adult population. This figure is three times the comparable figure for Great Britain (0.9%) and has more than doubled since 1998 (Kenway et al, 2006). In their study of Incapacity Benefit claimants in Northern Ireland, Green and Shuttleworth (2010) noted that poor health, low levels of skills and poor self-esteem were compounded with a widespread perception of limited employment opportunities.

Educational achievement

Northern Ireland presents an unusual profile of educational achievement with a high rate of academic achievement, with 63% in 2007 achieving five or more GCSEs at grades A–C or equivalent, compared to 59% in England and Scotland and 54% in Wales; but also a high rate of low achievement with, for example, 22% of the working population with no qualifications compared to 13% in England and Scotland and 15% in Wales. This profile is related to an education system in Northern Ireland based on academic selection. It does, however, leave the greater proportion of deprived children with unsatisfactory educational outcomes; 30% of 16-year-olds receiving free school meals do not get five GCSEs compared with 15% on average (NIA, 2008b).

Older people

The ageing of the population is a phenomenon common to almost every developed country, and for Northern Ireland society it is one of the most significant demographic changes of the 21st century. The population is becoming increasingly older and while this is a cause for celebration, it also presents a particular set of challenges for access to local services, housing, health and welfare services. Currently, Northern Ireland has the lowest percentage of older people in its population in the UK, however, since 1991 it has been ageing faster than other regions. It has been estimated that around 30% of Northern Ireland's population will be over current pensionable age by 2060, and almost 10% of the whole population will be over 85 by 2080. Poverty is associated with old age with almost 57,000 older people living in relative poverty (21% of the total), the third-highest rate of all UK regions. This can be partly explained by the fact that pensioners (particularly, single pensioners) are disproportionately dependent on pension income with fewer private sources such as investments. Almost one in every two older people living in relative poverty in Northern Ireland live in severe relative poverty (i.e. they earn an income below 50% of median household income after housing costs). Notwithstanding reductions in poverty levels between 1997 and 2003, the risk of falling into poverty for Northern Ireland's older population has increased since 2003 – in contrast to that of older people in the UK as a whole and the average Northern Ireland household (Iparraguirre, 2009). In contrast to other regions, excess winter mortality among older people has been growing since 2007. Significantly, in terms of health and social care, the region has the lowest percentages of disability-free life expectancy both for males and females in the UK. With life expectancy almost as high as in Wales, and higher than in Scotland, the short period of life spent free from disability draws attention to the relatively poor health outcomes.

The risk of poverty is defined as the percentage of a particular group (in this case, pensioners) that live in households experiencing relative income poverty. A household is in relative income poverty if the household income (in this case after housing costs) is less than 60% of the contemporary median income for all households. The risk of pensioners living in income poverty is related to the type of location in which they live. Specifically pensioners living in rural areas in Northern Ireland have a higher risk of poverty than those living in either urban areas in general or the Belfast Metropolitan Urban Area (BMUA) (see Table 8.4). Poverty in urban and rural settings has many common features, but it should be noted that rural poverty is distinct because of different physical and social characteristics. Specific aspects such as physical isolation, a dispersed population, limited access to services and a poor transport infrastructure result in older people living in rural communities experiencing a different form of poverty compared to their urban counterparts. Northern Ireland has been characterised as a rural region with 35% of the population living in rural areas. Agriculture plays a more significant role in the economy of Northern Ireland than is the case for the UK as a whole. Under the Noble Deprivation Index, the top most deprived wards in the 'access to services' categories are rural (DARD, 2007). Resource allocation and service delivery in these areas are largely dependent on the awareness and knowledge of social work managers. The rural dimension is often not well understood or evident in resource allocation (Turbett, 2009). Research by the Department of Agriculture and Rural Development in Northern Ireland showed that 48% of those living in isolated rural areas are in fuel poverty and 53% of dwellings that failed the housing fitness standard were located in isolated rural areas (DARD, 2009).

Relatively low incomes among older people are exacerbated by low levels of benefit uptake. For older people, who form the largest group experiencing low income in rural areas, receipt of welfare benefits is of crucial importance. However, there is clear evidence that take-up rates are lower in rural areas. In her examination of patterns of informal care in rural Northern Ireland, Heenan (2000) noted that despite the low incomes of many people, the uptake of benefits was much lower than would have been expected. Respondents found the benefit system complicated and were often confused about the benefits that were available and levels of entitlement. Access to advice in urban centres was an issue, with

Table 8.4: Pensioners at risk of poverty in different geographical locations

Urban/rural classification	Risk of poverty (%)
BMUA*	12
Urban	16
Rural	33
All	21

Note: * BMUA = Belfast Metropolitan Urban Area.
Source: Households Below Average Income (2004/05).

benefit offices considered daunting places. The stigma associated with claiming state welfare was deep-seated and prevalent in these rural communities. The culture of independence and self-reliance in rural areas is an important factor militating against the collection of state benefits. Individuals were reluctant to claim benefit as it was associated with shame and a loss of personal dignity (Heenan, 2006; 2010). For some, existing on a meagre income was infinitely preferable to claiming state benefits.

Fuel poverty

People in Northern Ireland are disproportionately affected by the relatively high fuel costs. Prices of individual fuels are significantly higher in Northern Ireland than in Great Britain. This is compounded by the fact that many households in Northern Ireland face a limited choice of fuels, and for many, therefore, the cheapest option may not actually be available. Northern Ireland has the highest rate of fuel poverty in the United Kingdom (defined as when a household has to spend more than 10% of their income on keeping their home at an acceptable temperature), with one in three households suffering its effects (NIA, 2009). Fuel poverty damages health and social well-being and those who are affected are often vulnerable groups, that is, the elderly, children, those who are disabled or have a long-term illness, and one in two households headed by a lone parent (Liddell, 2008). The most recent Northern Ireland House Condition Survey undertaken in 2006 reported that 34% of households were in fuel poverty. This survey was due to be repeated again in 2010, and is likely to confirm that fuel poverty has risen substantially. The impact of fuel poverty on older people in Northern Ireland has been highlighted by campaigns such as the Help the Aged 'Heat or Eat' campaign. It suggested that fuel poverty among older people is a particularly serious problem not only because older people are at greater risk from the cold, but also because they are more likely to spend more time within the home, and this is especially the case for those aged 85 and over.

Carers

Another key group of social work service users who are likely to experience poverty are carers. There is a strong relationship between the hours spent caring per week, the length of time caring and poverty. Data from the 2001 Census (NISRA, 2001) reveal that those caring for more than 20 hours per week are more likely to live in workless households than those who care for less than this period or non-carers. In a study of carers undertaken by the DHSSPS in 2006 to inform their policy development, a lack of awareness of assessments for the needs of carers was revealed. Just 43% of respondents were aware that they could have a separate assessment with less than 40% offered one (DHSSPS, 2006b). Voluntary organisations providing support to carers have voiced their concerns that there are a significant number of people who are entitled to carers' benefits and not claiming them. The role of social workers in signposting people towards the appropriate welfare support is patchy and depends on the context (DHSSPS and DSD, 2009). The need for a review of the services and support for carers of older people was identified in 2004 as part of the inspection process.

Housing

One key area of possible social disadvantage is housing. The relationship of housing disadvantage to poverty has been less clear in Northern Ireland than in other areas. Traditionally Northern Ireland has had lower housing costs than Great Britain, including house prices, social housing rents and private-sector rents. These lower housing costs have been particularly important in reducing poverty. Northern Ireland also had low rates of housing unfitness, which were achieved by the Northern Ireland Housing Executive making this a priority in expenditure and action. More recently, issues including the growth of homelessness, the lengthening of waiting lists and the lack of affordable housing have become more significant. Since 2003, Northern Ireland has had a *Supporting People* initiative similar to Great Britain. This offers support services to a range of vulnerable categories of people to enable them to live as independently as possible. The main categories include those likely to be engaged with a social work strategy. *Supporting People* is administered by the Housing Executive, often in partnership with Health and Social Care Trusts and voluntary bodies and has been regarded as a model of good practice in joint working.

Policy responses to poverty

Having drawn this profile of disadvantage it is possible to examine the scope and impact of policy developments aimed at alleviating key aspects of disadvantage. It should be noted that the tax and benefits system is of fundamental importance in addressing poverty, which is, in practice, the responsibility of the UK government and, therefore, uniform throughout Northern Ireland and Great Britain. This leaves the question as to what extent devolved powers, and/or the devolved administration during Direct Rule, were used to deal with poverty and disadvantage.

The policy responses to levels of disadvantage and deprivation in Northern Ireland have not been very effective or innovative in reducing many of the key aspects of poverty. This is indicated in little overall change in the high levels of deprivation in Northern Ireland or reducing comparative disadvantage with England, Scotland and Wales. Despite the high levels of child poverty and the lack of access to childcare in Northern Ireland many of the initiatives introduced in England have not been adopted and there is less public funding for childcare than in any other region of the UK. Spending on Sure Start introduced in 2001 is also much lower in Northern Ireland. In 2007/08, expenditure per child was £80, which compares unfavourably with the rest of the UK where it was nearly £600 per child in England, £380 in Scotland and between £270 and £350 in Wales. Even with the caveat that the Sure Start programme started later in Northern Ireland than in the rest of the UK, it is still a huge differential.

In 2006, the Northern Ireland Pre-School Playgroup Association (NIPPA) estimated that, at this level of funding, Sure Start could only deliver services to 20% of children aged 0–4 (NIPPA, 2006). Sure Start children's centres were designed to provide a holistic range of services to pre-school children and their families and these were earmarked for significant expansion. In 2000, there were 800 in England, and the target of 3,500 was achieved in April 2010. The former education secretary, Ruth Kelly, claimed children's centres were at the heart of the government's plans to eradicate child poverty. Their role in supporting families and addressing child poverty has been widely acknowledged by children's charities and advocacy groups. In Northern Ireland the government plans were to develop four such centres. To date these centres have not yet materialised and, even though a partnership working together to improve social and economic conditions in Northern Ireland has described it as 'vital' that government addresses the issue of childcare quality and provision (Concordia, 2007, p 27), this inadequate provision and neglect appears set to continue.

Further evidence of the underfunding of children's services in Northern Ireland was provided in 2010 by the voluntary group 'Early Years' in an election manifesto. They noted that in this region each child gets 12.5 hours of pre-school education per week for one year, compared to England and Wales where each child gets 20 hours of government funded pre-school education per week for two years. In Northern Ireland there is no training and development strategy for working with young children despite a commitment in 2006 by the Department of Education to the publication of an Early Years Strategy, whereas £200 million has been allocated for this type of training in England and Wales. The Department of Education now tends to define early years provision as pre-school, not including early years social care. The review recommends that there should be a reshaping of the childcare vision for Northern Ireland, including the allocation of mainstream funding to the childcare strategy. It also recommends that there should be clearer accountability for action relating to the implementation of childcare policy and that more robust leadership structures are required to drive forward an integrated childcare and early years service. Northern Ireland has seen an almost complete absence of extended schools and children's centres.

In Northern Ireland, the Executive has not yet agreed lead responsibility for childcare, which underscores the importance of developing a robust childcare strategy and implementation plan. Currently, four government departments – the Department for Health, Social Services and Public Safety, the Department for Employment and Learning, the Department for Social Development and the Department of Education – share responsibility for childcare. In 1999, the

Northern Ireland childcare strategy was set out in *Children First* (DHSSPS, 1999a). *Children First* envisaged an integrated approach to early childhood education and care in Northern Ireland, and identified three main challenges for childcare – variable quality, affordability and limited access. This strategy, however, did not have a clear implementation plan with agreed funding, targets and timescales and to a large extent was simply a paper exercise.

Save the Children (2009) produced an assessment of the extent to which public spending on primary and secondary education is weighted towards the poorest children in the UK, and whether or not there is a case for strengthening this poverty-focused link. It revealed that spending per pupil in Northern Ireland's primary and post-primary schools is the lowest in the UK: in 2006/07, spending ranged from less than £4,000 in Northern Ireland to nearly £6,000 in Scotland, with the average UK spend at just over £4,700. Since 2002/03, spending per pupil has grown slightly faster in England (29% in real terms) than in Scotland (27%), Wales (23%) and Northern Ireland (just 9%). This research also commented on spending on personal social services, focusing on children's and families' services. Spending was £311 per child in Northern Ireland in 2004/05, which was 30% below the UK average. Spending is highest in Wales (£544 per child in 2006/07), with spending in Scotland at £539 per child and £455 in England. The relatively low levels of spending associated with children's and families' services in Northern Ireland were described as striking. The authors commented that in the context of enduring levels of poverty, it was difficult to avoid the conclusion that children's services appear to be a relatively low priority. Later in 1999, the Department for Work and Pensions published its first *Opportunity for All* report. This was the Labour government's strategy for tackling poverty across the UK, and included a significant focus on child poverty. This has been followed by annual *Opportunity for All* reports, which outline actions taken and the indicators monitoring their impact on poverty. However, these reports only cover Northern Ireland in respect of tax and benefits, and the responsibility for all other areas falls under the remit of the devolved government.

In 2001, during the brief period of devolution, the Executive agreed to adopt a Targeting Social Need Strategy. This was a strategy to direct resources at those areas, groups and individuals in greatest need, but it had been criticised as having little influence on departmental spending, having no specific budget and not using deprivation statistics (Tomlinson, 2000). Five years on from this in November 2006, and following two consultations, Secretary of State for Northern Ireland Peter Hain published *Lifetime Opportunities* (OFMDFM, 2006b), the Northern Ireland Anti-Poverty and Social Inclusion Strategy. It was reviewed by the Preparation for Government Committee of the Transitional Assembly, which recommended in general that it should be adopted by the new Executive, albeit with a number of adjustments. A strategy for tackling poverty, social exclusion and areas of deprivation was to be one of the priorities for the newly restored devolved government after the St Andrews Agreement in 2006, but to date progress on reaching consensus on a strategy document has been extremely slow.

In 2006, the Northern Ireland Executive signed up to the UK-wide target of ending child poverty by 2020. To this end it pledged to halve the proportion of children living in relative poverty by 2010/11, this initial milestone involved lifting 67,000 children out of poverty. In its progress report on *Lifetime Opportunities* OFMDFM commented on progress in meeting targets. It noted that child relative income poverty rates have fallen from 29% in the baseline year (1998/99) to 25% in 2008/09. Progress has, as with the UK as a whole, not maintained the earlier momentum seen between 1998/99 and 2004/05. On the basis of current trends it is unlikely that the Northern Ireland Public Service Agreement target to halve child relative income poverty by 2010/11, that is, to achieve a child relative income poverty rate of around 15%, will be achieved (OFMDFM, 2010). Action to promote this agenda has been somewhat limited, dependent mainly on benefit uptake campaigns, improving deprived areas through neighbourhood renewal and the work of the Child Support Agency. There is little evidence of major initiatives in Northern Ireland to change significantly the persistence of child poverty. The key factors of benefit and work lie outside devolved powers, while government action on improved education, skills and childcare is negligible (Hirsh, 2008a).

The year 2006 also witnessed the publication of *Our Children and Young People – Our Pledge*, a 10-year strategy for children and young people in Northern Ireland produced by OFMDFM (2006c). This report proclaimed that partnership working was essential to transform the lives of children and this could solely be the concern of government. Child poverty and the impact of the conflict on the lives of children were identified as core issues. This document included eight pledges designed to transform children's services. The focus here was on a holistic, preventive approach informed by the UN Convention on the Rights of the Child. It has long been accepted that services for vulnerable children should be planned alongside services for all children. To this end, the four existing Health and Social Services Boards in Northern Ireland were required to create Area Children's and Young People's Committees (ACYPCs), to ensure Children's Service Plans were developed and implemented in an integrated, collaborative manner. These committees are made up of senior representatives from the statutory, voluntary and community sectors, and they recommended the production of a regional Northern Ireland Children's Services Plan 2008–11, based on the themes identified in the OFMDFM strategy for children and young people. The plan was published in November 2008 (ACYPC, 2008) and priority themes included safeguarding children and addressing the needs of young carers.

Following the re-establishment of devolution in May 2007, concerns that the Executive appeared willing to adopt the anti-poverty strategy *Lifetime Opportunities* (introduced by the Direct Rule government) in its entirety, with no updating or reviewing, led to an agreement to set up an Executive subcommittee on poverty and social exclusion. This subcommittee met for the first time almost two years later, at the end of March 2009. It agreed to meet again to formulate the terms of reference of a forum, which aims to enable a range of stakeholders to inform development and the implementation of actions. Progress here has, again, been painfully slow with little evidence of a genuine commitment to action.

Furthermore, when compared to other regions, mental health and learning disability provision in Northern Ireland is poorly developed and inadequate, with significant inequalities in access, treatment and opportunity, accompanied by major funding and legislative failures. Historically, mental health services in Northern Ireland have been under-resourced, overstretched and reactive (Heenan, 2009b). *The Bamford Review of Mental Health and Learning Disability (Northern Ireland)* (DHSSPS, 2005) was established in 2002 by the DHSSPS and represented the most comprehensive review of the future strategic direction and legislative changes required to improve mental health and learning disability services. Its main report in 2005 stressed the need for a root-and-branch review of provision that would necessitate a doubling of the amount spent on services over the next 20-year period (DHSSPS, 2005). It concluded that when compared to other areas of the UK, there was clear evidence of inequalities in the investment associated with mental health and learning disability over many years, and proposed that a target should be set for 50% of people with mental ill health or a learning disability to be in full-time employment. By 2010 there had been few if any discernible changes with mental health services still lagging behind the UK, and in the face of retreating services this looks likely to continue.

In March 2005, the government launched *Ageing in an Inclusive Society: A Strategy for Promoting the Social Inclusion of Older People* (OFMDFM, 2005). This document sets out six strategic objectives of government to promote the social inclusion of older people, including an action plan to achieve the objectives. It aims to tackle issues of financial and social exclusion, to deliver services that will improve the health and quality of life for older people, and ensure that they live safe and secure in their own homes and communities. The strategy acknowledges that a partnership approach with older people and organisations in the voluntary and community sector representing their needs is required to address the issues. At the time of publication there was some concern that the final strategy was a diluted version of the consultation document. The lack of targets or any robust system for monitoring and evaluation of progress were identified as key issues. There was no agreed action plan, timescale or departmental leads. In 2009, a review of the Ageing Strategy was undertaken by two leading charities for older people (Age Concern and Help the Aged NI, 2009). Their assessment of progress to date made for rather grim reading, with little or no change reported against the six strategic objectives. There was little headway in the area of poverty with the proportion of people experiencing poverty remaining constant and the numbers experiencing severe poverty increasing. The main initiatives to combat disadvantage were a series of benefit take-up initiatives. Whilst these were broadly welcomed, the reliance on this approach was deemed inadequate. Difficulties surrounding means-tested benefits including stigma and complexity meant that the impact was marginal. In terms of health and social care, the review used data from the Continuous Household Survey to reveal that, since 2005, progress had been negative. There had been an increase in both the percentage of older people reporting long-standing illnesses and the number of older people who were limited by these illnesses. The numbers of older people receiving care in their own homes increased slightly, but this progress was offset by a significant decrease in the number of those in receipt of home helps.

This assessment of the governmental strategy for older people also included comparative analysis of the four regional policy responses. The English, Welsh and Scottish strategies had all made considerable progress with improvements identified using a range of indicators. A notable feature of these documents was their clear implementation plans and measures. The nations of Great Britain demonstrated a willingness to develop and fund innovative approaches on healthy ageing, combating ageism and promoting intergenerational activities; however, the same cannot be said for Northern Ireland. Statements are largely visionary and generic with limited engagement and consultation with older people. The advisory panel set up by the OFMDFM to inform the delivery of the policy had a very limited impact and, with just two meetings to date, appeared to be just window-dressing. Responsibility for the implementation of the Northern Ireland strategy was split across a number of government departments and this lack of ownership meant that passing the buck was commonplace. This supports the findings of Trench and Jeffery (2007), who described Northern Ireland's approach to ageing as the most disjointed in the United Kingdom.

In May 2008, the Minister for Social Development established a Fuel Poverty Task Force, which included representatives from the statutory, voluntary and private sectors. The group made a number of recommendations, the key outcome of which was a one-off fuel payment for households in receipt of income support and pension credit in addition to the winter fuel payment. This has been welcomed, but has a limited impact as many older people in poverty are not in receipt of means-tested benefits. A warm homes scheme to assist people in private-sector housing to install better insulation and heating was also introduced.

The devolved government was hailed as the opportunity to shift the focus from constitutional to domestic, bread-and-butter politics. The Joseph Rowntree Foundation-sponsored evaluation of devolution's impact on low income and deprivation compared the trends in the four regions of the UK (McCormick and Harrop, 2010). Somewhat predictably perhaps, the story is a mixed one, but progress in Northern Ireland has been slow, with little evidence of the local administration having a transformational effect on social policies. Regional strategies on the skills agenda have the potential to address local issues and reverse negative trends. An examination of the numbers in the workforce without qualifications reveals that Wales has fared best under devolution, followed by Northern Ireland and Scotland. However, this indicator is a good illustration of the difficulties with comparison, as, while it appears that Northern Ireland is performing relatively well in terms of qualifications, it began from a particularly low base. Indeed, according to the report, one in five of Northern Ireland's working-age adults were still unqualified, a number higher than the rate in most parts of the UK a decade earlier. It also found that although regeneration had delivered a number of benefits to devolved regions, least progress had been made in Northern Ireland; this was disappointing but understandable given the segregated nature of many communities.

The implications of poverty and disadvantage for social work

Poverty is a major factor in determining which people are likely to become users of social work services. Severe poverty is likely to increase the risk of engagement with social intervention. Research tracking children who have grown up in poverty shows that they face later disadvantage, even after controlling for other characteristics. Many harmful phenomena are associated with child poverty and the costs impinge most on social services and education (Hirsch, 2008b). The numbers of referrals to social services in Northern Ireland can be viewed as a reflection of the levels of poverty in society (Gray and Horgan, 2009) and have grown by 50% in the last 10 years. The numbers on child protection lists have also grown. In 2008 there has been an increase of 29% from the same date in 2003 and, as Table 8.5 shows, Northern Ireland had the highest number of children on the Child Protection Register per 10,000 population aged under 18.

A Save the Children study (2010) identified categories of people more likely to require social work intervention as follows:

• the long-term unemployed who are totally dependent on benefits;
• those with poor educational achievements;
• single-parent families;
• those with a disability;
• those living in rented accommodation.

Research has shown that social and economic deprivation is a factor in identifying which children have characteristics requiring child protection (Devaney, 2008). At risk groups of children include children born prematurely, children with disabilities, adolescents, children in care, runaways and asylum-seeking children (NSPCC and Barnardos Northern Ireland, 2009). The Northern Ireland Anti-Poverty Network (NIAPN, 2007) identified groups at the greatest risk of poverty, and therefore groups most likely to be engaged with social workers, as: people from minority

Table 8.5: Children on the Child Protection Register, per 10,000 (2008)

Northern Ireland	48.0
England	26.6
Scotland	23.3
Wales	36.4

Source: DHSSPS (2008)

ethnic groups, Travellers, lone-parent families, the families of ex-prisoners, people with low or no educational qualifications, long-term unemployed people, people living in disadvantaged communities and people living in border areas. Despite the widespread view that an improvement in education and skills of those on low incomes lies at the heart of any long-term strategy to reduce child poverty (Hirsch, 2008b, p 7), positive action on education and skills has only developed slowly with limited additional expenditure to address low achievement. Improving the skills and qualifications of the workforce is generally viewed as a core component in tackling unemployment and worklessness, as those with the fewest qualifications also have the fewest opportunities.

While the lack of educational achievement may not necessarily lead to contact with social work services, nonetheless low levels of literacy and numeracy contribute to a disturbing profile of disadvantage. It is also the case that Northern Ireland has higher levels of children with special educational needs, 4% compared to 2.8% in Great Britain in 2006/07 and such needs can be part of a multiplicity of social care needs (Gray and Horgan, 2009, p 76). Northern Ireland's high rates of fuel poverty can contribute to mental and other health problems (Liddell, 2008) and put pressure on lone parents and older people. Government provision for worklessness and long-term unemployment has largely followed the 'Welfare to Work' and 'Pathways to Work' agendas of Great Britain. Under one of the few initiatives specific to Northern Ireland, subsidies were available to employers for up to six months for employing participants on the New Deal for Lone Parents (Birrell, 2009a, p 129). Another unique employment project involved the voluntary sector providing personal development training, childcare and advice (PDP, 2007).

Progressing the equality agenda has been a particular predilection of the devolved administrations in Northern Ireland, with the term attracting a high public profile. Indeed, it is difficult to find a discussion of policy development that does not refer to the equality agenda. Section 75 of the 1998 Northern Ireland Act requires the Northern Ireland Assembly and all public bodies to have due regard to promoting the principle of equality of opportunity, but not equality of outcomes, and this is stated in terms of horizontal equality (gender, disability and religion) rather than vertical equality (income). As Wilson (2007, p 151) noted, equality dominates political agendas and the 'e-word is frequently employed' by politicians, civil servants and officials. Unfortunately, it would seem that the fixation with identity politics and the fair treatment of the two communities has hindered attempts to focus on reducing inequality and deprivation. Equality is less about the impact of policies and initiatives on those who are socially excluded and more about whether 'we' get as much as 'them'. Despite the emphasis on equality and the rhetoric about a fairer deal for both communities, this is not reflected in the poverty statistics, which still reflect an unequal and unjust society (Burchardt and Holder, 2009).

Social work initiatives to address poverty

Have Northern Ireland's high levels of poverty seen the development of specific social work initiatives and strategies to alleviate disadvantage and help prevent intensive intervention? Although the strategy documents of existing Trusts may have general references to disadvantage, there is little detailed analysis or strategy. The *Corporate Management Plan* of the Belfast Health and Social Care Trust (2010a) referred to an overarching aim to reduce health and social inequalities, but no further specific detail on how this might be achieved and monitored was given.

Anti-poverty narratives often suggest that social care activities could be at the core of interventions. However, to date some of the more obvious areas for some form of social work intervention to alleviate poverty have produced few initiatives. In Northern Ireland the giving of welfare advice and information to promote benefit and tax credit take-up and income maximisation is relatively underdeveloped. Expenditure on early years provision is low at £80 per child compared to £600 in England and Wales (Save the Children, 2010). User and carer participation lags significantly behind Great Britain, and debt and financial exclusion work is left to voluntary organisations. Youth transitional work to assist young people at key points in their lives has been largely overlooked and has not operated beyond limited initiatives for those leaving the care system. Youth services are also administered totally separately from social care and form a relatively minor part of the work of large education bodies. Despite the rhetoric of using partnership working to tackle the root causes of deprivation and developing efficient and effective services, there are remarkably few examples of initiatives in this area producing tangible outcomes. Work by the NSPCC and Barnardos has referred to a Parents and Children Together Service (PACT), to re-engage young mothers with the needs of their children. It highlighted a dearth of research on the issue of neglect and in particular its link with deprivation and poverty (NSPCC and Barnardo's Northern Ireland, 2009).

Conclusion

In many respects poverty in Northern Ireland is broadly similar to poverty in other parts of the UK. It is disproportionately associated with disabled people, older people, families and economic inactivity. However, in Northern Ireland poverty is deeply ingrained, systemic and severe, but this has not been sufficient to move it to prominence on the local policy agenda. Despite the promises and the rhetoric there have to date been very few if any interventions with the potential to deliver social justice. Moving out of poverty requires a targeted, sustained, funded, long-term strategy with clear lines of responsibility, targets and timescales. Rather than take the opportunity to develop innovative, creative solutions to the persistent problem of poverty, government here has failed to reach a consensus on a core social policy. There is little commitment to user engagement, transparency, accountability and localism. Policymaking has been extremely limited and has deviated only marginally from Great Britain. The lack of evidence-based policymaking and a retreat into identity politics means progress in this area has been negligible.

While theoretically social workers should use their knowledge and values to influence the anti-poverty agenda, in Northern Ireland Boards and Trusts have preferred to concentrate on an approach based on casework and services, where there is only marginal involvement in pre-employment, transition to work and welfare rights programmes and advocacy approaches. It can be suggested that social work practice has failed to make the connections between the circumstances of vulnerable groups and the issues of protection and risk, and the significance of the poverty dynamic is often misunderstood or ignored. There is increasing support for the view that social change cannot be effected or promoted through detached, mechanistic ways of working. For some it can be hard to reconcile an increasingly interventionist, risk-averse, authoritarian, regulatory role with concepts such as partnership, collaboration and capacity-building.

NINE

Devolution and social work

Northern Ireland has had a long history of devolution within the United Kingdom, going back to 1921. In more recent times periods of devolution have alternated with periods of Direct Rule by the Westminster government, as Table 9.1 shows.

Table 9.1: Forms of government in Northern Ireland

1921	Devolution set up
1972	Direct Rule imposed
1999	Introduction of devolved government
2002	Direct Rule reintroduced
2007	Restoration of devolved government

The legislation establishing devolution, in both 1921 and 1998, set out the matters that remained the responsibility of the UK with all other matters being devolved, and this included social work services as they developed. This meant that legislative, executive and administrative powers, as well as the allocation of finance, rested with the devolved form of government. During Direct Rule executive responsibility passed to a Northern Ireland Office minister, and legislation on social policy was passed at Westminster as separate Northern Ireland legislation under an order in council procedure (Birrell, 2009b). The Northern Ireland Department, however, remained in place and Direct Rule did not produce major changes in social work practice in Northern Ireland, although there was a tendency to bring some social legislation into line with Great Britain, for example, on divorce. Legislation in 1998 saw devolution introduced to Scotland and Wales. Thus, from 1999 Scotland was similar to Northern Ireland in having an executive (cabinet) and parliament or assembly with comprehensive responsibilities for social work and social care, Wales originally had devolved powers over executive and administrative decisions regarding subordinate legislation only. Since the 2006 Government of Wales Act, the Welsh Assembly Government has had enhanced powers for primary legislation, including social care. The operation of devolution raises the question of whether devolution has been used in Northern Ireland to develop social policy innovations and initiatives that could be copied by, or have lessons to teach, the other devolved administrations. Policy copying in social care could also operate in the other direction with examples of Northern Ireland copying Scotland or Wales. This chapter examines the impact of devolution on social care in Northern Ireland since 1999 in terms of the analysis of programmes for government, the organisational arrangements for social care, policy and practice developments in distinct areas of social work, the extent of policy copying, and current reviews of the future of social work.

Programmes for government

The devolved governments in Northern Ireland have existed in the coalition or consociational format required under the Good Friday Agreement. On taking office they have produced programmes for government and to date two programmes for government for Northern Ireland have been produced. The first programme (NIE, 2001) did list a range of detailed actions in social care: hospital discharge arrangements, extra community care packages, resettlement of long-stay patients from hospitals, increased mental health provision, a new carers' strategy, new child protection guidance, an increase in foster places, and help for young people in moving from care into the community. The second programme for government (NIE, 2008) was much briefer, reflecting difficulties in the new four-party coalition reaching consensus. The programme contained only specific commitments on expanding community care for mental health and learning disability and on reducing the number of abused or neglected children on the child protection register or in care. The details in the list of public service agreements implementing the programme were more specific in relation to targets which covered: the numbers of children in care, children leaving care, resettlement from mental health hospitals and learning disability institutions, substance use, early years, social inclusion for vulnerable groups, and domiciliary care.

The programmes for government in Scotland and Wales have all had a stronger emphasis than Northern Ireland on social policies (Birrell, 2009b, p 10) and have tended to give priority to a range of policies and provision including social care. Particularly noticeable in Scotland have been free personal care for the elderly and social inclusion initiatives. The 2003 programme (Scottish Executive, 2003) had a strong emphasis on support for young people, child protection, youth work, early years, hospital discharge and social work reforms. The programmes for government of the new Scottish National Party (SNP) government have emphasised a comprehensive early years strategy and improved outcomes for vulnerable children, the promotion of foster care, and continuing support for free personal care (Scottish Government, 2007a). The early programmes in Wales following devolution had a strong emphasis on tackling social exclusion and promoting early years provision. Wincott (2005) identified a highly innovative approach to early childhood education and care. The One Wales Agenda (WAG, 2007a) of the new coalition government placed great importance on supporting social care, including domiciliary care, looking after children, a carers' strategy, and enhancing the social care workforce, as well as continuing early years strategies. Overall the Northern Ireland devolved administrations have not set out very highly specific or joined-up commitments in their various programmes for government for social care, although there has been continuing expression of support for the maintenance of the integrated structure of health and social care.

Organisational position of social care in the devolved administration

The introduction of devolution in 1999 led to an expansion of the number of Northern Ireland government departments to 11, but social care remained, as before, combined with health at government policy level within a new Department of Health and Social Services and Public Safety (DHSSPS). This represented a difference from England, Scotland and Wales in maintaining child protection as a function of a health and social services department. In the Northern Ireland Executive the Minister for Health, Social Services and Public Safety has responsibility for both children's and adults' social care although the Office of the First Minister and Deputy First Minister contains a Children's and Young People's Unit, which has a limited coordinating role across departments on a children's and young peoples' strategy. Two junior ministers in the Office of the First Minister and Deputy First Minister share responsibility for children and young people. The Scottish government has separate senior cabinet ministers for health, which includes adult social care, and for education, which covers children's services, children's hearings, social work and the social work inspectorate. There is also a junior minister for children and early years. Wales has a deputy minister responsible for all social services including child protection, and a deputy minister for children who is responsible for child care, early years and the youth service.

Within the Department of Health and Social Services and Public Safety at Stormont is an Office of Social Services, which is the main policy-related body, whose task is to support ministers, the department and other bodies working in the field of social work and social care. Formally the Office of Social Services has the role of:

- promoting the quality of social work and social care services;
- providing professional advice and expertise on social care services to ministers, departments, agencies, other statutory bodies and voluntary, community and private-sector organisations in the formulation, implementation and efficient delivery of social work and social care services;
- giving professional advice to the Northern Ireland Assembly, particularly in the scrutiny of new legislative proposals;
- developing policies on training, qualifications and staff development for the social services workforce;
- sponsoring and holding to account related non-departmental public bodies;
- facilitating the conducting of business between the DHSSPS, commissioners and providers of social work and social care; and
- evaluating targeted voluntary organisations that receive funding from the DHSSPS.

The Office of Social Services has ten areas of responsibility: adoption, disabled children and ethnic minority issues; safeguarding children; looked-after children;

the social care workforce; children's services reform; community care and older people; mental health, dementia and disability; modernisation and quality; policy training; and relevant aspects of criminal justice (DHSSPS, 2010).

In Scotland and Wales, the central administrative structure does not align totally with ministerial responsibility. Scotland has abolished departments since 2007 and has a structure of 35 directorates, which includes one for primary and community care and one for children, young people and social care. In Wales there is a Department for Health and Social Services with a Social Services Directorate and a separate department responsible for children, education and lifelong learning. Thus there are different configurations between the devolved administrations and also with Whitehall. Each has different underpinning principles and the extent of policy learning or copying is limited. Scotland's configuration is based largely on a separation of health and adult social care services from children's services and child protection, in a similar principle to England. Wales has had a more integrated structure of health and social care, which includes child protection. The Northern Ireland structure of central administration has also opted for this principle. In Northern Ireland, social work and social care is not strongly represented at ministerial level, with only one minister for the large DHSSPS and two junior ministers in the Office of the First Minister and Deputy First Minister, but with only a few functions relating to children and young people. The effectiveness of the Northern Ireland central administration has also been influenced by the operation of ministerial departments in 'silo' mode. This is not only a consequence of the adoption of a 'mini-Whitehall' model, but also of the fact that ministers have been able to make their own executive decisions rather than implement collective government decisions as the Northern Ireland Executive is not bound by collective responsibility. If there is a positive lesson from the central organisation for social care in Northern Ireland it would, again, relate to the integration of health and social care in the central policymaking and delivery structures.

Delivery by quangos

It is some 30 years since there was local government involvement in the delivery of social care in Northern Ireland. Social work and social care services have been delivered in conjunction with health services through a structure of non-departmental public bodies or quangos. Since 2007, there have been only five quangos in social care delivery, and prior to that 11 in total. The restoration of devolution and the Review of Public Administration (RPA) did raise the possibility of a change in this structure. The underpinning values of the RPA (RPA, 2006, p 13) were put forward as including democratic accountability, community responsibility, the integration of services, subsidiarity and a move towards strong and effective local government, and there were also references to reductions in the powers of quangos and increasing democratic accountability. However, the outcome as endorsed by the devolved administration in 2007 was for the continuation of the delivery of social care and health by five Trusts, operating as non-departmental public bodies with a nominated Board appointed by the minister and sponsored by the government department. This stands in sharp contrast to the long-standing location of social work and social care in local government in England, Scotland and Wales. A lesson from Northern Ireland might relate to some of the disadvantages of the role of quangos, of a top-down approach, of little public participation and of Board members being unelected, unrepresentative and largely anonymous and inaccessible to users and the public. There has been a suggestion in one analysis (Greer, 2004) that quangos have encouraged a permissive managerialist approach with a conservative ethos, and the model has been described by Houston (2008, p 29) as very bureaucratic and top down.

The creation of five new Trusts has not removed such criticisms of the role of quangos. With the Trusts having very large populations of between 250,000 and 400,000, which are among the largest health-related bodies in the UK, issues of a lack of local responsiveness and accountability have continued. Arguments may be presented that the use of the quango model has brought more professional expertise and financial knowledge, and encouraged specialisation and a less party political approach. It is highly unlikely that this Northern Ireland model would be copied in Great Britain, although the Care Trust model, introduced in England with very limited impact had some similarities. Care Trusts meant moving social services, by agreement, from local government to the NHS. In practice the structure in Northern Ireland is somewhat ambiguous on this question. Although fully integrated with health, social services in Northern Ireland are still not normally seen as formally part of the NHS. The lack of empathy with the quango model in Northern Ireland can also be demonstrated by the move in Scotland towards direct elections for part of the membership of health quangos. Directly elected members and councillors nominated by local authorities would form a majority of Board members. Also, Glasby (2009) has suggested a fundamental rethink to examine the case for local government-led systems of health care delivery, not just for social care. However, Northern Ireland's structure can be interpreted as a lean or streamlined bureaucracy, which may attract some attention from Great Britain given pressures to reduce administrative cost as part of public expenditure cuts.

Structures for registration, training and inspection

The introduction of devolution saw the establishment of new separate devolved structures for registration, education and inspection. Four distinct bodies came into operation in 2001, the Scottish Social Services Council, the Care Council in Wales, the Northern Ireland Social Care Council and the General Social Care Council in England. The councils in Scotland, Wales and Northern Ireland have similar responsibilities for a registration scheme, the promotion and development of education and training for the social services workforce, the accreditation of social work qualifying and post-qualifying training, codes of practice for social care workers and employers, and social work bursaries.

England has had a slightly different structure since 2005, with responsibility for the development of a national training standards and qualifying framework and workforce development needs for social care workers in England resting with two bodies: Skills for Care, which covers adult services, and the Children's Workforce Development Council, which covers the children's workforce including early years professionals. All five training bodies come together as part of a UK Alliance of Skills for Care. One consequence of the territorial bodies has been the facilitation of some discretion, for example, over the phasing in of different groups for registration. The Northern Ireland Social Care Council is likely to continue in existence despite the abolition of the English body.

The degrees in social work in England, Scotland, Wales and Northern Ireland can be amended to suit local conditions. The development of the post-qualifying education and training framework for social workers has also seen differences, with England committed to three different academic levels while Northern Ireland has only one level. Northern Ireland has also chosen a different route in restricting access to post-qualifying or specialist training to registered social workers. Success there was greater for assessed continuing professional development and partnership arrangements with employers than elsewhere in the UK (Taylor et al, 2010, p 483).

The systems for inspection and improvement of social services provision have undergone considerable change in each country since devolution. Since 2000, Northern Ireland has had a single body, the Northern Ireland Regulation and Quality Improvement Authority, which governs health and social care, but this structure still covers child protection and children's residential homes. England previously had a single social care body, the Commission for Social Care Inspection, but in 2009 a new body came into existence, the Care Quality Commission, as an independent regulator of health and social care. This body also took over the regulation of mental health services including Mental Health Tribunals, a development that was copied by the Northern Ireland Regulation and Quality Improvement Authority. The Care Quality Commission differs from the Northern Ireland body in not having responsibility for child protection and children's services.

Scotland has maintained a number of separate bodies. A social work inspection agency had carried out performance reviews of social work services in local government. The Scottish Commission for the Regulation of Care was a separate body for the regulation of care services and reported on the quality of care in institutions and agencies and dealt with complaints. Changes were made following *The Crerar Review* (Scottish Government, 2007b) into the scrutiny section and complaints handling system in Scotland. In 2008 the Scottish government announced that from 2011 a new body, Social Care and Social Work Improvement Scotland (SCSWIS), would come into operation in place of the Social Work Inspection Agency and the Care Commission. However, there would be a separate body, Health Care Improvement Scotland (HIS), which would scrutinise health care services. Wales, following devolution, had a similar structure to Scotland of a Social Services Inspectorate for Wales and a Care Standards Inspectorate for Wales, but in 2007 the Welsh Assembly Government announced that the two bodies would amalgamate. There is now a Care and Social Services Inspectorate for Wales that carries out regulation and inspection for all social care and early years provision, deals with complaints and enforcement, and also has the role of encouraging improvement by service providers for social care, but not health care, which is the responsibility of the Healthcare Inspectorate for Wales.

What can be noted is the general apparent lack of policy learning or transfer in published deliberations about reconfigurations. The Crerar inquiry in Scotland made no reference to systems of inspection in the other devolved institutions. Northern Ireland has ended up with a similar configuration as England yet, in the emergence of these bodies, there seems no acknowledgement of the similarities or, as the new bodies have been fully operative for some time, any evidence of policy transfer or learning. The likely abolition of the General Social Care Council in England did not involve discussion with the relevant devolved bodies. Also set up following devolution was a Social Care Institute for Excellence (SCIE), to promote and disseminate good practice, guidance and provide resources for practitioners, students, managers, commissioners, educators and policymakers. SCIE has a wide remit and has been funded by the Department of Health and Social Services and Public Safety to carry out some work for Northern Ireland. Its publications are mainly oriented to England although it has published some Northern Ireland material. The different countries have also launched projects to improve practice. Wales introduced an innovative Social Services Improvement Agency to support and improve local authority services by providing research and information on policy, legislation, good practice and performance management. Officially the Northern Ireland Regulation and Quality Improvement Authority was given an improvement role, but the organisation has very little research capacity.

Policy innovation and development

Has devolution in Northern Ireland led to innovative policies reflected in legislation other than in the long-standing area of integration of social care with health? Are there policy developments that have the potential to be copied from the Northern Ireland experience? Three types of decision-making at the level of government can be examined: legislation, expenditure and assembly inquiries and actions. The 2000–02 period of devolution did produce six devolved Acts relating to social care. These included a response to the UK Royal Commission on Long-term Care Law, and an Adoption Act required to conform with the Hague Convention on Adoption, while legislation on carers and direct payments both mirrored UK legislation. Since 2007, there have been only two bills relating to social care enacted: one dealing with emergency protection for children and required under the European Convention on Human Rights; the other dealing with the total restructuring and integration of social care with primary and secondary health care. This has to be viewed in the context that the actual legislative output in discretionary policy areas, as opposed to parity, financial and externally determined legislation, has not been large, some 13 Acts in all. The legislative output since 2007 in Scotland has also not been large with three social care Acts, and two legislative measures in Wales. Apart from integrated restructuring, there have been no major legislative innovations in Northern Ireland.

It is possible to examine patterns of expenditure between the devolved administrations to check for initiatives in prioritising or expanding expenditure on social care. The overall expenditure per head on health and social services (Table 9.2) shows Northern Ireland positioned below Scotland and Wales.

Table 9.2: Expenditure on health and personal social services

	Expenditure per head (£)
Northern Ireland	2,006
Scotland	2,313
Wales	2,109
England	1,915

Source: HM Treasury (2008)

An analysis of public expenditure on children in Northern Ireland showed that, in regards to social services expenditure on children in particular, Northern Ireland spent less per child than England, Scotland and Wales, indeed, approximately 28% less than England (Table 9.3).

Table 9.3: Expenditure per child on personal social care

	Expenditure per child (£)
Northern Ireland	287
Scotland	513
Wales	429
England	402

Source: HM Treasury (2008)

The allocations to health and social care by the Northern Ireland Executive since 2007 from UK funding, as determined by the Barnett formula, have not been generous. An analysis of the generation of the 'Barnett consequences' shows that some 58% of the additional money for 2010 was generated by health and adult social care expenditure in England, while the Northern Ireland Executive in total spent 48% of its budget on this area (Heald, 2009). The Northern Ireland Assembly did discuss the possible introduction of free personal care for older people and declared itself in favour of the innovative Scottish system, but no further action was taken to introduce or fund such a measure. There are also criticisms of low levels of expenditure in Northern Ireland on early years provision, mental health and learning disability. Consequently, there is, thus, little evidence from Northern Ireland of any major commitment to high levels of expenditure in any area of social care.

The Northern Ireland Assembly has a system of statutory committees to align with the departmental structure, and they have a role in assisting with policy formulation, pre-legislative scrutiny and analysis of policy, provision and budgets. Consequently, there is an Assembly Committee for Health, Social Services and Public Safety, which, as its first major devolved activity, produced a major report on residential and secure accommodation for children in Northern Ireland (NIA, 2000). Since 2007, however, the Committee has only produced two scrutiny reports on health topics and some shorter responses on autism and suicide. Following a visit to Glasgow it complained that mother and baby mental health services lag behind Scotland. However, there has been little engagement with core adult or children's social care services or social work for detailed scrutiny. The Assembly Public Accounts Committee has been critical at times of social care provision, of the resettlement of learning disability patients and the shift in care to domiciliary settings for older people.

Departmental strategies

The main source of strategies and guidance from government in Northern Ireland lies with the DHSSPS. The Office of Social Services within the DHSSPS, since changing from its inspection role, does not itself publish much material. It has published a review practice guide on the Children Order in 2008 and on defining day care in 2010. The practitioner review of the Children Order mainly suggested an initiative similar to that outlined in a 2006 Department of Health report in England (Larkin et al, 2008). The defining day care report was based on research by McVicker (2004), which noted a refocusing of day services from traditional building-based models of service provision and reported progress in support for adults with learning disabilities, but that the pace of change within other programmes, particularly of older people, had been slower than traditional forms of day care. The main plans, guidance and strategies are produced in the name of the DHSSPS, and these can be categorised under a number of thematic headings.

Child protection reforms

Reform has focused mainly on a 'change agenda' for children's services, which has seen the development and implementation of a single assessment framework, including risk assessment and mental health needs components, called UNOCINI (Understanding the Needs of Children in Northern Ireland). This agenda also included the development of common thresholds to determine when services are needed, standards of practice that underpin a children's pathway model and mechanisms to facilitate high-quality performance and training. Child referrals and the number on the child protection register have grown over the last 10 years. The UNOCINI assessment framework provides an assessment model that is capable of meeting the requirements of professionals from all agencies working with children. It has three areas of assessment: first, the needs of the child; second, the capacity of the parents or carers to meet needs; and, third, wider family and environmental factors. Once a referral is judged appropriate for a social services intervention by a threshold standard this leads to a UNOCINI pathway assessment and then a more comprehensive assessment. While UNOCINI is stated to have been specifically designed for Northern Ireland's unique system of providing health and social services, it does draw on a number of sources, including the UK Department of Health's assessment framework, family health needs assessment, the Connexions youth assessment framework and others (DHSSPS, 2010a), which raises some issues about its applicability or potential 'uniqueness'. The DHSSPS has also published child protection standards to assist with planning, delivery, audit and inspection services and a framework for best practice for all organisations and practitioners (DHSSPS, 2010c).

Some concern with a number of individual cases involving child protection, issues about a residential home and the background of allegations of child abuse going back in time concerning clergy have created pressure for further reform to delivery, earlier interventions and more efficient safeguarding arrangements. In 2006 it was proposed that the existing area Child Protection Committees and Panels be replaced by Safeguarding Boards. The arrangement is similar to that adopted in England and Wales under the 2004 Children Act with local Safeguarding Children Boards. It is proposed that the Board will represent the statutory, voluntary and community sectors. There was also a local system of Safeguarding Panels in each Trust.

Concern at difficulties across a number of Boards and Trusts over failures in timely and appropriate interventions led to the development of a gateway service within each Health and Social Care Trust. This is a process for receiving referrals and completion of an initial assessment for children's services and family support services. In 2010, as part of a reaction to a number of cases where children have been seriously injured or died, a project was launched into improving communication and joint working between mental health services and children's services. The project was established as part of a UK-wide national initiative on working with parents with mental illness and their children. The need for such a project did raise issues about the lack of use of the integrated structure of health and social services.

The underlying themes of the development of child protection can be seen as:

• determined strongly in overall organisational shape by the primacy of the integrated structure in Northern Ireland, so the structures of the *Every Child Matters* (DfES, 2003) reforms in England for integrated children's services were not replicated;

- adopting aspects of practice and detailed policy from strategies and guidelines in Great Britain;
- having a tendency towards uniform and top-down strategies and guidelines imposed on all delivery bodies (again there will be only one centralised Safeguarding Board for all of Northern Ireland); and
- based on a tendency to use the quango model of governance.

Older people and care

Devolution meant that each country can determine its own policies and eligible criteria for social care. Given the decision not to follow the Scottish example of free personal care, other trends can be identified. There has still not been a significant shift away from institutional care and progress has been slow (NIA, 2009) even though the *People First* (DHSS, 1991) strategy for community care has been in place since 1990. A key element of this strategy depends on the development of domiciliary care, which covers traditional home help services, overnight and 24-hour services, routine household tasks, and home care in sheltered housing. However, progress has been slow in the move away from hospitals, residential care homes and nursing homes to domiciliary settings. The Northern Ireland Audit Office report (NIAO, 2007) found that the percentage of older people cared for in their own homes had increase by 32% in 10 years. However, the balance with institutional care had remained relatively static. It also appeared that resources are increasingly being directed towards those with the most severe needs and levels of dependency and withdrawn from older people with low and moderate levels. The report did note, however, that the scope and range of provision varied across Trusts. While noting mixed performance on hospital discharge and intermediate care into the community, it did not discuss the impact or influence of the integrated service. The Northern Ireland Public Accounts Committee (2008), in examining this report, expressed the view that there had been a failure to develop sufficient capacity in the domiciliary care sector to fully realise the 'People First' strategy.

A research study (Iparraguirre, 2009) noted that personal social services under the elderly programme of care experienced the lowest percentage increase in terms of planned expenditure between 2003 and 2009 compared to other areas of social care. The DHSSPS's policy adopted by all five Trusts was for the increased use of the independent sector both for domiciliary care and residential care. This can be seen as catching up with England where the independent sector provides over three quarters of public funded home care; in 2008/09 the corresponding figures for Northern Ireland were approximately 60% statutory and 40% independent (NIAO, 2009, p 5). The rationale for this strategy, although called modernisation and reform, gave little consideration to issues of user preference and regulation and the quality of community care.

In 2009 the Northern Ireland Single Assessment Tool (NISAT) was launched, designed as a person-centred assessment of the health and social care and housing needs of older people. NISAT has seven components: contact screening, core housing assessment, complete needs assessment, carers assessment, specialist referral if needed, specialist summary, and GP/or medical practitioner report. NISAT has been described as the first of its kind in the UK, as other regions of the UK have used off-the-shelf tools whereas NISAT is tailor-made for Northern Ireland to underpin the assessment process. While the new NISAT may be noted as a positive and innovative outcome of integration, some weak performances in the number of delayed discharges, closing of institutions and development of intermediate care give a more negative perspective. Devolution has not brought any change in the payment system for domiciliary care. Means-tested services are free to pensioners assessed in need aged 75 or over and those in receipt of income support or family credit. The lack of change in the charging system since devolution contrasts with Scotland's free care and also with Wales, which introduced more support and reduced costs for those on lower incomes.

Mental health and learning disability

Mental health and learning disability have had a significant interaction with social work in Northern Ireland for four main reasons. First, there are persistent patterns of higher rates of mental illness in Northern Ireland than in England and Scotland. Second, the desirability of moving people from hospitals into community care settings had started in the 1980s (Prior, 1995), but by the late 1990s progress in closing mental hospitals and learning disability hospitals had slowed down. In 2003 there were some 600 people being treated in the six traditional psychiatric hospitals that date back to the 1880s (DHSSPS, 2003b). In 2002 Northern Ireland also had the highest proportion of people with learning disabilities in long-stay hospitals (NIAO, 2009). Third is the continuing emphasis on a medical model with too much reliance on acute provision in psychiatric hospitals, rather than developing social care models. In 2000, 58% of the total mental health budget was spent on hospitals, compared to England's 40% (DHSSPS, 2003b, p 23). Fourth, there had been a lack of progress in fully utilising the integrated health and social care structure.

In the first period of Direct Rule, these considerations led to the establishment of a major review of mental health and learning disability, which was headed up by a professor of social work, David Bamford. The main reasons given for the review were: the existing focus on hospital care, the need to update legislation, human rights, equality and European requirements, changes in treatment and care, and the fact that there had been similar reviews in neighbouring jurisdictions. The Bamford Review set out principles, values, strategies and recommendations in a series of reports between 2003 and 2007. Many of the 11 reports had a strong social work/social care emphasis including promoting social inclusion, enhancing lives, treating dementia and mental health in older age, including human rights and equality dimensions, developing comprehensive child and adolescent mental health services, and new strategies for learning disability and alcohol and substance abuse. The response to the recommendations became the responsibility of the restored devolved Assembly and Executive. The Department of Health did publish a strategy, *Delivering the Bamford Vision* (DHSSPS, 2008b), which has been seen as falling short of the recommendations. The change to community care has still not been progressed quickly. In 2008 the aim was for only a 10% reduction in the numbers residing long term in psychiatric hospitals by 2011, and the aim of closing all learning disability hospitals had been pushed back to 2013. There had, however, been an increase in community mental health teams and the development of children and young people's mental health teams. Amended mental health legislation and new mental health capacity legislation is still pending. Legislation has not been changed since 1986 and this contrasts with the priority given to new incapacity legislation by the Scottish Executive and Parliament in 2000 (Birrell, 2009b, pp 60–3). Support was expressed in *Delivering the Bamford Vision* for more advocacy work, but there was not support for a statutory right to advocacy as developed in Scotland.

The Bamford Review endorsed user participation with user advocacy as a new principle, despite controversy over the late involvement in the review process of user groups (Heenan, 2009b). In practice, Northern Ireland has not developed major initiatives in user participation, although there are probably more local initiatives in the mental health field than other areas, and user groups in this area have become more critical and vocal. Wilson and Daly (2007) cite a technical and competence-based training agency culture and the continuing influences of biomedical approaches as composing obstacles. There are still questions in Northern Ireland concerning social workers adapting to user participation and the task for social workers of involving users remains challenging (Heenan, 2009b). The implementation process for Bamford led to some increases in resources for some areas, for example, dementia. Overall, expenditure has lagged behind Britain and was judged to be 26% lower on community-based services than in England (Wilson and Daly, 2007, p 426). Expenditure on learning disability was the lowest per head in the UK (NIAO, 2009, p 3). A Bamford monitoring board, which was set up to have a challenge function to the implementation process, expressed concern at the lower proportion of expenditure on mental health compared with England (McClelland, 2007). Although integrated working in mental health has developed further, the full potential of the opportunity provided by the reorganisation of services and the devolved administration has not been fully taken. There is still a reluctance among policymakers to share power and there are still elements of professional protectionism.

Personalisation

Personalisation became the relatively new term to describe the move towards self-directed support and personal budgets as the way forward for adult social care, and has become part of the transformation of social care in Britain. In particular, the strategy has had a strong focus on direct payments to individuals who have been assessed as needing support. The personal budget-holder devises a support plan to meet personal outcomes, and support can be purchased from statutory social services, voluntary, private-sector and user organisations, community groups or carers (Carr, 2010). Pilot studies have also taken place in England with the more widely based 'individual budgets'. Direct payments were introduced in Great Britain and Northern Ireland in 1996 and social services trusts could make payments to users to then purchase their own community care rather than receive services from the Trusts. Direct payments fall under devolved services and in Northern Ireland Trusts now have a duty to allow people to choose a direct payment. However, an individual can choose not to accept a direct payment and have the service provided by the Trust. Direct payments have been slow to develop in Northern Ireland, with only 132 in total in 2003 and under 1,000 by 2008. A four-country study of direct payments in the UK found that, of the 59 authorities which reported more direct payments than the mean average, only one was in Northern Ireland (Riddell et al, 2006). The Centre for Independent Learning is the main organisational source of support in Northern Ireland, whereas support in England is channelled through a wide range of organisations (Pearson, 2006). A study by the DHSSPS in Northern Ireland found a lack of knowledge among staff, that staff were ill equipped to promote the uptake of direct payments, that it was not a topic in their professional training and that often confused information was given to the public. Riddell et al (2006, p 9) also found that payment rates were lower in Northern Ireland and there was an absence of direct payment support posts. A further analysis (Priestley et al, 2007) suggested that there was little evidence of community ownership for policy development in Northern Ireland, and that there was a focus on people with physical disabilities rather than on other groups with little involvement of the new groups. Direct payment remains largely a minority service within social work in Northern Ireland indicating a slow response to the personalisation strategy. It can be noted that the report on the review of roles and tasks of social work saw the move towards personalisation as presenting both opportunities and threats (Bogues, 2008, p 24).

User and public involvement

User and public participation has developed in Great Britain as a key element of social care modernisation, stemming in part from self-help and advocacy organisations, from social inclusion and equality agendas, and from the strong emphasis on public and patient involvement in the health services from the late 1990s. Social care has been seen as leading the way in engaging with services users (Newman et al, 2008). It involves all groups, but has been especially influential in the fields of mental illness and learning disability. User involvement has developed as a high-profile issue (Beresford and Croft, 2004) and has embraced carer involvement as well. User involvement has moved beyond consultation and focus groups, surveys and public/user panels to user participation in policy planning and decision-making, co-production and co-delivery of services, self-management, and user participation in education and training, regulation and inspection, and research. Further developments have seen the training of users or experts by experience, payment of users and the growth of user organisations and networks. The experience of user participation in Northern Ireland has again not kept up with modernisation agendas in Great Britain. A research project (Duffy, 2008) found the development of service user involvement in Northern Ireland was uneven across agencies and most of the involvement policies quoted for the four Boards only really related to consultation. A study (Roulstone and Hudson, 2007) specifically on comparing carer participation between England, Wales and Northern Ireland found that research evidence was sparse.

In 1991 four Health and Social Service Councils were set up to provide a voice for the consumer as local committees for each Board area. The appointed quangos model was used and their function was mainly to represent the interests of the public and to keep the operation of services under review. The restructuring of health and social care provided an opportunity for an infrastructure to promote the modernisation of service user and public involvement. Despite some claims that in health and social services in Northern Ireland there was a commitment to the values of democratic participation and 'having a say' (Campbell, H., 2007), there was to be little evidence of a commitment to making user participation and public involvement a major value in the restructuring. A single quango, the Patient and Client Council, was established for the whole of Northern Ireland. It has fewer powers, for example, no visiting powers, and fewer members than the old social service councils, which had a more representative composition. A centrally appointed body, its role is to promote public involvement, provide advice and information, and represent the interests of the public, but its public profile and impact has been limited. Individual delivery Trusts have produced public involvement strategies, but, again, these are limited in detail to consultation rather than progressing to co-production or self-management and all five Trusts have produced documents that appear to confuse user, carer and public participation with community development.

The one area where development in user participation has kept in alignment with Britain relates to user involvement in education and training in social work. There are requirements by the Northern Ireland Social Care Council for user involvement. Duffy (2006) describes user involvement covering student selection, curriculum design, course review and practical assessment in Northern Ireland as similar to Britain. In contrast, user involvement in health and social care research, which is controlled by the DHSSPS, Research and Development Office and Trusts, is very underdeveloped. Northern Ireland has not experienced many of the benefits of user participation in terms of improvements in the quality and standard of services, the inputs from lived experience, greater user satisfaction, the generation of new knowledge, a contribution to social capital, and as a means to improve education, inspection and research. The limited development of user participation in social care also sits alongside the limited involvement of local councillors. Elected councillors do not have even a representative role on Trusts as in Scotland and Wales and there is no development similar to local involvement networks (LINKs) in England. The only lesson that might be drawn from the Northern Ireland experience to date relates again to the integration of health and social care in the limited structures that do exist for user and public participation, and that has some resonance for the rationale for the local involvement networks which have combined health and social care.

Policy copying

There has been an amount of policy copying into Northern Ireland of some significant policy innovations, which have had an impact on social care. Particularly noteworthy has been the Children's Commissioner, initiated in Wales in 2002. The Northern Ireland Commissioner for Children and Young People was set up in 2003, but with more extensive powers than all the other Commissioners, including more unique powers of investigating individual complaints, with the power to enter premises. The Northern Ireland Commissioner is also better funded and staffed, proportionally, than the Commissioners in England, Scotland and Wales. The Commissioner has been influential in Northern Ireland in lobbying government on the numbers of unallocated child protection cases, underinvestment in children's services and the mental health needs of children. Northern Ireland is also copying the Welsh model of an Older People's Commissioner. This Commissioner may serve to better promote social care provision for older people and raise awareness of issues, such as elder abuse. However, in terms of the key issue of free personal care Northern Ireland has not been so good at learning lessons from the Scottish or Welsh policy developments (Bell, 2010).

The formal mechanism for the devolved administrations and the UK government to meet, the Joint Ministerial Council (JMC), is not fully operational. However, the British–Irish Council (BIC), which was set up after the Good Friday Agreement, became a mechanism for exchanging policy ideas and information and comparing practice. The BIC consists of representatives of three devolved governments, the UK government, the Irish government and the governments of the Isle of Man, Guernsey and the Channel Islands. The work streams of the BIC have included social inclusion, misuse of drugs, youth justice, early years work, disability and access to services, and the role of credit unions. BIC activity was particularly significant in obtaining the agreement of all the devolved administrations to the UK 2010 Child Poverty Act.

The role of social work

Since 2006, all four countries of the UK have decided to carry out separate fundamental reviews of the future role and task of social workers. The General Social Care Council in England (2008) report, *Social Work at its Best*, followed a review on raising the standards of social care (Platt, 2007). Later another taskforce, headed by Moira Gibb, produced a report on *Building a Safe, Confident Future* (Social Work Taskforce, 2009).

With devolution, Scotland and Wales were able to produce their own reports. In 2006 a review group report, *Changing Lives*, was published in Scotland (Scottish Executive, 2006). The Welsh review, *Fulfilled Lives, Supportive Communities* (Welsh Assembly Government, 2007b), followed a previous review report, *Social Work in Wales, A Profession to Value* (SSIA, 2005), which had concentrated on reviewing tasks and workforce issues.

The analysis in these reports has much in common. The *Changing Lives* review found social work in Scotland to be lacking in confidence in its skills and distinctive contribution, and the *Social Work in Wales* report had noted that social workers felt undervalued. The Social Work Taskforce in England also noted the poor public image and understanding of social work. The papers recognised the significance of similar demographic and socio-economic factors and gave a commitment to support the socially excluded and vulnerable in both Scotland and Wales. A similar four-tier pyramid of intervention was used to describe the tasks of social workers. In looking at the way ahead the main recommendations stressed three main principles. First was engaging users and carers in working together. In Scotland this was described as building on the capacity of individuals and communities and ending top-down approaches (Watson and West, 2008), and in Wales as delivering social work in partnership with users. Second was the theme of personalisation of services through direct payments and individual budgets. Third was the importance of collaboration: *Challenging Lives* urged the exploration of the potential of partnership working in Scotland. In the Welsh paper there was a commitment to address the barriers to better collaboration. Some differences did emerge, for example, the Scottish paper recommended that social work should remain a single generic profession whereas the English *Social Work at its Best* raised the issue of loosening boundaries between professional disciplines. The Welsh document proposed maintaining the integration between children's and adult's social care.

In Northern Ireland the changing context of social work was recognised (Martin, 2007) but an equivalent review was not initiated until 2008 and it copied the example of England in that the review was carried out by the Northern Ireland Social Care Council. The Northern Ireland Chief Social Services Officer, at the launch of the project on the role and tasks of social work, had expressed some similar views to those expressed in other countries; these views suggested it was time for social workers to stop taking themselves down and take pride in the profession, and referred to values of fairness and social justice, the need to be person-centred and the protection of those at risk of harm. The Chief Social Services Officer did state that social work 'cannot be defined as a special skill or a specific body of knowledge' (Martin, 2008, p 8). This statement also saw the review as an opportunity to proactively influence social work's role within the integrated system and to improve its professional standing.

The statement gave primacy to ensuring clarity about the contribution social work can have in a wide range of roles. It also stated that it was important to be clear about what is particularly distinctive about social work in Northern Ireland, where it operated in a uniquely integrated model of health and social services (Martin, 2008, p 9).

Table 9.4: Strategic points

England	Scotland	Wales	Northern Ireland
Power in hands of people	Personalised services	Users and citizens at centre	Social work to be valued
Extend personalisation	Participation/citizen leadership	Contribution of carers	Develop strong profession leadership
Integrated working with other professions and agencies	Management leadership	More accountable leadership	Validate number of social workers
Assessing people's situation	Collaboration and integration	Collaborative working	Deliver services around users need
Arranging advocacy	Performance measures	Performance outcomes	Culture of continuous improvement
Acting as broker to obtain support people want	Supporting carers	Effective commission framework	Ensure professional governance arrangements
Promote social justice	Building workforce capacity	Plan for workforce	
Sharing of social work tasks with other workers	Early intervention	Use of research	Promote public understanding of social work
National career structure	Use of technology	Use of technology in care	
Training for front-line social workers		Personalisation	
Improve public understanding			

The key themes of the review were clearly related to Northern Ireland society and listed as follows:

- stating what social work can do and achieve;
- advocating on behalf of others;
- meeting demographic, economic and technological change;
- integrated working;
- reform of children's services and new safeguarding arrangements;
- empowerment;
- emerging rights agenda; and
- reducing dominance of individual casework. (NISCC, 2008)

The outcome of a consultation process by the review on the roles and tasks of social work endorsed some of the above themes, sometimes with qualifications (Bogues, 2008). Particularly noteworthy was support for:

- involving carers and users, but there was a belief that the relationship with service users had been diluted;
- increasing the advocacy and broker role, but the review noted pressure on social workers to meet organisational targets worked against best interests of individuals;
- reclaiming community development credentials;
- the personalisation agenda, but this was seen as offering both opportunities and threats;
- integrated working, but there was a perceived threat of domination by the health agenda;
- accepting the requirements of technological and demographic changes;
- an improved understanding of the political agenda.

However, the consultees also raised a number of issues that the official documentation had not flagged as major concerns:

- the social worker as a gatekeeper of resources;
- relating to people and unequal relationships;
- the need for more resources;
- resistance to a mechanical listing of tasks;
- promotion of rights for effective social work practice;
- the dilution of the therapist role;
- the need for social work to be more politically aware;
- promoting social change; and
- the need for a social work champion.

The final strategy document (DHSSPS, 2010b), *A 10 Year Strategy for Social Work in Northern Ireland 2010–2020*, had a major focus on the social work profession, but this meant the strategy rather neglected policy, services, user and governance issues. The report recommended seven areas for action:

- supporting social workers to feel valued and confident to do their jobs;
- developing strong professional leadership to support and empower social workers to deliver an effective service;
- creating an effective system to identify the right number of social workers;
- designing and delivering social work services around the needs of people who use them;
- developing a culture of continuous improvement and building a knowledge base;

- ensuring professional governance arrangements; and
- promoting greater understanding by the public of the contribution of social work.

The proposal for implementing the strategy was expressed very briefly, mainly in relation to establishing a government-led steering group (DHSSPS, 2010c, p 42). The strategy lacked a focus on key issues for social provision in Northern Ireland including: using full powers of integration, promoting personalisation and service user agendas, critically examining the impact of governance and commissioning strategies, making comparisons with England, Scotland and Wales, dealing with continuing issues of violence and communal conflict, and the future difficult resource questions.

Conclusion

A number of the social work policies examined can be seen as a response by the devolved administration to distinctive Northern Ireland needs, in terms of identity divisions and the consequences of conflict. In practice, relatively few of the responses have been totally distinctive. Otherwise the social characteristics of Northern Ireland society are not totally different from the rest of the UK or the Republic of Ireland. There is nothing uniquely Northern Irish about the levels of disadvantage. Devolved policies representing a social work response are largely similar or less developed with few examples of innovations.

It has been suggested that an examination of what has been distinctive about social work policies in Wales since devolution, apart from bilingualism, has been that many social policies are intended to alter the nature of social work and broader social care services (Scourfield et al, 2008). A range of key strategies can be cited: on child poverty, early years, mental health, older people, learning disability and community care. The Scottish Parliament has a strong profile of mainstream initiatives with the themes of poverty and child poverty occupying a major role, accompanied by a strong youth justice agenda. These have covered a wide range of health and social care (Mooney et al, 2006a). Major initiatives by the Scottish devolved administration have covered free personal care for older people, early years, mental health and learning disability.

Overall, Northern Ireland's performance in producing social policies to specifically impact on social care is weak. There has been a failure in the Northern Ireland Executive to reach a consensus on a new anti-poverty strategy, on a new Single Equality Bill, on academic selection, a community relations strategy and a voluntary sector strategy, while there has been a lack of commitment to developing early years provision, an older people's strategy and pushing ahead with resettlement.

A major explanation for the relatively few mainstream policy innovations in Northern Ireland lies in two factors. First is the prevailing view in Scotland that social policy was the main concern and function of the Scottish Parliament and

Executive (Mooney et al, 2006b), and that the Welsh Assembly Government was also seen as a social policy assembly for Wales (Chaney and Drakeford, 2004). This view was seen as justified by the nature of devolved powers, devolved expenditure and the thrust of the Barnett formula. However, this view has received very little support in the Northern Ireland Executive or Assembly. The second factor is the values that underpin policymaking in the Northern Ireland administration. In Scotland and Wales there has been a continuing emphasis on the principles of social justice and progressive universalism (Fawcett, 2004; Drakeford, 2007) underpinning policymaking, but Northern Ireland government narratives have been lacking in reference to social justice as a specific value (Birrell, 2009a). An analysis by the Joseph Rowntree Foundation of the impact of devolution tends to attribute Northern Ireland performance on welfare to stop–go devolution, but does not address the different value base in Northern Ireland (McCormick and Harrop, 2010). This is crucial in explaining the lack of innovative policies in social care following devolution.

TEN

Conclusion

The contention that social work in Northern Ireland over the last 40 years has unique features had greater salience for the first half of that period. In the last 15 years some of these features have taken on a greater resonance for social work development in Great Britain. These particular features are: the structural integration of health and social care, coping with political and communal violence and emergencies, revisiting community development approaches, cooperating across land borders, social work in acutely disadvantaged areas, and the impact of devolved government. Social work in Northern Ireland has had sustained exposure to each of these contexts compared to rather less engagement in England, Scotland and Wales. However, in recent years some of these issues have received a higher profile in Great Britain and this analysis has focused on what lessons have been, or might be, learnt from the Northern Ireland experience.

Social work in Northern Ireland, as well as operating with these features, has continued to deliver services and practice in the more mainstream areas, broadly similar to the rest of the UK. This includes addressing social needs in terms of childcare and child protection, children leaving care, fostering and adoption, providing a range of adult social care in the community, domiciliary day care and residential care, and responding to demographic changes. Social work in Northern Ireland has also faced similar issues to the rest of the UK in recruitment, retention, workloads, workforce development and the pressures on resources and standards following the high profile of, in particular, child abuse cases. The impacts of the requirements of performance management, efficiency drives, public expenditure cuts and welfare retrenchment have been similar to those in Great Britain. Social work education has also largely kept in line with modern developments in the rest of the UK; notable strengths include an assessed year in employment, strong agency partnerships and a reformed and updated post-qualifying framework.

However, social work in Northern Ireland has not totally engaged in what can be called the UK social work modernisation agenda. This applies particularly to a relatively conservative and gradual approach to the personalisation and participation agendas. Historically, social work in Northern Ireland has been slow to adapt to modernisation agendas, for example, direct payments and user and carer participation. There has been very limited support among professional social workers or social care managers of Trusts and Boards for any radical social work approaches. This implies an ongoing value base for social work based on conservatism, managerialism and technocratic approaches, which have presented obstacles to any extensive innovation.

In the last 10 years, social work in Northern Ireland has been subject to major restructuring with the amalgamation of Trusts and further structural integration with former Hospital Trusts. This reorganisation has led to uncertainties for staff, retirements, relocation and job changes, which has been expressed as 'change is the normal state' (Dornan, 2009). The process raised major issues about the available resources for managing the change process (Martin, 2007, p 262), as well as social work concerns about the outcomes of the restructuring for the future of the profession if placed in a subordinate and possibly competitive position with health.

We have identified the key areas where social work in Northern Ireland has demonstrated a more unique experience and where this long-standing engagement has provided lessons in policy, practice and delivery for social work in Great Britain. This should be placed in a context where the full potential of strategies and opportunities was not always realised. This would apply in particular to the integration of health and social care, community development, and cross-border working. The analysis and extraction of lessons also has to be put in the context of a relatively limited amount of research and analysis by government agencies, delivery Boards and Trusts, the voluntary sector, and academics.

Our analysis has focused on identifying the social work strategies and responses in settings with unique salience to Northern Ireland. The difficulties facing social work in dealing with sectarianism were multidimensional and did lead eventually to responses particularly in education and training with the adoption of anti-discriminatory practice, the equality agenda and good relations issues. Such developments have made more connections possible with anti-oppressive practice and statutory equality duties in Britain. The relative downplaying of the significance of anti-sectarianism, however, may not necessarily reflect post-conflict changes, but a more general desire on the part of social workers, managers and Trust board members and civil servants to avoid controversy. Initially, the social work response to the social and psychological effects of violence and emergencies was noteworthy for its inadequate, unplanned and ad hoc nature. Subsequently, practitioners and statutory bodies moved to a more planned response and to some significant innovative work in emergency responses and in relation to trauma. This work has had some impact on appraisals of the role of social care emergency planning in Britain and also on the relevance of a wider and more socially oriented model of trauma and its treatment. The focus within Northern Ireland has in the last decade shifted to care and support for victims and survivors. Examples of good practice have to be extracted from the many political considerations and divisions that affect the discourses on assisting the victims of the conflict.

The integrated structure of health and social care is the most unique aspect of social work in Northern Ireland and one that attracted substantial interest from policymakers, academics, practitioners and managers in Great Britain. A difficulty arises with the limited number of detailed research studies and evaluations of the system and the limited analysis in department, Trust and Board documents in Northern Ireland. Some information can be gleaned from research, commentaries and descriptions of the working of the integrated system. This provides a base of knowledge and information that is highly relevant to the continuing debates in Great Britain on greater integration of health and social care. This material is particularly important in casting further light on many issues concerning problems and difficulties with the operation of collaboration, cooperation and partnership working in Great Britain. The approach of practitioners, policymakers and managers to Northern Ireland being a laboratory for the study of structural integration of health and social care has been low-key. Integrated structures have professional, managerial, administrative and political support, but they remain largely unacknowledged and overlooked. The achievements of the integrated structures are rarely analysed, nor is the system in Northern Ireland compared to the non-integrated structures in Great Britain.

Community development approaches have retained a powerful appeal in social work and social care in Northern Ireland. This can be seen as a reflection of the enduring appeal of community groups which are widely viewed as more acceptable, innovative and dynamic than the statutory sector. Community development is acknowledged as a key component of social work practice, but despite this it has largely been relegated to the margins of practice and education. Achievements in community development practices can be identified and they provide case studies and working examples that contribute to and provide a rationale for an increased role for community development approaches in social work.

Northern Ireland is unique in the UK in having a land frontier, and a study of cross-border cooperation and linkages demonstrates specific practical issues that emerge between the two different jurisdictions. Cross-border cooperation in social work is of some significance in Northern Ireland and is of small but increasing significance along Scotland–England–Wales boundaries because of devolution. Cross-border cooperation in Ireland in social work is also significant in its EU setting, demonstrating that while there are barriers that have to be dealt with, there are also substantial benefits to cooperation, and scope for cooperation between different welfare systems. It is clear that cross-border working is not very extensive and again conservative influences and political attitudes have an influence on social work cooperation across the border.

Social work in Northern Ireland has long experience of operating in one of the most socially disadvantaged areas of the UK. The implications for social work delivery can be listed and debated, particularly the high level of children living in persistent poverty, high rates of worklessness and high rates of disability. There is strong evidence about the relationship between poverty and social work interventions, but historically practice in this area has not been particularly innovative. Early years social care and welfare advice services and advocacy have not been developed in many social work offices. Statutory social work strategies, corporate management plans and business plans at department, agency or Trust level have failed to engage with social work's role in alleviating disadvantage. There is little connection made between social work interventions and tackling the root causes of poverty, helping to reduce the impact and lift people out of poverty.

Social work policies and strategies have developed in Northern Ireland under a devolved system of government, not only since 1999, but also under the previous Stormont system of devolution between 1921 and 1972. The main impact has been major patterns of divergence in administrative and delivery structures, rather than in details of practice. Historically there have been some innovations, such as a comprehensive regional special care service for learning disability, but broadly in terms of social work practice, education and training there has been convergence with the rest of the UK. Devolution has meant that Northern Ireland has its own legislation, administrative structures, policies, strategies, priorities and control over expenditure, and also has the legal capacity to mould social work provision to its needs. The devolution of power has also resulted in separate registration, professional and inspection bodies. However, devolution has not resulted in the development of distinctive or innovative social work services. Social work and social care issues have not been given a high priority by the Executive or in Assembly Committees, and expenditure on both children and adult social care is below levels in England, Scotland and Wales. Some of the explanation for this rests with broader deficits in the operation of devolution, the political system, political attitudes and the organisation of the public sector in Northern Ireland. Unlike Scotland and Wales, there is limited acceptance that social policy is the main policy function of devolution and a limited commitment among politicians to the pursuit of values such as social justice (Birrell, 2009a). There have also been difficulties with developing a strong policymaking capacity in the devolved administration and in Northern Ireland generally there has been an absence of policy networks, policy forums and research institutes on social affairs and particularly social work. This has changed a little with lobbying by some pressure groups in relation to child poverty, childcare, early years provision, lone parents and older people. The large-scale governance of social work by quangos has also resulted in dominance by a managerialism that does not encourage innovative ideas.

Social work in Northern Ireland has been different from the rest of the UK. The book has focused on the themes grounded in these differences and the perspectives and strategies used to address these. A number of lessons can be drawn from the unique context and practice of social work in Northern Ireland, which may encourage more policy transfer and learning across the UK.

References

Acheson, N., Harvey, B. and Williamson, A. (2004) *Two Paths, One Purpose: Voluntary Action in Ireland, North and South*, Dublin: Institute of Public Administration.

Acheson, N., Cairns, E., Stringer, M. and Williamson, D. (2007) *Voluntary Action and Community Relations in Northern Ireland*, Coleraine: Centre for Voluntary Action Study.

Adelman, L., Middleton, S. and Ashworth, K. (2003) *Britain's Poorest Children: Severe and Persistent Poverty and Social Exclusion*, London: Save the Children.

Age Concern and Help the Aged NI (2009) *Positive Ageing: Is the Government's Ageing Strategy Fit for Purpose?*, Belfast: ACNI.

Anderson, M. (1998) 'Social Work and the Integrated Service', in M. Anderson,, S. Bogues, J. Campbell, H. Douglas and M. McColgan (eds) *Social Work and Social Change in Northern Ireland*, Belfast: CCETSW.

Appleby, J. (2005) *Independent Review of Health and Social Services in Northern Ireland*, Belfast: DHSSPS.

Area Children and Young People's Committees (2008) *Northern Ireland Children's Services Plan 2008–2011*, Belfast, ACYPC.

Barclay, P. (1982) *Social Workers: Their Roles and Tasks*, London: Bedford Square Press.

Barnardo's (2007) *'It Doesn't Happen Here': The Reality of Child Poverty in the UK*, Essex: Barnardo's.

Barr, A., Hashagen, S. and Purcell, R. (1996) *Monitoring and Evaluation of Community Development in Northern Ireland*, Belfast: Voluntary Activity Unit, DHSS.

Barron, C. and Taylor, B.J. (2010) 'The Right Tools for the Right Job: Social Work Students Learning Community Development on Placement', *Social Work Education*, vol 29, no 4, pp 372–85.

Belfast Health and Social Care Trust (2008) 'Troubles Research Published'. Available at: www.belfasttrust.hscni.net/new/troubles/20research

Belfast Health and Social Care Trust (2009a) *Excellence and Choice: A Consultation on the Future Delivery of Adult Mental Health Services in Belfast*, Belfast: HSCNI.

Belfast Health and Social Care Trust (2009b) 'Annual Report 2008–2009'. Available at: www.belfasttrust.hscni.net

Belfast Health and Social Care Trust (2010) 'Corporate Management Plan'. Available at: www.belfasttrust.hscni.net

Bell, D. (2010) 'The Impact of Devolution on Long-Term Care Provision in the UK'. Available at: www.jrf.org.uk

Beresford, P. and Croft, S. (2004) 'Service Users and Practitioners Reunited: The Key Component for Social Work Reform', *British Journal of Social Work*, vol 34, no 1, pp 53–68.

Birrell, D. (1993) 'The Management of Civil Emergencies in Northern Ireland', *Journal of Contingencies and Crisis Management*, vol 1, no 2, pp 79–89.

Birrell, D. (1999a) 'Cross-Border Co-operation Between Local Authorities in Ireland', *Local Governance*, vol 25, no 2, pp 109–18.

Birrell, D. (1999b) 'North–South Cooperation in Social Policy Areas', *Administration*, vol 47, no 2, pp 3–30.

Birrell, D. (2009a) *Direct Rule and the Governance of Northern Ireland*, Manchester: Manchester University Press.

Birrell, D. (2009b) *The Impact of Devolution on Social Policy*, Bristol: The Policy Press.

Birrell, D. and Heenan, D. (2010) 'Devolution and Social Security: The Anomaly of Northern Ireland', *Journal of Poverty and Social Justice*, vol 18, no 2, pp 203–15.

Birrell, W.D. and Murie, A. (1980) *Policy and Government in Northern Ireland*, Dublin: Gill and Macmillan.

Birrell, W.D. and Williamson, A.P. (1983) 'Northern Ireland's Integrated Health and Personal Social Service Structure', in A. Williamson and G. Room (eds) *Health and Welfare States of Britain*, London: Heinemann.

Bloomfield, K. (1998) 'We Will Remember Them. Report of the Northern Ireland Victims Commission'. Available at: www.cain.ulster.ac.uk

Bogues, S. (2008) 'People Work Not Over Paperwork: What People Told Us During the Consultation Conducted for the NISCC Roles and Tasks of Social Work Project'. Available at: www.niscc.gov.uk

Bolton, D. (2005) *Catastrophe Mental Health, Emergency Planning, Mental Health and Catastrophic Events: Policy and Practice Implications*, Omagh: The Northern Ireland Centre for Trauma and Transformation.

Bolton, D. (2010) Information supplied by Director of Northern Ireland Centre for Trauma and Transformation.

Bolton, D. and Duffy, M. (1999) 'The Immediate Community Services Response to the Omagh Bombing', Presentation in Draperstown, 28 June.

Boyd, F.I. (1988) *Social Work in the Royal Victoria Hospital 1938–1988*, Belfast: Eastern Health and Social Services Board and GPS Graphics.

Boyle, L. (1978) 'The Ulster Workers Council Strike May 1974', in J. Darby and A. Williamson (eds) *Violence and the Social Services in Northern Ireland*, London: Heinemann.

Brodie, I., Nottingham, C. and Plunkett, S. (2008) 'A Tale of Two Reports: Social Work in Scotland from *Social Work and the Community* (1966) to *Changing Lives* (2006)', *British Journal of Social Work*, vol 38, no 4, pp 697–715.

Buckland, P. (1981) *A History of Northern Ireland*, New York: Holmes and Meier.

Burchardt, T. and Holder, H. (2009) 'Towards a More Equal Society': Inequality and the Devolved Administrations: Scotland, Wales and Northern Ireland', in J. Hills, T. Sefton and K. Stewart (eds) *Poverty, Inequality and Policy Since 1997*, Bristol: The Policy Press.

Burgess, P., Caul, B., Heaslett, A. and O'Neill, P. (1998) *Access to Higher Education in Northern Ireland and the Republic of Ireland*, Standing Conference for North/South Co-operation in Further and Higher Education, Coleraine: Coleraine Printing Company.

Cabinet Office (2010) *Meeting the Needs of those Affected by an Emergency*, London: Cabinet Office.

Cairns, E. and Wilson, R. (1989) 'Mental Health Aspects of Political Violence', *International Journal of Mental Health*, vol 18, no 1, pp 38–56.

Campbell, H. (2007) '"Nothing about Me, Without Me": NHS Values Past and Future in Northern Ireland', in S.L. Green and P. Rowland (eds) *Devolving Policy, Diverging Values*, London: The Nuffield Trust.

Campbell, J. and Christie, A. (2005) 'Editorial: Crossing Borders', *Social Work Education,* no 5, August, pp 483–4.

Campbell, J. and McCrystal, P. (2005) 'Mental Health Social Work and the Troubles in Northern Ireland: A Study of Practitioner Experience', *Journal of Social Work*, vol 5, no 2, pp 173–90.

Campbell, J. and Pinkerton, J. (1997) 'Embracing change as opportunity: Reflections on social work from a Northern Ireland Perspective', in B. Lesnk (ed) *Change in Social Work: International Perspectives in Social Work*. Aldershot: Ashgate.

Campbell, S. (2007) 'Social Work, Political Violence and Historical Change', *Social Work and Society*, vol 5. Available at: www.socwork.net/2007/festschriff/arsw/campbell

Carr, S. (2010) 'Personalisation: A Rough Guide', Adult Services Report 20. Available at: www.scie.org.uk/resources

Caul, B. and Herron, S. (1992) *A Service for People. Origins and Development of the Personal Social Services of Northern Ireland,* Belfast: Universities Press.

CAWT (Cross Border and Working Together) (2002) *Partnership in Action: CAWT Business Plan 2002–2006*, Derry: CAWT.

CCETSW (1999) *Getting off the Fence: Challenging Sectarianism in Personal Social Services*, London, CCETSW.

CCETSW/NSWQB (1998) *Crossing Borders: Resource Pack for Social Workers (NI) Social Work Context (Education, Training and Practice)* Belfast: Northern Ireland Social Care Council.

Central Emergency Planning Unit (1998) 'Northern Ireland Standards in Civil Protection'. Available at: www.ofmdfmni.gov.uk/index/making–government-work/emergencies

Central Emergency Planning Unit (2004) 'A Guide to Emergency Planning Arrangements in Northern Ireland'. Available at: www.ofmdfmni.gov.uk/index/making-government-work/emergencies

Centre for Cross Border Studies (2008) *Your Guide to Co-operation in Health Services*, Armagh: CCBS.

Challis, D., Stewart, N., Donnelly, M., Weiner. N. and Hughes, J. (2006) 'Care Management for Older People: Does Integration have a Difference', *Journal of Interprofessional Care*, vol 20, no 4, pp 335–48.

Chaney, P. and Drakeford, M. (2004) 'The Primacy of Ideology: Social Policy and the First Term of the National Assembly for Wales', in N. Ellison, L. Bauld and M. Powell (eds) *Social Policy Review 16*, Bristol: The Policy Press.

Chapman, P. (1998) 'The Same but Different: Probation Practice in Northern Ireland', in CCETSW (ed) *Social Work and Social Change in Northern Ireland*, Belfast: CCETSW.

Child, C., Clay, D., Warrington, G. and Das, J. (2008) *Caring in a Crisis: The Contribution of Social Care to Emergency Response and Recovery*, London: Social Care Institute for Excellence.

Clarke, P. (2007) 'Institutional Cooperation: The Health Sector', in J. Coakley and L. O'Dowd (eds) *Crossing the Border*, Dublin: Irish Academic Press.

Clarke, S. (1996) *Social Work as Community Development: A Management Model for Social Change,* Aldershot: Avebury Press.

Clarke, P and Jamison, J. (2001) *From Concept to Realisation: An Evaluation of CAWT,* Armagh: Centre for Cross Border Studies.

Coakley, J. (2001) 'North–South Co-operation', in D. Wilson (ed) *A Guide to the Northern Ireland Assembly*, Belfast: The Stationery Office.

Coakley, J., O'Caoindealbhain, B. and Wilson, R. (2007) 'Institutional Cooperation, The North-South Implementation Bodies', in J. Coakley and L. O'Dowd (eds) *Crossing the Border*, Dublin: Irish Academic Press.

Community Relations Council (2004) *Good Relations Framework*, Belfast: CRC.

Concordia (2007) *Childcare that Works*, Dungannon: Concordia.

Cooke, J., Owen, J. and Wilson, A. (2002) 'Research and Development at the Health and Social Care Interface in Primary Care: A Scoping Exercise in One National Health Service Region', *Health and Social Care in the Community*, vol 10, no 6, pp 435–44.

Co-operation Ireland (1999) *Border Crossings: Lessons from the Peace Programme*, Belfast, Co-operation Ireland.

Craig, J. (1934) *Parliamentary Debates, Northern Ireland House of Commons*, vol XVI, cols 1091–5, Unionist Party, 24 April.

Curran, P.S., Bell, P., Murray, D., Loughrey, G., Roddy, R. and Roche, G. (1990) 'Psychological Consequences of the Enniskillen Bombing', *British Journal of Psychiatry*, vol 156, no 4, pp 479–92.

Curry, J. (1980) *The Irish Social Services,* Dublin: Institute of Public Administration.

Daly, M. (1984) *Dublin, the Deposed Capital – A Social and Economic History, 1860–1914*, Cork: Cork University Press.

Darby, J. and Williamson, A. (eds) (1978) *Violence and the Social Services in Northern Ireland*, London: Heinemann.

DARD (Department of Agriculture and Rural Development) (2007) *Northern Ireland Strategy Plan for Implementation of the EU Rural Development Regulation in 2007–2013*, Belfast: DARD.

DARD (2009) *Rural Anti-Poverty and Social Inclusion Framework Consultation*, Belfast: DARD.

Department for Education and Skills (DfES) (2003) *Every Child Matters*, London: DfES.

Department for Work and Pensions (1999) *Opportunity for All*, London: DWP.

Devaney, J. (2008) 'Inter-Professional Working in Child Protection with Families with Long Term and Complex Needs', *Child Abuse Review*, vol 17, pp 242–61.

Devlin, P. (1981) *Yes We Have No Bananas: Outdoor Relief in Belfast 1920–39*, Belfast: Blackstaff Press.

DH (Department of Health) (1989) *Caring for People: Community Care in the Next Decade and Beyond*, Cm 849, London: HMSO.

DH (2000) *The NHS Plan*, London: The Stationery Office.

DH (2008) *The Evidence Base for Integrated Care*, London: DH.

DHSS (Department of Health and Social Services) (1972) *Health and Personal Social Services (Northern Ireland) Order*, Belfast, DHSS.

DHSS (1991) *People First*, Belfast: HMSO.

DHSS (1993) *Strategy for the support of the voluntary sector and for community development in Northern Ireland*, Belfast: HMSO.

DHSS (1997a) *Health and Wellbeing into the next Millennium: Regional Strategy for Health and Social Wellbeing 1997–2002*, Belfast: DHSS.

DHSS (1997b) *Well into 2000*, Belfast: DHSPSS.

DHSSPS (Department of Health and Social Services and Public Safety) (1999a) *Children First*, Belfast: DHSSPS.

DHSSPS (1999b) *Mainstreaming Community Development in Health and Personal Social Services*, Belfast: DHSSPS.

DHSSPS (2000) *A Better Future: Fifty Years of Child Care in Northern Ireland 1950–2000*, Belfast, DHSSPS.

DHSSPS (2001) *Health and Wellbeing in Northern Ireland*, Belfast: DHSSPS.

DHSSPS (2002a) *Developing Better Services*, Belfast: DHSSPS.

DHSSPS (2003a) *Evaluation of Health and Social Services for Victims of the Conflict Final Report*, Belfast: DHSSPS.

DHSSPS (2003b) *Planning Priorities and Actions for the Health and Personal Social Services*, Belfast: DHSSPS.

DHSSPS (2005) *The Bamford Review of Mental Health and Learning Disability (Northern Ireland): A Strategic Framework for Adult Mental Services*, Belfast: DHSSPS.

DHSSPS (2006a) *Review of Public Administration: Consultation on Draft Legislation to Establish New Integrated Health and Social Services Trusts*. Available at: www.dhssps. gov.uk/hpssreview-trust-consultation-document

DHSSPS (2006b) *Survey of Carers of Older People in Northern Ireland*, Belfast, DHSSPS.

DHSSPS (2008a) *Evaluating Healthy Living Centres*, Belfast, DHSSPS.

DHSSPS (2008b) *Delivering the Bamford Vision*, Belfast, DHSSPS.

DHSSPS (2009) *Children Order Statistical Bulletin*, Belfast, DHSSPS.

DHSSPS (2010a) *Office of Social Service. Standards For Child Protection Services*. Available at: www.dhssps.gov.uk/index/ssi/oss-children's-services

DHSSPS (2010b) *A Ten Year Strategy for Social Work in Northern Ireland 2010–2020*, Belfast: DHSSPS.

DHSSPS (2010c) *Office of Social Services, Key Roles and Responsibilities*, Belfast, DHSSPS.

DHSSPS and DSD (2009) *Review of the Support Provision for Carers*, Belfast: DHSSPS.

Dickson, B. and Osborne, R. (2007) 'Equality and Human Rights since the Belfast Agreement', in P. Carmichael, C. Knox and R. Osborne (eds) *Devolution and Constitutional Change in Northern Ireland*, Manchester: Manchester University Press.

Dignam, T. (2003) *Low-Income Households 1990–2002: Methodology and Statistics Tables*, Belfast: OFMDFM.

Dillenburger, K. (1992) *Violent Bereavement: Widows in Northern Ireland*, Aldershot: Avebury Press.

Dillenburger, K., Akhonzada, R. and Fargas, M. (2007) 'Community Services for People Affected by Violence: An Exploration and Categorisation', *Journal of Social Work*, vol 8, no 1 pp 7–27.

Disasters Working Party (1991) *Disasters: Planning for a Caring Response*, London: HMSO.

Ditch, J. (1988) *Social Policy in Northern Ireland between 1939–1950*, Aldershot: Avebury Press.

Doherty, P. and Poole, M. (1997) 'Ethnic Residential Segregation in Belfast, Northern Ireland 1971–1991', *Geographical Review*, vol 87, no 4, pp 520–36.

Dominelli, L. (2002) 'Anti-Oppressive Practice in Context', in R. Adams, L. Dominelli and M. Payne (eds) *Social Work Themes, Issues and Critical Debates*, Basingstoke: Palgrave Macmillian.

Dornan, B. (1999) *Teamwork in Integrated Primary Health and Social Care Teams, Research Report,* Lisburn: Down Lisburn Trust.

Dornan, B. (2009) 'Service Improvement in Northern Ireland', conference presentation, 23 September. Available at: www.niscc.info/2009sep23-socialwor katitsbestspeakerspresentations.pdf

Dowling, B., Powell, M. and Glendinning, C. (2004) 'Conceptualising successful partnerships', *Health and Social Care in the Community*, vol 12, no 4, pp 309-17.

Drakeford, M. (2007) 'Social Justice in a Devolved Wales', *Benefits*, vol 15, no 2, pp 171–8.

Duffy, J. (2006) 'Participation and Learning: Citizen Involvement in Social Work Education in the Northern Ireland Context: A Good Practice Guide'. Available at: www.scie.org.uk/publications

Duffy, J. (2008) 'Looking out from the Middle: User Involvement in Health and Social Care in Northern Ireland', Report 18. Available at: www.scie.org.uk/ publications/reports

Duffy, M., Gillespie, J. and Clarke, D.M.(2007) 'Post Traumatic Stress Disorder in the Context of Terrorism, and Other Civil Conflict in Northern Ireland: Randomised Controlled Trial', *British Medical Journal*, vol 334, no 1147.

Eames, R. and Bradley, D. (2009) 'Report of the Consultative Group on the Past'. Available at: www.cgpni.org

ECNI (Equality Commission for Northern Ireland) (2003) *Racial Equality in Health and Social Care: Good Practice Guide*, Belfast: ECNI.

ECNI (2005) *Promoting Equality in intra Work Places*, Belfast, ECNI.

ECNI (2006) *Good Relations in Practice. A Report of Progress on the Good Relations Duty*, Belfast: ECNI.

ECNI (2007) *Section 75, Keeping it Effective*, Belfast: ECNI.

ECNI (2010) *Section 75 of the Northern Ireland Act 1998: A Guide for Public Authorities*, Belfast, ECNI.

ESRC (Economic and Social Research Council) (2005) *Poverty and Income Distribution in Northern Ireland*, Belfast: ESRC, OFMDFM.

Etzioni, A. (1993) *The Spirit of Community: The Reinvention of American Society*, New York: Touchstone.

Evans, D. and Forbes, R. (2009) 'Partnerships in Health and Social Care', *Public Policy and Administration*, vol 24, no 7, pp 67–83.

Evason, E., Darby, J. and Pearson, M. (1976) *Social Need and Social Provision in Northern Ireland. Social Security, Personal Social Services, Health and Education. Occasional Papers in Social Administration*, Coleraine: University of Ulster.

Fahey, T. and McLaughlin, E. (1999) 'Family and State, North and South', in A.F. Heath, R. Breen and C.T. Whelan (eds) *Ireland North and South: Perspectives from Social Science*, Oxford: Oxford University Press.

Fair Employment Commission (1995) *A Profile of the Northern Ireland Workforce*, Belfast: FEC.

Fawcett, H. (2004) 'The Making of Social Justice Policy in Scotland: Devolution and Social Exclusion', in A. Trench (ed) *Has Devolution Made a Difference? The State of the Nations 2004*, Exeter: Imprint Academic.

Fay, M., Morrissey, M. and Smyth, M. (1999]) *Northern Ireland's Troubles: The Human Costs*, London: Pluto Press.

Fee, E. and Corrigan, M. (1999) *Omagh Bombing, Sperrin Lakeland's Response. A Review*, Omagh: Sperrin Lakeland Health and Social Care Trust.

Ferry, F., Bolton, D., Bunting, B., Devine, B., McCann, S. and Murphy, S. (2008) *Trauma, Health and Conflict in Northern Ireland*, Omagh: The Northern Ireland Centre for Trauma and Transformation.

Field, J. and Peck, E. (2003) 'Mergers and Acquisitions in the Private Sector: What are the Lessons for Health and Social Services', *Social Policy and Administration*, vol 37, no 7, pp 742–55.

Frazer, H. (ed) (1981) *Community Work in a Divided Society*, Galway, Ireland.

Freeman, I. and Moore, M. (2008) 'Community Health and Care Partnerships in Scotland', *Journal of Integrated Care*, vol 16, no 3, pp 38–47.

French, D. (2009) 'Residential Segregation and Health in Northern Ireland', *Health and Place*, vol 15, no 3, pp 888–96.

Fulton, B. and Webb, B. (2009) 'The Emergence of the Probation Services in North East Ireland', *Irish Probation Journal*, vol 6, pp 32–48.

Gaffikin, F. and Morrissey, M. (1990) *Northern Ireland: The Thatcher Years*, London: Zed Books.

Garrett, P.M. (1999) 'The Pretence of Normality: Intra-Family Violence and the Response of State Agencies in Northern Ireland', *Critical Social Policy*, vol 19, no 1, pp 31–55.

General Social Care Council (2008) *Social Work at its Best*. Available at: www.gscc. org.uk/cmsFiles/policy/roles

Gibson, M. (1991) *Order from Chaos. Responding to Traumatic Events*, 1st edn, Birmingham: Venture Press.

Gibson, M. (1996) 'Paper Given to CCETSW Council on 21 February 1996', *Child Care in Practice*, vol 3, no 1, pp 87–91.

Gibson, M. (2006) *Order from Chaos: Responding to Traumatic Events*, 3rd edn, Bristol: The Policy Press.

Gibson, M. and Iwaniec, D. (2003) 'An Empirical Study into the Psychosocial Reactions of Staff Working as Helpers to those Affected in the Aftermath of Two Traumatic Incidents', *British Journal of Social Work*, vol 33, no 7, pp 851–70.

Gibson, F., Michael, G. and Wilson, D. (1994) *Perspectives on Discrimination and Social Work in Northern Ireland*, London: CCETSW.

Glasby, J. (2004) 'Discharging Responsibilities: Delayed Hospital Discharges and the Health and Social Care Divide', *Journal of Social Policy*, vol 33, no 4, pp 593–604.

Glasby, J. (2009) 'Creating NHS Local – The Relationship between Local Government and the NHS', paper presented at the Social Policy Association conference, Edinburgh, July.

Glendinning, C. and Coleman, A. (2003) 'Joint Working: The Health Service Agenda', *Local Government Studies*, vol 29, no 3, pp 51–72.

Goldsworthy, J. (2002) 'Resurrecting a Model of Integrating Individual Work with Community Development and Social Action', *Community Development Journal*, vol 37, no 4, pp 327–37.

Gray, A.M. and Horgan, G. (2009) *Figuring it Out: Looking Behind the Social Statistics in Northern Ireland*, Belfast: ARK (Social and Political Archive for Northern Ireland at the University of Ulster).

Green, A.E. and Shuttleworth, I. (2010) 'Local Differences, Perceptions and Incapacity Benefit Claimants: Implications for Delivery', *Policy Studies*, vol 31, no 2, pp 233–43.

Greer, S. (2004) *Territorial Politics and Health Policy*, Manchester: Manchester University Press.

Griffiths, H. (1975) 'Paramilitary Group and Other Community Action Groups in Northern Ireland Today', *International Review of Community Development*, vol 33, no 4, pp 189–206.

Griffiths, H., Boland, V., Gilliland, D., McKernan, B. and Shields, L. (2007) 'An Evaluation of the Child and Parent Support Service Within the Magherafelt and Cookstown Areas', *Child Care in Practice*, vol 13, no 2, pp 125–35.

Griffiths, R. (1998) *Community Care: Agenda for Action*, London: The Stationery Office.

Grounds, A. and Jamieson, R. (2003) 'No Sense of an Ending', *Theoretical Criminology*, vol 7, no 3, pp 347–62.

Hadden, T. and Boyle, K. (1989) *The Anglo-Irish Agreement*, London: Sweet-Maxwell.

Ham, C. (2009) *Only Connect. Policy Options for Integrating Health and Social Care*, London: Nuffield Trust.

Harvey, B. (2010) 'Community Development along the Border: An Instrument for the Development of the Cross-Border Region?' *The Journal of Cross Border Studies in Ireland*, no 5, Spring, pp 33–46.

Harvey, C. (2001) 'Human Rights and Equality in Northern Ireland', in C. Harvey (ed) *Human Rights, Equality and Democratic Renewal in Northern Ireland*, Oxford: Hart Publishing.

Haverty, T. (1983) 'Delivery of Personal Social Services in Derry', MSc dissertation, University of Ulster.

Hayes, P. and Campbell, J. (2000) 'Dealing with Post Traumatic Stress Disorder: The Psychological Sequence of Bloody Sunday and the Response of State Services', *Research on Social Work Practice*, vol 10, no 6, pp 705–21.

Heald, D. (2009) 'Should Northern Ireland Wish the Abolition of the Barnett Formula?', Lecture at University of Ulster, 2 April.

Heenan, D. (2000) 'Informal Care in Farming Families in Northern Ireland: Some Considerations for Social Work', *British Journal of Social Work*, vol 30, no 2, pp 855–66.

Heenan, D. (2004) 'Learning Lessons from the Past or Revisiting Old Mistakes: Social Work and Community Development in Northern Ireland', *British Journal of Social Work*, vol 3, no 6, pp 793–809.

Heenan, D. (2006) 'The Factors Influencing Access to Health and Social Care in the Farming Communities of County Down, Northern Ireland', *Ageing and Society*, vol 26, no 3, pp 378–91.

Heenan, D. (2009a) 'Working across Borders to Promote Positive Mental Health and Well-Being', *Disability and Society*, vol 24, no 6, pp 715–26.

Heenan, D. (2009b) 'Mental Health Policy in Northern Ireland: The Nature and Extent of User Involvement', *Social Policy and Society*, vol 8, no 4, pp 451–62.

Heenan, D. (2010) 'Social Capital and Older People in Farming Communities', *Journal of Aging Studies*, vol 24, no 1, pp 40–6.

Heenan, D. and Birrell, D. (2002) 'Re-evaluating the Relationship between Social Work and Community Development: The Northern Ireland Experience', *Social Work and Social Sciences Review*, vol 9, no 2, pp 42–57.

Heenan, D. and Birrell, D. (2005) 'The Nature and Context of Cross-Border Social Work in Ireland', *European Journal of Social Work*, vol 8, no 1, pp 63–77.

Heenan, D. and Birrell, D. (2006) 'The Integration of Health and Social Care: The Lessons from Northern Ireland', *Social Policy and Administration*, vol 40, no 1, pp 47–66.

Heenan, D. and Birrell, D. (2009) 'Organisational Integration in Health and Social Care: Some Reflections on the Northern Ireland Experience', *Journal of Integrated Care*, vol 17, no 5, pp 3–12.

Higgins, G. and Brewer, J. (2003) 'The Roots of Sectarianism in Northern Ireland', in O. Hargie and D. Dickson (eds) *Researching the Troubles*, Edinburgh: Mainstream Publishing.

Hillyard, P., Kelly, G., McLaughlin, E., Parsius, D. and Tomlinson, M. (2003) *Bare Necessities: Poverty and Social Exclusion in Northern Ireland*, Belfast: Democratic Dialogue.

Hirsch, D. (2008a) *What is Needed to End Child Poverty in 2020?* York: Joseph Rowntree Foundation.

Hirsch, D. (2008b) *Estimating the Costs of Child Poverty*, York: Joseph Rowntree Foundation.

HMSO (1929) *Report on the Administration of Local Government Services, 1928/29*, Cmnd 110, Belfast: HMSO.

HMSO (1948) *Report of the Mental Health Services Advisory Committee 1948*, Belfast: HMSO.

HMSO (1968) *Report of the Committee on Local Authority and Allied Personal Social Services* (the Seebohm Report), London: HMSO.

HMSO (1969) *The Administrative Structure of the Health and Personal Services in Northern Ireland*, Belfast: HMSO.

HMSO (1970) *Review Body on Local Government in Northern Ireland 1970* (the Macrory Report), Belfast: HMSO.

HMSO (1979) *Legislation and Services for Children and Young People in NI: Report of the Children and Young Persons Review Group* (the Black Report), Belfast: HMSO.

HMSO (1995) *The Framework Document*, London: HMSO.

HM Treasury (2008) *Public Expenditure Statistical Analysis of Public Experiment by Country*, London: The Stationery Office.

Horgan, G. (2005) 'Child Poverty in Northern Ireland: The Limits of Welfare-to-Work Policies', *Social Policy and Administration*, vol 39, no 1, pp 49–64.

Horgan, G. and Monteith, M. (2009) *What Can We Do to Tackle Child Poverty in Northern Ireland?*, York: Joseph Rowntree Foundation.

Houston, S. (2008) 'Transcending Ethnoreligious Identities in Northern Ireland: Social Work's Role in the Struggle for Recognition', *Australian Social Work*, vol 61, no 1, pp 25–41.

Hudson, B. (2007) 'Partnerships Through Networks: Can Scotland Crack It?', *Journal of Integrated Care*, vol 16, no 1, pp 3–13.

Hudson, B. and Henwood, M. (2002) 'The NHS and Social Care: The Final Countdown?' *Policy and Politics*, vol 30, no 2, pp 153–66.

Hughes, J., Campbell, A., Hewstone, M. and Cairns, E. (2007) 'Segregation in Northern Ireland. Implications for Community Relations Policy', *Policy Studies*, vol 28, no 1, pp 35–53.

Iparraguirre, J.L. (2009) Public Expenditure on Older People in Northern Ireland, Belfast: Economic Research Institute of Northern Ireland.

Jamison, J., Clarke, P. and O'Neill, M. (2001) *Cross Border Co-operation in Health Services in Ireland*, Armagh: Centre for Cross Border Studies.

Jarman, N. (2004) 'From War to Peace? Changing Patterns of Violence in Northern Ireland 1990–2003', *Terrorism and Political Violence*, vol 16, no 3, pp 420–38.

Jarman, N. (2005) *No Longer a Problem? Sectarian Violence in Northern Ireland*, Belfast: Institute of Conflict Research.

Joseph Rowntree Foundation (2009) *Monitoring Poverty and Social Exclusion in Northern Ireland 2009*, York: Joseph Rowntree Foundation.

Kapur, R. and Campbell, J. (2004) *The Troubled Mind of Northern Ireland*, London: Karnac.

Kee, M., Bell, P., Loughrey, G., Rood, R. and Curran, P. (1987) 'Victims of Violence: A Demographic and Clinical Study', *Medicine, Society and the Law*, vol 27, pp 214–47.

Kelleher, C.C. (2003) 'Mental Health and the Troubles in Northern Ireland: Implications of Civil Unrest for Health and Wellbeing', *Journal of Epidemiology and Community Health*, vol 57, pp 474–5.

Kenny, S. (1999) *Developing Communities for the Future: Community Development in Australia*, Melbourne: Thomas Nelson.

Kenway, P., MacInnes, T., Kelly, A. and Palmer, G. (2006) *Monitoring Poverty and Social Exclusion in Northern Ireland*, York: Joseph Rowntree Foundation.

Laird, S.E. (2008) *Anti-oppressive Social Work*, London: Sage.

Larkin, E., McSherry, D. and Murphy, C. (2008) *Research Report: Practitioner Review of the Children Order Advisory Committee. Best Practice Guide*, Belfast: DHSSPS.

Lawrence, R. (1965) *Government of Northern Ireland*, Oxford: Oxford University Press.

Lee, S. (1995) 'Abortion Law in Northern Ireland: The Twilight Zone', in A. Furedi (ed) *The Abortion Law in Northern Ireland: Human Rights and Reproductive Choice*, Belfast: Family Planning Association Northern Ireland.

Liddell, C. (2008) 'The Impact of Fuel Poverty on Children, Policy Briefing'. Available at: www.savethechildren.org.uk/northernireland

Lister, R. (1997) *Citizenship, Feminist Perspectives*, Basingstoke: Macmillan.

Loughrey, G., Bell, P., Kee, M., Roddy, R. and Curran, P. (1988) 'Post Traumatic Stress Disorder and Civil Violence in Northern Ireland', *British Journal of Psychiatry*, vol 153, pp 554–60.

Luce, A., Firth-Cozens, J., Midgley, S. and Burges, C. (2002) 'After the Omagh Bomb: Post Traumatic Stress Disorder in Health Service Staff', *Journal of Traumatic Stress*, vol 15, no 1, pp 27–30.

Luddy, M. (1995) *Women and Philanthrophy in Nineteeth-Century Ireland*, Cambridge: Cambridge University Press.

Macbeath, A.A. (1957) *Fifty Years of Social Work 1906–1956: A Brief History of the Work of Belfast Council of Social Welfare*, Belfast: Nicholson and Bass.

Manktelow, R. (1998) 'Political Conflict, Mental Ill-health and Social Work', in CCETSW (ed) *Social Work and Social Change in Northern Ireland*, Belfast: CCETSW.

Manktelow, R. (2007) 'The Needs of Victims of the Troubles in Northern Ireland: The Social Work Contribution', *Journal of Social Work*, vol 7, no 1, pp 31–50.

Mantle, G. and Backwith, D. (2010) 'Poverty and Social Work', *British Journal of Social Work*, advance access online.

Martin, P. (2007) 'The Times They Are a Changing: The Challenges Facing Social Work in Northern Ireland', *Child Care in Practice*, vol 13, no 3, pp 261–9.

Martin, P. (2008) 'Social Work: A Profession Fit for the Future', Speech on 16 January, Belfast: NISCC.

Maucher, M. and Rotzinger, C. (2002) *Challenges and Options in the Crosscountry Provision of Social Services – A Good Example of More Integrated European Social Policy, Discussion Paper from the Observatory for the Development of Social Services in Europe*, Germany: Frankfurt am Main.

McCall, C. and Williamson, A. (2000) 'Fledgling Social Partnership in the Irish Border Region: European Union Community Initiatives and the Voluntary Sector', *Policy and Politics*, vol 28, no 1, pp 397–410.

McClelland, R. (2007) 'Letter to OFMDFM from Board for Mental Health and Learning Disability', 21 December. Available at: www.pfgbudgetni.gov.uk/boardformentalhealthandlearningdisability.pdf

McCormick, S. and Harrop, A. (2010) *Devolution's Impact on Low-Income People and Places*, York: Joseph Rowntree Foundation.

McCoy, J. (1993) *'Integration – A Changing Scene in Social Services Inspectorate'. Personal Social Services in Northern Ireland: Perspectives on Integration*, Belfast: Department of Health and Social Services.

McCready, S. (2001) *Empowering People: Community Development and Conflict – 1999*, Belfast: The Stationery Office.

McCrudden, C. (2001) 'Equality', in S. Harvey (ed) *Human Rights, Equality and Democratic Renewal in Northern Ireland*, Oxford: Hart Publishing.

McGuigan, K. and Shevlin, M. (2010) 'Longitudinal Changes in Post Traumatic Stress in Relation to Political Violence (Bloody Sunday)', *Traumatology*, vol 16, no 1, pp 1–6.

McKay, S. (2009) 'Dealing with Cross-Border Sex Offenders: Learning from the North's Multi-Agency Approach', *The Journal of Cross-Border Studies*, no 4, pp 67–78.

McLaughlin, E. (1993) 'Catholic Corporatism', in A. Cochrane and J. Clarke (eds) *Comparing Welfare States: Britain in International Context*, London: Sage.

McLaughlin, E. (1998) 'The View from Northern Ireland', in H. Jones and S. McGregor (eds) *Social Issues and Party Politics*, London: Routledge.

McLaughlin, E. (2007) 'From Negative to Positive Equality Duties: The Development and Constitutionalism of Equality Provisions in the UK', *Social Policy and Society*, vol 6, no 1, pp 111–21.

McLaughlin, J. and Kelly, B. (1998) 'The Physical Disability Content and Crisis Support Services in Northern Ireland', in CCETSW (ed) *Social Work and Social Change in Northern Ireland*, Belfast: CCETSW.

McNamara, F. (2001) 'North and South Unite over Abuse', *Irish News*, 4 January.

McQuade, J. (2001) 'Tackling the Issues of Sectarianism', *Childcare in Practice*, vol 1, no 3, pp 21–5.

McShane, L. and O'Neill, M. (eds) (1999) *Community Development in Health and Social Services*, Craigavon: Craigavon and Banbridge Trust.

McVeigh, R. (2007) 'The "Final Solution": Reformism, Ethnicity Denial and the Politics of Anti-Travellerism in Ireland', *Social Policy and Society*, vol 7, no 1, pp 91–102.

McVicker, H. (2004) 'Defining Day Care'. Available at: www.dhsspsni.gov.uk/oss-defining_day_care.pdf

Mendes, P. (2004) 'Competing Visions of Community Development in Australia: Social Inclusion vs Social Exclusion', paper presented at the Proceedings of Community Development Human Rights and The Grassroots Conference, Deakin University: Geelong.

Mendes, P. (2008) 'Teaching Community Development to Social Work Students: A Critical Reflection', *Community Development Journal*, vol 44, no 2, pp 248–62.

Miller, M. (2008) 'Anti-Oppressiveness: Critical Comments on a Discourse and its Contexts', *British Journal of Social Work*, vol 38, no 2, pp 362–75.

Monteith, M. and McLaughlin, E. (2004) *The Bottom Line: Children and Severe Poverty in Northern Ireland*, Belfast: Save the Children.

Monteith, M., Lloyd, K. and McKee, P. (2008) 'Persistent Child Poverty in Northern Ireland'. Available at: www.savethechildren.org.uk/northernireland

Mooney, G., Scott, G. and Williams, C. (2006a) 'Rethinking Social Policy Through Devolution', *Critical Social Policy*, vol 26, no 3, pp 483–97.

Mooney, G., Sweeney, R. and Law, A. (2006b) *Social Care Health and Welfare in Contemporary Scotland*, Paisley: Kynoch and Blaney.

Morrissey, M. and Smyth, M. (2002) *Northern Ireland After the Good Friday Agreement*, London: Pluto Press.

Mowbray, M. (2004) 'Community Development the Third Way: Mark Latham's Localist Policies', *Urban Policy and Research*, vol 22, no 1, March, pp 107-15.

Mowbray, M. and Meekosha, H. (1990) 'Reconstruction to Deconstruction: The Transformation of Community Work in Australia', *Community Development Journal*, vol 25, no 4, pp 337–44.

Moyle Report (1975) *Report of the Joint Working Party on Sporting and Recreational Provision of District Councils*, London: HMSO.

Muldoon, O., Schimd, N., Downs, G., Kremer, J. and Trew, K. (2003) *The Legacy of the Troubles, Mental Health and Social Attitudes*, Belfast: Queen's University.

Murtagh, B. (2001) 'Integrated Social Housing in Northern Ireland?' *Housing Studies*, vol 16, no 6, pp 771–89.

National Social Work Qualifications Board (2001) *Crossing Borders: Social Work Mobility Study*, Dublin: NSWQB.

Newman, J., Glendinning, C. and Hughes, M. (2008) 'Beyond Modernisation: Social Care and the Transformation of Welfare Governance', *Journal of Social Policy*, vol 37, no 4, pp 531–57.

NHS (National Health Service) (2000) *The NHS Plan*, Cm 4818–1, London: The Stationery Office.

NIA (Northern Ireland Assembly) (2000) *Inquiry into Residential and Secure Accommodation for Children in Northern Ireland*, Belfast: NIA.

NIA (2008a) *Comparing Child Poverty in Northern Ireland with Other Regions*, Briefing Note 23/08, Belfast: NIA.

NIA (2008b) *Tackling Severe Childhood Poverty*, Briefing note 09/08, Belfast: NIA.

NIA (2008c) *Childcare Provision in the UK and Republic of Ireland*, Research Paper 16/08, Belfast: NIA.

NIA (2009) *Fuel Poverty in Northern Ireland*, Belfast: NIA.

NIAO (Northern Ireland Audit Office) (2007) 'Older People and Domiciliary Care', NIA 45/07–08. Available at: www.niauditoffice.gov.uk/pubs

NIAO (2009) *Resettlement of Long-Stay Patients from Learning Disability Hospitals*, Belfast: The Stationery Office.

NIAPN (Northern Ireland Anti-Poverty Network) (2007) 'Fact Sheet on Poverty in Northern Ireland, 17 October', Belfast: NIAPN.

NICDRG (Northern Ireland Community Development Review Group) (1991) *Community Development in Northern Ireland: Perspectives for the Future*, Belfast: CDRG.

NIE (Northern Ireland Executive) (2001) *Programme for Government Making A Difference*, Belfast: OFMDFM.

NIE (2008) 'Programme for Government 2008–11 Building a Better Future'. Available at: www.northernireland.gov.uk

NIO (Northern Ireland Office) (1974) *Finance and the Economy, Northern Ireland Discussion Paper*, Belfast: HMSO.

NIO (1998) *Partnership for Equality*, Cm 3890, Belfast: The Stationery Office.

NIPPA (2006) *Response to the Draft Budget Statement by Peter Hain from NIPPA – The Early Years Organisation*, Belfast: NIPPA.

NISCC (Northern Ireland Social Care Council) (2002) *Code of Practice for Social Care Workers and Employers of Social Care Workers*, Belfast: NISCC.

NISCC (2003) *Northern Ireland Framework Specification for the Degree in Social Work*, Belfast: NISCC/DHSSPS.

NISCC (2005) *Curriculum Guidance for the Degree in Social Work: The Northern Ireland Context*, Belfast: NISCC.

NISCC (2008) 'The Role and Tasks of Social Workers in Northern Ireland in the 21st Century. Discussion Paper'. Available at: www.niscc.gov.uk

NISCC (2009) *The Northern Ireland Degree in Social Work Partnership: Practice Learning Handbook*, Belfast: NISCC.

Northern Health and Social Care Trust (2010) 'Northern Area Trauma Advisory Panel'. Available at: www.nhssb.n-i.nhs.uk/partnerships/tot/php

Northern Ireland Affairs Committee (2005) *The Challenge of Diversity: Hate Crime in Northern Ireland*, HC 548, London: House of Commons.

Northern Ireland Public Accounts Committee (2008) *Report into Older People and Domiciliary Care*, Belfast: Northern Ireland Assembly.

Northern Ireland Statistics and Research Agency (2001) *Northern Ireland Census of Population 2001*, Belfast, NISRA.

NSPCC and Barnardo's Northern Ireland (2009) 'Briefing Paper on Neglect', Contribution to a debate in Northern Ireland Assembly, 24 November, Belfast: NSPCC/Barnardo's.

O'Connor, I., Wilson, J. and Setterlund, D. (1998) *Social Work and Welfare Practice*, Frenchs Forest: Pearson.

O'Dowd, L. and Corrigan, J. (1995) 'Buffer Zone or Bridge: Local Responses to Cross-Border Economic Co-operation in the Irish Border Region', *Administration*, vol 42, no 4, pp 335–51.

O'Dowd, L. and McCall, L. (2007) 'The Voluntary Sector: Promoting Peace and Cooperation', in J. Coakley and L. O'Dowd (eds) *Crossing the Border*, Dublin: Irish Academic Press.

OFMDFM (1998) *New Targeting Social Need: An Agenda for Promoting Social Inclusion in Northern Ireland*, Belfast: OFMDFM.

OFMDFM (2005) *Ageing Inclusive Society*, Belfast: OFMDFM.

OFMDFM (2006a) *First Annual Implementation Action Plan for the Racial Equality Strategy for Northern Ireland*, Belfast: OFMDFM.

OFMDFM (2006b) *Lifetime Opportunities, Government's Anti-Poverty and Social Inclusion Strategy for Northern Ireland*, Belfast: OFMDFM.

OFMDFM (2006c) *Our Children and Young People – Our Pledge: A Ten Year Strategy for Children and Young People in Northern Ireland 2006–2016*, Belfast: OFMDFM.

OFMDFM (2008) *Report on Inquiry into Child Poverty in Northern Ireland*, Report 07/07/08R, Belfast: NIA.

OFMDFM (2009a) 'Central Emergency Planning Unit – Background'. Available at: www.ofmdfmni.gov.uk/index/making-government-work/emergencies

OFMDFM (2009b) 'Strategy for Victims and Survivors'. Available at: www.ofmdfm.ni.gov.uk

OFMDFM (2010) *Lifetime Opportunities Monitoring Framework: Baseline Report*, 14 October. Available at www.ofmdfmni.gov.uk/annex_3_lifetime_opportunities_monitoring_framework_oct_2010_pdf.pdf

Oliver, J.A. (1978) *Working at Stormont*, Dublin: Institute of Public Administration.

O'Leary, B. and McGarry, J. (1993) *The Politics of Antagonism: Understanding Northern Ireland*, London: Athlone Press.

O'Mahony, O. and Chapman, T. (2007) 'Probation, the State and Community: Delivering Probation Services in Northern Ireland', in L. Gelsthorpe and R. Morgan (eds) *Handbook on Probation*, Cullompton: Willan Publishing.

O'Maolain, C. (2000) *North–South Co-operation in Tourism: A Mapping Study*, Armagh: Centre for Cross Border Studies.

O'Neill, M. (1999) 'A Community Work Team in a Health and Social Services Trust', in L. McShane and M. O'Neill (eds) *Community Development in Health and Social Services*, Craigavon: Craigavon and Banbridge Trust.

O'Neill, M. and Campbell, J. (2005) *Curriculum Guidance for the Degree in Social Work, Community Social Work and Community Development*, Belfast: NISCC.

O'Neill, M. and Douglas, H. (1999) *The Re-emergence of Community Development in Health and Social Services*, Craigavon: Craigavon and Banbridge Community Health and Social Services Trust.

O'Reilly, D. and Stevenson, M. (2003) 'Mental Health in Northern Ireland: Have the Troubles Made it Worse?', *Journal of Epidemiology and Community Health*, vol 57, no 7, pp 488–92.

Osborne, R. (2003) 'Progressing the Equality Agenda in Northern Ireland', *Journal of Social Policy*, vol 32, no 2, pp 339–60.

Osborne, R. (2007) 'Evidence and Equality in Northern Ireland', *Evidence and Policy*, vol 3, no 1, pp 79–97.

Osborne, R.D. (2008) 'Emerging Equality Policy in Britain in Comparative Context: A Misused Opportunity?', *Public Money and Management*, vol 28, no 5, pp 305–12.

PDP (Possibilities Development Partnership) (2007) *Equalities of Opportunity for Lone Parents*, Belfast: Northern Ireland Executive.

Pearson, C. (ed) (2006) *Direct Payments and Personalisation of Care*, Edinburgh: Dunedin Academic Press.

Philpot, T. (2001) 'The Promised Land', *Community Care*, 8–13 March, pp 22–3.

Pinkerton, J. and Campbell, J. (2002) 'Social Work and Social Justice in Northern Ireland: Towards a New Occupational Space', *British Journal of Social Work*, vol 32, no 6, pp 723–37.

Platt, D. (2007) 'The Status of Social Care – A Review 2007'. Available at: www.dh.gov.uk/en/Publicationsandstatistics/Publications/ PublicationsPolicyAndGuidance/DH_074217

Pollock, A. (2000) *North–South Co-operation in Education: A Mapping Study*, Armagh: Centre for Cross Border Studies.

Pollock, A. (2009) 'The Centre for Cross Border Studies and its Work in the Irish Border Region', address to an IBAN meeting, Omagh, 21 October. Available at: www.crossborder.ie/cbnews/icban.pdf

Popple, K. (1995) *Analysing Community Work: Its Theory and Practice*, Buckingham: Open University.

Powell, F. and Guerin, D. (1997) *Civil Society and Social Policy*, Dublin: A. and A. Farmar.

Priestley, N., Jolly, D., Pearson, C., Rideel, S., Barnes, C. and Mercier, G. (2007) 'Direct Payments and Disabled People in the UK: Supply, Demand and Devolution', *British Journal of Social Work*, vol 37, no 7, pp 1189–1204.

Prior, P.M. (1993) *Mental Health and Politics in Northern Ireland*, Aldershot: Avebury Press.

Prior, P. (1995) 'The Impact of Recent Health Policy Change on Mental Health Social Work in Social Services Inspectorate', in **[missing ed?]** (Inspectorate) (ed) *Personal Social Services in Northern Ireland: Social Work in Mental Health*, Belfast: Department of Health and Social Services.

Putnam, R.D. (2000) *Bowling Alone: The Collapse and Revival of American Community*, New York: Simon and Schuster.

Quinlivan, E. (1999) *Forging Links: A Study of Cross Border Co-operation in the Irish Border Region*, Belfast: Co-operation Ireland.

Ramon, S., Campbell, J., Lindsay, J., McCrystal, P. and Baidoun, N. (2006) 'The Impact of Political Conflict on Social Work: Experiences from Northern Ireland, Israel and Palestine', *British Journal of Social Work*, vol 36, no 3, pp 435–50.

Ramsey, A. and Fulop, N. (2008) *Integrated Care Pilot Programme: The Evidence Base for Integrated Care*, London: DH.

Rea, E. (2008) *Messages from Legislation and Policy in Northern Ireland*, Belfast: NISSC.

Reilly, S., Challis, D., Donnelly, M., Hughes, J. and Stewart, R. (2007) 'Care Management in Mental Health Services in England and Northern Ireland: Do Integrated Organizations Promote Integrated Practice?', *Journal of Health Services Research and Policy*, vol 12, no 4, pp 236–41.

Reynolds, J. (2006) '*Order from Chaos: Responding to Traumatic Events* (Third Edition). Marion Gibson. Book Review', *British Journal of Social Work*, vol 36, no 5, pp 870–2.

Richards, J. (2000) *The Northern Ireland Model – Unifying Health and Social Services: What Can Be Read Across?*, Belfast: QMW Public Policy Seminar.

Riddell, S., Priestly, M., Pearson, C., Morgan, G., Barnes, C., Jolly, D. and William, V. (2006) *Disabled People and Direct Payments: A UK Comparative Study*, Swindon: Economic and Social Research Council Report.

Robson, T. (2000) *The State and Community Action*, London: Pluto Press.

Roof, M. (1972) *A Hundred Years of Family Welfare: A Study of the Family Welfare (Formerly Charity Organisation Society) 1869–1969*, London: Michael Joseph.

Rose, R. (1971) *Government without Consensus: An Irish Perspective*, London: Faber.

Rosen, R. and Ham, C. (2008) *Integrated Care: Lessons from Evidence and Experience*, London: Nuffield Trust.

Roulstone, R. and Hudson, V. (2007) 'Carer Participation in England, Wales and Northern Ireland: A Challenge for Interprofessional Working', *Journal of Interprofessional Care*, vol 21, no 3, pp 303–17.

Royal College of Psychiatrists (2009) 'Reduction in Psychiatric Beds'. Available at: www.rcpsych.ac.uk

Royal Commission on the NHS (1979) Cmnd 7615, London: HMSO.

RPA (Review of Public Administration) (2005) *Further Consultation*, Belfast: RPA.

RPA (2006) *Better Government for Northern Ireland*, Belfast: RPA.

Save the Children (2009) 'A Child's Portion: An Analysis of Public Expenditure on Children in the UK', Northern Ireland Briefing.

Save the Children (2010) 'Measuring Severe Child Poverty in Northern Ireland'. Available at: www.savethechildren.org.uk

Scottish Executive (2003) 'A Partnership for a Better Scotland: Partnership Agreement'. Available at: www.scotland.gov.uk/publications/2003

Scottish Executive (2006) 'Changing Lives: Report of the 21st Century Social Work Review'. Available at: www.scotland.gov.uk

Scottish Government (2007a) 'Principles and Priorities: The Government's Programme for Scotland'. Available at: www.scotland.gov.uk

Scottish Government (2007b) *The Crerar Review: The Report of the Independent Review of Regulation, Audit, Inspection and Complaints Handling of Public Services in Scotland*. Available at: www.Scotland.gov.uk/publications/2007

Scottish Government (2010) *Financial Integration Across Health and Social Care Evidence Review*, Edinburgh: Scottish Government Social Research.

Scourfield, J., Holland, S. and Young, C. (2008) 'Social Work in Wales since Democratic Devolution', *Australian Social Work*, vol 61, no 1, pp 42–56.

Shevlin, M. and McGuigan, K. (2003) 'The Long-Term Psychological Impact of Bloody Sunday on Families of the Victims as Measured by the Revised Impact of Event Scale', *British Journal of Clinical Psychology*, vol 42, no 4, pp 427–32.

Shirlow, P. and Murtagh, B. (2006) *Belfast: Sectarian Violence and the City*, London: Pluto Press.

Shuttleworth, I. and Lloyd, C. (2009) 'Are Northern Ireland Communities Dividing? Evidence from Geographically Consistent Census of Population Data 1971–2001', *Environment and Planning*, vol 41, no 1, pp 213–29

Skehill, C. (1999) *The Nature of Social Work in Ireland*, New York: Edwin Mellen Press.

Smale, G., Tuson, G. and Stratham, D. (2000) *Social Work and Social Problems*, Basingstoke: Palgrave.

Smyth, L. (2006) 'The Cultural Politics of Sexuality and Reproduction in Northern Ireland', *Sociology*, vol 40, no 4, pp 663–80.

Smyth, M. (1994) *Social Work Sectarianism and Anti-Discriminatory Social Work Practice in Northern Ireland*, Derry: University of Ulster.

Smyth, M. and Campbell, J. (1996) 'Social Work, Sectarianism and Anti-Sectarian Practice in Northern Ireland', *British Journal of Social Work*, vol 26, no 1, pp 77–92.

Smyth, M., Morrisey M. and Hamilton, M. (2001) *Caring Through the Troubles. Health and Social Services in North and West Belfast*, Belfast: North and West Belfast Health and Social Services Trust.

Social Work Task Force (2009) 'Building a Safe, Confident Future'. Available at: http://publications.dcsf.gov.uk

South-Eastern Health and Social Care Trust (2008) *Annual Report 2007–2008*, Belfast: HSCNI.

SSI (Social Services Inspectorate) (1998) *Living With the Trauma of the Troubles*, Belfast: SSINI.

SSI (2002) *Key Indicators of Personal Social Services for Northern Ireland*, Belfast: Department of Health, Social Services and Public Safety.

SSI (2004a) *Social Work Research in Northern Ireland 1998–2003*, Personal Social Services in Northern Ireland, No 61, Belfast: DHSSPS.

SSI (2004b) *Inspection of Social Work in Mental Health Services*, Belfast: DHSSPS.

SSIA (Social Services Improvement Agency) (2005) 'Social Work in Wales: A Profession to Value'. Available at: www.wlga.gov.uk/english/meeting-documents

Summerfield, D. (2000) 'War and Mental Health: A Brief Overview', *British Medical Journal*, no 321, pp 232–5.

Tannam, E. (1999) *Cross Border Co-operation in the Republic of Ireland and Northern Ireland*, Basingstoke: Macmillan.

Taylor, B., Mullinevy, J. and Gleming, G. (2010) 'Partnership, Service Needs and Assessing Competence in Post Qualifying Education and Training', *Social Work Education*, vol 29, no 5, pp 475–89.

Teahen, B., Gaffney, B. and Yarnell, J. (2002) 'Community Development: Knowledge, Attitudes and Training Needs Amongst Professionals in Northern Ireland', *Health Education Journal*, vol 61, no 1, pp 32–43.

Thompson, N. (2006) *Anti-Discriminatory Practice*, Basingstoke: Palgrave Macmillan.

Tomlinson, M. (2000) 'Targeting Social Need, Social Exclusion and Social Security Statistics', in N. Yeates and E. McLaughlin (eds) *Measuring Social Exclusion and Poverty*, Belfast: Department for Social Development.

Traynor, C. (1998) 'Social Work in a Sectarian Society', in CCETSW (ed) *Social Work and Social Change in Northern Ireland*, Belfast: CCETSW.

Trench, A. and Jeffery, C. (2007) *Older People and Public Policy: The Impact of Devolution*, London: Age Concern.

Turbett, C. (2009) 'Tensions in the Delivery of Social Work Services in Rural and Remote Scotland', *British Journal of Social Work*, vol 39, pp 506–21.

Verba, S., Scholozman, K. and Brady, H. (1996) *Voice and Equality: Civic Voluntarism in American Politics*, Cambridge, MA: Harvard University Press.

Waddington, P. (1994) 'The Values Base of Community Work', in S. Jacobs and K. Popple (eds) *Community Work in the 1990s*, Nottingham: Spokesman.

WAG (Welsh Assembly Government) (2007a) 'One Wales: A Progressive Agenda for the Government of Wales'. Available at: www.wales.gov.uk/about/programme for government/onewales

WAG (2007b) 'Fulfilled Lives, Supportive Communities: A Strategy for Social Services in Wales over the Next Decade'. Available at: www.wales.gov.uk/about/strategy/publications

Watson, D. and West, J. (2008) 'The Report of the 21st Century Social Work Review: Reviewing the 'Transformative' Aspirations of a Major Public Policty Initiative in Scotland', *Public Policy and Administration*, vol 23, no 3, pp 302-18.

WAVE Trauma Centre (2010) 'Services Available. Belfast'. Available at: www.wavetraumacentre.org.uk

Weeks, S. (2007) *Report on the Integration of Health and Social Care Services in England*, London: Unison. Available at: www.unison.org.uk

Williamson, A. and Darby, J. (1978) 'Social Welfare Services', in J. Darby and A. Williamson (eds) *Violence and Social Services in Northern Ireland*, London: Heinemann.

Wilson, R. (2007) 'Rhetoric Meets Reality: Northern Ireland's Equality Agenda', *Benefits*, vol 15, no 2, pp 151–62.

Wilson, C. and Daly, M. (2007) 'Shaping the Future of Mental Health Policy and Legislation in Northern Ireland: The Impact of Service User and Professional Social Work Discourses', *British Journal of Social Work*, vol 37, no 3, pp 423–39.

Wilson, G., O'Connor, E., Walsh, T. and Kirby, M. (2009) 'Reflections on Practice Learning in Northern Ireland and the Republic of Ireland: Lessons from Student Experiences', *Social Work Education*, vol 28, no 6, pp 631–45.

Wincott, D. (2005) 'Reshaping Public Space? Devolution and Policy Change in British Early Childhood Education and Care', *Regional and Federal Studies*, vol 15, no 5, pp 453–70.

Wistow, G. (2000) *The Modernized Personal Social Services: NHS Handmaiden or Partnerships in Citizenship*, paper commissioned by ADSS, Leeds: Nuffield Institute for Health.

Younghusband, E.L. (1959) *Report of the Working Party on Social Services in the Local Authority Health and Welfare Services*, London: HMSO.

Yu, P. (1998) 'Racism and Anti-Racist Practice in Northern Ireland. Implications for Social Work', in M. Anderson, S. Bogues, J. Campbell, H. Douglas and M. McColgan (eds) *Social Work and Social Change in Northern Ireland*, Belfast: CCETSW.

Index

Note: *n* = note; *t* =table

A

abortion 28
Acheson, N. 12, 14, 26
active citizenship 75
Active Communities Initiative 84
Adelman, L. 111
The Administrative Structure of the Health and Personal Social Services in Northern Ireland (1969) (HMSO) 55–6
Age Concern 123
Ageing in a Inclusive Society: A Strategy for Promoting the Social Inclusion of Older People (OFMDFM) 123–4
Agriculture and Rural Development in Northern Ireland, Department of (DARD) 117
All-Ireland Suicide Prevention Plan 97
almoner service 15, 16–17
Almoners, Institute of *see* Institute of Medical Social Workers
Anderson, M. 63
Anglo-Irish Agreement (1985) 94
Appleby, J. 64, 70
Area Children's and Young People's Committees (ACYPCs) 122
Assembly Committee for Health, Social Services and Public Safety 137

B

The Bamford Review of Mental Health and Learning Disability (Northern Ireland) (DHSSPS) 123, 140–1
Barclay Report (1982) 81, 86
Bare Necessities (Hillyard et al) 109–10
Barnado's 26, 115, 127
Barr, A. 83
Belfast 25, 33, 38, 39, 40, 55, 117*t*
Belfast Christian Civic Union 13
Belfast Council for/of Social Welfare (formerly Charity Organization Society (COS)) 12–15
Belfast Council for Voluntary Work 13
Belfast Health and Social Care Trust 43, 47, 66, 127
Belfast Welfare Authority 22
BIC (British-Irish Council) 144
Birrell, D. 8, 63, 64, 70, 96, 101–2
Black Report (1979) (HMSO) 20
Bloody Sunday (1972) 47
Bloomfield Report (1998) 50

border region *see* cross border social work
Boyd, F.I. 16, 17
Brewer, J. 23
Britain's Poorest Children (Adelman et al) 111
British Abortion Act 28
British Association of Social Workers 28
British-Irish Council (BIC) 144
Brodie, I. 1
Buckland, P. 9
Building a Safe, Confident Future (Social Work Taskforce) 144

C

Campbell, J. 24, 39, 63, 76–7, 81
Care Council (Wales) 133
Care Quality Commission (England) 134
Care and Social Services Inspectorate (Wales) 135
carers 118–19, 127
Catholic community 7, 11, 12, 17, 24, 25, 27, 31, 80, 110
Caul, B. 8, 15, 16, 20–1, 56, 79
CAWT *see* Co-operation and Working Together
Central Council for Education and Training in Social Work (CCETSW) 24, 29, 105–6
Central Emergency Planning Unit 51
Centre for Cross Border Studies 92
Centre for Independent Learning 142
CERT (Community Emergency Response Team) 44–5
Challenge project 102, 103
Challis, D. 64
Changing Lives (Scottish Executive) 145
Charity Organization Society (COS) *see* Belfast Council of Social Welfare
child poverty 111, 112*t*, 113*t*
Child Poverty Act (2010) 113, 144
child protection 60, 68–9, 96–7, 99–100, 125, 131, 144
Childcare Act (2006) 113
childcare services 100, 101, 103, 113, 127
Children First childcare strategy 121
Children Order initiative 84
Children and Young Persons Act (1950, 1968) 19–20, 22
Children's Workforce Development Council 134
Chronically Sick and Disabled Persons Act (1970) 22
Citizens Advice Bureau 13

Clarke, S. 77, 98, 99
Co-operation Ireland 103–4
Co-operation and Working Together (CAWT) 97–9, 104, 105
Colwyn Committee (1925) 8
Commission for Racial Equality for Northern Ireland 34
Commission for Victims and Survivors (1997, 2009) 50, 51
Commissioner for Complaints (ombudsman) 30–1
community development 2–3, 26–7, 73–4, 89–90, 152, 153
    community social work 76–8
    community-oriented services 86–9
    definition 74–6
    historical background 77–83
    policy developments since 1990s 83–5
The Community Development Challenge (DCLG) 85
Community Development Programme (1969) 79
Community Emergency Response Team (CERT) 44–5
Community Relations, Ministry of 80
Community Relations Commission (1969) 79–80
Community Relations Council 33
community social work 76–8
Community Worker Research Project 80
community-oriented services 86–9
community/institutional care 67–8
Craig, J. 7, 8
The Crerar Review (Scottish Government) 134, 135
Cross Border Childminding Alliance 100, 101, 103
Cross Border Elderly Needs project 100, 101
Cross Border Rural Childcare project 99–100, 101, 102, 103
cross-border social work 2, 4, 85, 91–2, 106–7, 152, 153
    background to cooperation 93–4
    classification of 96–101
    compatibility of professional qualifications 104–5
    context 92
    development of collaboration 94–5
    funding of work 103–4
    nature and focus of projects 101–3
    obstacles to cooperation 105–6
    social services and 95
Cross Border Studies, Centre for 92
Cross Border Women's Health Network 102
Curtis Committee 19

D

Daly, M. 141
Darby, J. 10, 37, 39

DARD (Department of Agriculture and Rural Development in Northern Ireland) 117
Delivering the Bamford Vision (DHSSPS) 141
Department of Agriculture and Rural Development in Northern Ireland, (DARD) 117
Department of Education 120
Department of Health (UK) 65, 66
Department of Health and Social Services and Public Safety (DHSSPS)
    anti-racism 34
    cross border work 97, 105
    devolution 131, 132, 137, 138, 139, 141, 142
    integration with social work 56, 57
    poverty 119–20 121, 123
    violence 37, 45
Department for Social Development (DSD) 111–12, 124
Department for Work and Pensions (DWP) 121
Dergfinn Partnership 100, 103
Developing Better Services (DHSSPS) 57–8
Devlin, P. 11
devolution 2, 4, 7, 121, 122, 148–9, 153–4
    childcare reforms 137–9
    delivery of care by quangos 132–3
    departmental strategies 137
    historic background 129t, 130
    key strategic points 146t
    mental health and learning disability 140–1
    older people and care 139–40
    organisational position of social care 131–2
    personalisation 141–2
    policy copying 130, 144
    policy innovation and development 135, 136t 137
    programmes for government 130
    registration, training and inspection structures 133–5
    role of social work 145, 146t, 147–8
    user and public involvement 142–4
DHSSPS see Department of Health and Social Services and Public Safety
Dillenburger, K. 39
Direct Rule 80, 83, 119, 129t, 140
disability 98, 99, 101, 102
Disasters Working Party (1989) 50–1
discrimination 30–3, 34–5, 36
Ditch, J. 8, 17
Dominelli, L. 35
Dornan, B. 60, 64
Douglas, H. 79
Dowling, B. 65
DSD (Department for Social Development) 111–12, 124
Duffy, J. 143
DWP (Department for Work and Pensions) 121

E

'Early Years' (voluntary group) 120
Eastern Health and Services Board 33, 34, 42
ECNI *see* Equality Commission for Northern Ireland
Economic and Social Research Council (ESRC) 109, 111
education 26, 116, 126
Education (Administrative Provisions) Act (1907) 9
Education, Department of 120
Education (Provision of Meals) Act (1906) 9
Education and Training in Social Work, Northern Ireland Central Council for 104
education and training of social workers 21–2, 87, 104–5, 134, 143
educators/trainers, response to sectarianism 29–30
Embracing Diversity (ECNI) 34
Emergency Planning College 50
employment 30–3, 35
empowerment and community development 75
Enniskillen Remembrance Day bombing 43–4
Equality Commission for Northern Ireland (ECNI) 31, 32–3, 34
ESRC (Economic and Social Research Council) 109, 111
European Union 85, 95, 99, 103–4, 106
Evason, E. 11, 20
'Every Child Matters' 71, 138
Extra Care Domiciliary Dementia Night Help service 102

F

Fahey, T. 17–18
Fair Employment Commission 31
Fair Employment Office 30–1
Fay, M. 43
Field, J. 66
fostering and adoption 28
Frazer, H. 79
fuel poverty 118, 126
Fuel Poverty Task Force 124
Fulfilled Lives, Supportive Communities (Welsh Assembly Government) 145
Fulop, N. 69

G

Garrett, P.M. 25
General Health Services Board 18
General Social Care Council (England) 133, 135, 144
Getting off the Fence, Challenging Sectarianism in Personal Social Services: Standards of Good Practice (CCETSW) 29
Gibb, M. 144
Gibson, M. 42, 43, 49, 50

Glasby, J. 65, 133
Good Friday Agreement 25, 31, 94–5, 130, 144
Good Relations Strategy (2006) 35–6
Government of Ireland Act (1920) 7, 9
Green, A.E. 115–16
Griffiths Report (1998) 82

H

Harvey, B. 93
Health Care Improvement Scotland (HIS) 135–6
Health and Community Trusts 57
Health, Department of (UK) 65, 66
Health, Social Services and Public Safety, Assembly Committee for 137
Health and Personal Social Services Order (1972, 1994) 57, 79
Health Service Executive (ROI) 96
health services 2, 3, 71–2, 152
  development of integrated services 55–8, 59t, 152–3
  integration and innovation 68–70
  internal assessment 63–5
  key policy outcomes 66–8
  operation of integrated services 59–63
  protecting social services 70–1
  UK perceptions 65–6
  welfare state and 17–18
Health and Social Care Trusts 59, 86, 88, 92, 95, 107, 138, 139, 152
  Belfast Health and Social Care Trust 43, 47, 66, 127
  Northern Health and Social Care Trust 66
  South-Eastern Health and Social Care Trust 68
  Southern Health and Social Care Trust 88–9
Health and Social Service Boards 80, 81, 82, 86, 92, 95, 107, 122, 152
  Eastern Health and Services Board 33, 34, 42
  Western Health and Social Services Board 31
Health and Social Service Councils 143
Health and Social Services and Public Safety, Department of *see* Department of Health and Social Services and Public Safety (DHSSPS)
Healthy Living Centres 84
Heenan, D. 63, 64, 70, 96, 101–3, 117
Help the Aged 118, 123
Henwood, M. 66
Herron, S. 8, 15, 16, 20–1, 56, 79
Higgins, G. 23
Hillyard, P. 109–10
Homefirst Community Trust 68–9
homelessness 101
hospital discharge policy 66–8
Hospital Trusts 56, 57
housing 30, 41, 71, 119

Houston, S. 133
Hudson, B. 66
Human Rights Commission (Northern Ireland) 31

I

Independent Learning, Centre for 142
Independent Safeguarding Authority (ISA) 97
Institute of Medical Social Workers (formerly Institute of Almoners) 16, 17
institutional/community care 67–8
integrated health and social services development 55–8, 59*t*, 71–2
  England 64
  innovation and 68–70
  internal assessment 63–5
  key policy outcomes 66–8
  operation of 59–63
  protecting social services 70–1
  UK perceptions 65–6
International Fund for Ireland (IFI) 103
INTERREG IVA programme (EU) 99, 100, 103
Ireland, Republic of *see* cross-border social work
Irish Poor Law system (1838) 10–11, 18–19
Irish Society for the Prevention of Cruelty to Children (ISPCC) 97
ISA (Independent Safeguarding Authority) 97

J

Jamison, J. 98
Jeffery, C. 124
Joint Ministerial Council (JMC) 144
Joseph Rowntree Foundation 110–11, 112, 113, 114*t*, 124, 149

K

Kegworth air crash 42

L

Labour Exchanges and Trade Boards Act (1909) 9
Lawrence, R. 9
Lifestart project 103
Lifetime Opportunities (Northern Ireland Anti-Poverty and Social Inclusion Strategy) (OFMDFM) 121–2
Living with the Trauma of the Troubles (SSI) 45
local involvement networks (LINKs) 143–4
Long-term Care Law, Royal Commission on (UK) 135
low pay 115, 126
Luce, A. 48
Lynn Committee (1938) 15–16

M

Macbeath, A.A. 14
McCall, C. 100

McCready, S. 78, 80, 82
McCrystal, P. 24, 39
McLaughlin, E. 17–18, 63, 105, 111, 112*t*
McQuade, J. 28
Macrory Report (1970) 56
McShane, L. 86
McVicker, H. 137
Mainstreaming Community Development in Health and Personal Social Services (DHSSPS) 84, 86
management of integrated services 62–3
Manktelow, R. 37
Martin, Paul (Chief Inspector of Social Services) 90
Maucher, M. 96
Measuring Severe Child Poverty in Northern Ireland (Save the Children) 125
Medical Social Workers, Institute of (formerly Institute of Almoners) 16, 17
Mental Health Act (Northern Ireland) (1948) 20–1
mental health services 20–1, 54, 38, 60, 64, 68, 123, 126, 138
  devolution and 140-1, 142
  poverty and 115–16
  trauma and 43–5, 49–50
  voluntary groups 100–1
Middleton Centre for Autism 97
Miller, M. 35
Ministry of Community Relations 80
Monteith, M. 111, 112*t*
Mowlem, M. 50
Moyle Report (1975) 80
Murie, A. 8
Murtagh, B. 25

N

National Assistance Act (1948) 18
National Association of Probation Officers, 27
National Insurance Act (1911) 9–10
National Insurance (Industrial Injuries) Act (Northern Ireland) (1946) 18
National Insurance (Northern Ireland) Act (1946) 18
National Social Work Qualifications Board (ROI) 104, 105
National Society for the Prevention of Cruelty to Children (NSPCC) 97, 127
Nationalists 7, 25
New Deal for Communities Programme 86
New Deal for Lone Parents 126
New Targeting Social Need initiative 84
NHS, Royal Commission on the (1979) 63–4
The NHS Plan (DH) 65
NIA (Northern Ireland Assembly) 112, 136–7
NIAO (Northern Ireland Audit Office) 139
NIAPN (Northern Ireland Anti-Poverty Network) 125, 126

NICDRG (Northern Ireland Community Development Review Group) 74–5
NICTT (Northern Ireland Centre for Trauma and Transformation) 47, 49, 50
NIHA (Northern Ireland Hospital(s) Authority) 18, 20
NIHE *see* Northern Ireland Housing Executive
NIPPA (Northern Ireland Pre-School Playgroup Association) 120
NISAT (Northern Ireland Single Assessment Tool) 140–1
NISCC *see* Northern Ireland Social Care Council
NIVT (Northern Ireland Voluntary Trust) 80
Noble Deprivation Index (DARD) 117
North-South Ministerial Council (NSMC) 95, 96, 97
Northern Health and Social Care Trust 66
Northern Ireland 6*n*, 7–8
Northern Ireland Act (1998) 31–3, 35–6 126
Northern Ireland Anti-Poverty Network (NIAPN) 125, 126
Northern Ireland Assembly (NIA) 112, 136–7
Northern Ireland Audit Office (NIAO) 139
Northern Ireland Central Council for Education and Training in Social Work 104
Northern Ireland Centre for Trauma and Transformation (NICTT) 47, 49, 50
Northern Ireland Children's Services Plan (2008–11) 122
Northern Ireland Commissioner for Children and Young People 144
Northern Ireland Community Development Review Group (NICDRG) 74–5
Northern Ireland Community Relations Strategy 35–6
The Northern Ireland Context (NISCC) 30
Northern Ireland Council of Social Service 13
Northern Ireland Executive 122, 131, 132, 136, 148
Northern Ireland Health and Well-being Survey (2001) (DHSSPS)
Northern Ireland Hospital(s) Authority (NIHA) 18, 20
Northern Ireland House Condition Survey (2006) 118
Northern Ireland Household Panel Survey (NIHPS) 112
Northern Ireland Housing Executive (NIHE) 25, 30, 41, 119
Northern Ireland Human Rights Commission 31
Northern Ireland Memorial Fund 50
Northern Ireland Office 41, 43
Northern Ireland Pre-School Playgroup Association (NIPPA) 120

Northern Ireland Public Accounts Committee 139
Northern Ireland Regulation and Quality Improvement Authority 134, 135
Northern Ireland Single Assessment Tool (NISAT) 140–1
Northern Ireland Social Care Council (NISCC) 29–30, 105, 133, 134, 143, 145
Northern Ireland Voluntary Trust (NIVT) 80
NSPCC (National Society for the Prevention of Cruelty to Children) 97, 127
Nuffield Trust 65, 66, 70

O

Office of the First Minister and deputy First Minister (OFMDFM) 50, 121–2, 123–4, 131, 132
Office of Social Services 131–2, 137
Old Age Pensions Act (1908) 9
older people 60, 69, 99, 100, 101, 102, 116, 117*t*, 118, 123–4, 126, 139–40
Older People's Commissioner 144
Oliver, J.A. 7
Omagh bombing 44, 47, 48
One Wales Agenda (Welsh Assembly Government) 130
O'Neill, M. 76–7
Opportunity for All (DWP) 121
O'Reilly, D. 43
Osborne, R. 32

P

paramilitarism 27, 37
Parenting Initiative 101, 102
Parents and Children Together Service (PACT) 127
partnership 76
Partnership Care West 100, 102–3
Partnership for Equality (NIO) 83
Patient and Client Council 143
peace walls 25
Peck, E. 66
PECS (Pre-Employment Consultancy Register) 97
People First (DHSS) 56–7, 139
Philpot, T. 66
Pinkerton, J. 63, 81
Poor Man's Lawyer Service 13
Popple, K. 74
post-traumatic stress disorder (PTSD) 43–4, 47, 48, 49
poverty 3, 9–10, 92, 109–10, 127–8, 153
implications for social work 125–6
main indicators 110–12, 113*t*, 114*t*, 115–16, 117*t*, 118–19
policy responses 119–25
social work initiatives 127
Poverty and Income Distribution in Northern Ireland (ESRC) 109, 111

Pre-Employment Consultancy Register
(PECS) 97
Prevention of Cruelty to Children, Irish
Society for the (ISPCC) 97
Prior, P.M. 68
Probation Act (1950) 16
Probation Officers, National Association of 27
probation service 15–16, 27, 33
professional forums 63
programme of care approach 60–1
Protestant community 7, 9, 12, 25, 27, 31, 110
Public Accounts Committee (Northern
Ireland) 139
public expenditure 136t, 139, 141
Public Health and Local Government
(Administrative Provisions) Act (Northern
Ireland) (1946) 18

Q

Queen's University Belfast 14, 21
Quinlivan, E. 94–5

R

Race Relations Order (1995) 34
*Racial Equality in Health and Social Care: Good
Practice Guide* (ECNI) 34
Racial Equality for Northern Ireland,
Commission for 34
racism 34–5
Ramsey, A. 69
*Regional Strategy for Health and Social Wellbeing
1997–2002* (DHSS) 84
Regional Strategy for the Northern Ireland
Health and Social Services (1987–92)
Regulation of Care, Scottish Commission for
the 134
Regulation and Quality Improvement
Authority (Northern Ireland) 134, 135
*Report on the Administration of Local Government
Services 1928/29* (HMSO) 10
Report of the Mental Health Services
Advisory Committee (1948) (HMSO)
20–1
*Report of the Working Party on Social Services in
the Local Authority Health and Welfare Service*
(Younghusband) 78
Republic of Ireland *see* cross-border social
work
Review of Public Administration (RPA)
(2005) 58, 59t, 88, 132
Riddell, S. 142
Robson, T. 79
Roof, M. 13
Rotzinger, C. 96
Royal Commission on Long-term Care Law
(UK) 135
Royal Commission on the NHS (1979) 63–4
Rupert Stanley College of Further Education
21

S

Safeguarding Boards 138, 139
Safeguarding Vulnerable Groups Act
(Northern Ireland Order) (2006) 97
Save the Children 26, 111, 112, 113t, 121, 125
SCIE (Social Care Institute for Excellence)
52–3, 135
Scotland 6n, 129, 130, 132, 133, 134–5, 136t,
137, 139, 140, 145, 148–9
Scottish Commission for the Regulation of
Care 134
Scottish Social Services Council 133
Scourfield, J. 1
SCSWIS (Social Care and Social Work
Improvement Scotland) 135
sectarianism
anti-discriminatory measures 30–3, 36, 152
anti-oppressive social work and 35–6
anti-racism 34–5
educators/trainers response to 29–30
good relations strategy 33–4
impact of attitudes 23–4
paramilitarism and 27
as segregation 25–7
social work agencies response to 28
social workers and 24–5
values of 27–8
Seebohm Report (1968) 21, 78
segregation and sectarianism 25–7
sex offenders 96, 97
Shankill Road bombing 42, 48–9
'Shared Frontiers' (mental health consortium)
100, 101
Shirlow, P. 25
Shuttleworth, I. 115–16
Skills for Care 134
Smale, G. 109
Smyth, M. 24, 39
social care 6n
Social Care Institute for Excellence (SCIE)
52–3, 135
Social Care and Social Work Improvement
Scotland (SCSWIS) 135
Social Development, Department for (DSD)
111–12, 124
Social Needs Act (Northern Ireland) (1969)
80
Social Service, Northern Ireland Council of
13
Social Services, Office of 131–2, 137
Social Services Financial Agreement (1949) 55
Social Services Improvement Agency (SSIA)
135, 145
Social Services Inspectorate (SSI) 37, 45, 48
Social Services Inspectorate (Wales) 135
Social Welfare, Belfast Council for/of
(formerly Charity Organization Society
(COS)) 12–15

social work
  anti-oppressive 35–6, 85–6
  devolution and 2, 4, 7
  distinctive context 1–3
  historical context 7–22
  similarities/differences with rest of UK 151
  unique features in Northern Ireland 151–2
Social Work at its Best (General Social Care
  Council) 144
Social Work Qualifications Board, National
  (ROI) 104, 105
Social Work Taskforce 144
Social Work in Wales, A Profession to Value (SSIA)
  145
Social Workers, British Association of 28
Society of St Vincent de Paul 12, 26, 101, 106
South and East Belfast Health and Social
  Services Trust 49
South-Eastern Health and Social Care Trust
  68
Southern Health and Social Care Trust 88–9
Special Support Programme for Peace and
  Reconciliation (SSPPR) 100, 103
Sperrin Lakeland Health and Social Services
  Trust 44
SSI *see* Social Services Inspectorate
SSIA (Social Services Improvement Agency)
  135, 145
St Vincent de Paul see Society of St Vincent
  de Paul
Staffcare 49, 50
state welfare 8–11
STEER mental health (voluntary group)
  100–1
Stevenson, M. 43
*Strategy for the Support of the Voluntary Sector
  and for Community Development in Northern
  Ireland* (DHSS) 82, 84
Summary Jurisdiction and Criminal Justice
  Act (Northern Ireland) (1935) 15
Supporting People initiative 71, 119
Sure Start programme 120

T

Tannam, E. 93
Targeting Social Need (TSN) programme 83,
  121
*10 Year Strategy for Social Work in Northern
  Ireland 2010–2020* 147–8
Thompson, N. 35
Trauma Advisory Panels (TAPs) 45–7
Trauma Resource Centre (Belfast) 47
travellers 34, 69, 92, 97
Trench, A. 124
The Troubles 25, 37, 38–9, 40–1, 43–4, 45, 48,
  49, 50, 78, 80, 93

U

UK Alliance of Skills for Care 134

UK Civil Contingencies Act (2004) 41, 51
Ulster Workers Council 40
Understanding the Needs of Children in
  Northern Ireland (UNOCINI) 137–8
unemployment 113, 114*t*
Unionists 7, 12, 22, 106
United Kingdom 6*n*
user participation 76, 141, 142–4

V

victim support 50–3, 152
Victims and Survivors, Commission for (1997,
  2009) 50, 51
Victims and Survivors Service 50–1
Victims Unit (Office of the First Minister and
  Deputy First Minister) 50
violence
  deaths 38
  mental health and trauma 43–5, 49–50, 54
  nature of 37–40
  operation and delivery of social work 39–40
  research into 37, 53–4
  social services response 2, 3-4, 45–8, 53–4
  social workers response to civil emergencies
    40–3, 53, 54, 78
  trauma and staff 48–9
  victim support 50–3
voluntary sector 11–15, 26, 28, 45–7, 51, 79,
  99–101, 119

W

Wales 6*n*, 129, 130, 131, 132, 135, 136*t*, 140,
  145, 148–9
WAVE (voluntary organisation) 51
Welfare Services Act (1949, 1954) 18–19, 21
welfare state 17–20
Well into 2000 (DHSS) 84
Well-being and Treatment Centres (Belfast) 62
Western Health Action Zone 34
Western Health and Social Services Board 31
Williamson, A. 10, 37, 39, 100
Wilson, C. 141
Wilson, G. 105
Wilson, R. 126
Wincott, D. 130
Wistow, G. 65–6
Wootton, B. 77
Work and Pensions, Department for (DWP)
  121
'Working for Patients' 56
Workman's Compensation Act (1897) 9

Y

Younghusband, E. 77–8
youth services 127